THE
ICE HOUSE
MURDER

Also by Robin Schiller and Pat Marry

Murder at Lordship: Inside the Hunt for a Detective's Killer

*

Robin Schiller is a journalist for Mediahuis Ireland covering Independent.ie, the *Irish Independent* and the *Sunday Independent*.

After being turned away by An Garda Síochána at 17 for being too young, **Pat Marry** joined the force eight years later. He went on to investigate some of Ireland's most high-profile cases, including the killings of Rachel O'Reilly and Garda Adrian Donohue. He retired in 2018 at the rank of Detective Inspector. In 2019 he published a memoir, *The Making of a Detective*.

THE ICE HOUSE MURDER

The Killing of Irene White

Robin Schiller & Pat Marry

ALLEN&UNWIN

First published in Great Britain in 2025 by Allen & Unwin

A CIP catalogue record for this book is available from the British Library.

Trade paperback ISBN 978 1 80546 384 9
E-Book ISBN 978 1 80546 385 6

Allen & Unwin
An imprint of Atlantic Books Ltd
Ormond House
26–27 Boswell Street
London WC1N 3JZ

www.atlantic-books.co.uk

Printed by CPI Group (UK) Ltd, Croydon CR0 4YY

10 9 8 7 6 5 4 3 2 1

Product safety EU representative: Authorised Rep Compliance Ltd., Ground Floor, 71 Lower Baggot Street, Dublin, D02 P593, Ireland. www.arccompliance.com

MIX
Paper | Supporting responsible forestry
FSC® C171272
FSC
www.fsc.org

CONTENTS

AUTHORS' NOTE

Certain witnesses in this case who have not appeared in court have been given pseudonyms to protect their identities.

PROLOGUE

6 APRIL 2005 – 'WHY ARE YOU DOING THIS?'

The menacing figure crept up the garden of Ice House, stealthily making his way through the hedges and across the well-kept grass. He had just scaled the seven-foot rear wall and didn't want to alert anyone to his presence in the garden. Not yet anyway. Passing a yellow toy digger and plastic football left out on the concrete patio, the man couldn't have been in any doubt that children lived in the house. Reaching the back door, he gave it a loud knock, sure to expect an answer. He'd been informed only moments earlier that Irene White was now at home.

It was shortly after 10 a.m. and Irene had just returned from dropping her three children to school. The day was only start-ing, though, and there was lots to do. She stood at the kitchen sink wearing orange gloves as she rinsed the dishes left over from the breakfast rush. Music blared from the radio perched on the counter, while the white curtain was pulled across the kitchen window. She wouldn't have heard or seen the man creeping up her back garden, and only noticed someone was outside from the loud knock at the door. Her mother Maureen lived in a mobile home in the back garden and would call over every morning. Irene was security conscious, and as she walked to the back door, she called out to her mother. 'The gate is swinging open,' a male voice replied from the other side of the wooden door. The two timber gates at the side of the house had swung outwards in the past but had only recently been fixed. Irene unlocked the back door to inspect what had happened for herself. As the door creaked open, she was greeted by an ominous figure towering over her. The gates hadn't swung open – it was only a ruse to lure Irene out from the safety of her home.

Suddenly the man raised his left hand, holding a large knife which he had concealed by his side. He lunged at Irene and, without saying a word, plunged the knife into her chest. She was pushed backwards and fell through the doorway, stumbling through the utility room and into the kitchen. Raising the knife above his head, the man forcefully brought the serrated blade down onto Irene's chest once more. She tried to grab hold of him but, standing at just five feet four inches tall, she was overpowered by his larger physique. The violent struggle continued in the kitchen; a glass jug shattered into pieces as it was knocked over, while two kitchen chairs also went crashing to the floor.

Panicked and bewildered by what was happening, Irene cried out, 'Stop, why are you doing this?' The man remained silent as he thrust the knife into Irene again. And again. And again. From the very moment Irene had opened the back door, she never stood a chance. As she lay motionless on the kitchen floor, the man leaned over her, breathing heavily from the frenzied attack and taking in what he had done. Irene was dead, that he was sure of. He kneeled beside Irene's body and muttered the 'Our Father' prayer before getting back to his feet. Stepping through the pool of blood, he made his way out of the back door, and vaulted over the rear garden wall. The killer had left a trail of bloody footprints in his wake as he fled. He had also left three children without their mother, having viciously taken the life of a much loved and caring woman. The hunt was about to begin for the man who had murdered Irene White. But he hadn't acted alone.

1

HAPPY BEGINNINGS

By April 2005, Irene White knew that her life was in danger. Her fears had been well documented through conversations with friends, counsellors, and the gardaí, as well as private diaries she kept. Despite being just 43 years old, she was considering making a will, believing that her death could be imminent. A bright and intelligent woman, she knew to tell people close to her about her concerns. She felt it was a case of not if it would happen, but when. Life hadn't always been like this for Irene, though, and most of her years had been spent living a normal and peaceful existence, free from the worry that someone was after her.

Born on 22 October 1961 in the rural Louth village of Omeath, she was the youngest of Maureen and Matthew McBride's three children. She grew up in the family cottage at Knocknagoran, known as Ceol, which had been willed to Maureen by her father. Irene's older siblings were Anne and Michael, but tragedy struck the McBride family on 26 June 1963. Michael, then aged six, was knocked down by a car in front of the family home. He later passed away from his injuries, and the driver of the vehicle was charged with dangerous driving causing death and driving with no insurance. It was the first of several tragedies to impact the family; in 1972, Matthew McBride passed away following a battle with cancer.

Irene was enrolled in St Laurence's National School in Omeath and then moved to the nearby St Michael's College in 1974 to begin her second-level education. She was a studious teenager, receiving seven honours in her Inter Cert before sitting her Leaving Cert in 1979. Irene was sociable during her time in school, with friends saying she always looked at the funny side of things in life. She was an enthusiastic badminton player and was also known for her distinctive hobbies: she raised goats and chickens at the family cottage. Her first job, while still studying for her Leaving Cert, was as a receptionist at Dundalk Aluminium, before later being employed by a coal company on Quay Street in the town. She would spend most of her twenties with that company, while also taking up a variety of educational courses in the 1980s, including one in mechanics and one in psychology. A gifted student who shone at English in her school years, she also became involved with the Omeath Development Association and helped in organising the local Gala Festival for several years.

In 1986 she began her first serious relationship when she met George Bannister, a customs official from Dublin who had relocated to Omeath for work. He encountered Irene one night and was smitten with her charm and beauty. The romance developed and they began renting a property together at Chapel Hill in Omeath, with Irene falling pregnant a short time later. On 23 February 1988, their daughter Jennifer McBride was born in Newry, County Down. Shortly after Jennifer came along, Irene took up work as a barmaid in Carlingford, then later moved to Fyffes in Dundalk, where she worked as a secretary. An extrovert, Irene returned to the more sociable pub work at the Century Bar in Dundalk. The owner, Tony O'Kane, had worked with Irene at the coal company on Quay Street, and she became good friends with his wife Dympna.

Above all, Irene was dedicated to raising Jennifer, and soon the late-night pub work didn't suit her commitments as a mother. She gave up her part-time work at the Century Bar but remained close friends with Dympna O'Kane. The relationship between Irene and George had also become fraught, and the couple agreed to amicably go their separate ways. One friend would say of this: 'Irene said that George was spending his time in the pub and leaving her at home alone with Jenny. She always wanted to better herself and knew this wouldn't happen with George.' After the split, Irene and Jennifer moved back in with her mother, Maureen, affectionately known as 'Mo' by her family, before Irene bought a house in Ashbrook, a quiet residential estate in Dundalk. Irene continued to pursue different educational courses, and in 1994 she obtained a practitioner's diploma in reflexology, later providing treatments from her home. Her enthusiasm for English and the arts also led her to taking part in amateur dramas put on by the Century Bar during the Maytime Festival in 1996. Through these shows a local businessman caught her eye. His name was Alan White.

A year younger than Irene, he was born on 11 October 1962 and grew up in the family home in St Malachy's Villas in Dundalk, later training as an electrician upon leaving school. After several years of apprenticeships and work in that trade, he became involved in the security business, setting up his own company called Classic Security in 1994. To Irene and her friends, he was a charming man whose business success suited Irene's driven personality. They began dating but there were some minor disagreements at the outset, with claims that Alan was still seeing another local woman. A friend of Irene's said of this: 'She put it to Alan about seeing [the other woman]. He denied it and said he had finished with her. He moved into Irene's house in Ashbrook and then his relationship with [the other woman] ended. Things were okay between Irene and Alan. She was in love with him and, as far as I could see, everything was fine.'

The security work was going well for Alan, and in December 1995 he bought Ice House on Demesne Road in Dundalk with a mortgage of £66,000. His relationship with Irene was also becoming more serious, so much so that she decided to sell her house in Ashbrook and move into Alan's home with Jennifer. Irene also began working as a secretary for Classic Security, which was being run from a spare room in Ice House, and a portion of the sale of the Ashbrook house was invested into the company. The role Irene had taken on was previously that of Alan's sister, and the decision to replace his sibling with his partner irked Alan White's family, creating a bad feeling towards her. While working with the business, Irene also set about taking further courses in first aid, physiotherapy, and aromatherapy.

Life appeared to be going well for her. The business was profitable, and to her friends she seemed happy with Alan White. One friend, recounting this stage of her life, explained: 'On meeting Alan I thought he was handsome and pleasant, and he chatted away about everyday things. I remember feeling happy that Irene had met someone nice and who had his own business and seemed comfortable financially. I remember Alan bought a blue Micra car for Irene. She used this car to visit her mother in Omeath. Irene was thrilled with this car, she had it for a couple of years. Over the years meeting Irene, she was always happy and seemed content.' Another acquaintance said that Irene seemed 'extremely happy' and was 'mad about' Alan, while 'looking forward to a great future' with him.

The couple took the next step in their relationship soon after, when Alan asked for Irene's hand in marriage. She happily accepted the proposal and a date was soon set for the wedding. While her friends said she was delighted at the prospect of marrying Alan, there were issues within the four walls of Ice House that weren't obvious to those on the outside. Her daughter Jennifer would later tell gardaí of one occasion when she saw Irene upset in the lead-up to the wedding: 'I woke up and heard my mother crying in the kitchen,' Jennifer said. 'The kitchen was upstairs and directly across from my room. I got up and asked Alan what was wrong with mam. He sent me in to her in the kitchen. When I saw mam crying, I started crying, and when I asked mam what was wrong, she said that Alan had kissed another girl. By that I know she was saying Alan cheated on her.'

Despite the alleged infidelity, the couple ironed out these issues, and the wedding went ahead as planned, with Irene marrying Alan on 23 June 1998 at St Patrick's Church in Dundalk. It was a low-key affair with only a handful of people present. Irene's family wasn't invited apart from Jennifer and, despite Alan's mother living in Dundalk and him having six siblings, only his brother Derek and his wife were present as witnesses. The secretive nature of the ceremony annoyed members of the White family, who believed it was Irene's decision to have a discreet wedding. Describing the White family's view on the small ceremony, a friend of Irene's said: 'They never warmed to her after this, they felt it was Irene's idea to have a small wedding and they couldn't understand why Alan's sisters couldn't be there.' The wedding party later went to Fitzpatrick's restaurant in the town for the reception meal before the newly-weds celebrated their honeymoon on a Mediterranean cruise.

While her mother and stepfather were celebrating their nuptials, Jennifer went to stay with her aunt Anne, who by this stage had relocated to England. (In 1979, Anne had met Kenneth Corbett from Newry, later marrying him and moving to Manchester in 1983. They had two daughters and had changed their surnames to Delcassian.) Dympna O'Kane, despite being a close friend of Irene's, also hadn't been invited to the wedding and would later tell gardaí: 'Irene rang me the same night to tell me she had great news. I told her I already knew that she had got married that day. Irene told me that Alan specifically said he didn't want me or any of her friends at the wedding. Her sister Anne wasn't asked. We weren't in as much contact after the wedding as before. I knew Alan didn't like me, so I saw Irene when she came to see me.'

While on the face of it Irene appeared happy with newly married life, cracks began to develop in the marriage within a year. A significant factor, Irene told her friends, was Alan's drinking. After one particularly nasty row, Irene and Jennifer left Ice House and went to live with Maureen in Omeath. Irene was making efforts to move out permanently, even having her friends accompany her to view a property in the Avondale area of Dundalk in the hope of leaving Alan. 'She was in a terrible emotional state,' one friend recalled. 'She was with a young child and had nowhere to live.' They also claimed that Alan 'threw her out', and no sooner was she gone than he 'was ringing her telling her he loved her and blaming his bad temper and drinking' on his past relationship with his father. But another confidant said Irene 'was crazy in love with Alan and she agreed to go back to live with him in Ice House'. It was also around this time that she discovered she was pregnant with the couple's first child.

Her friends said that Irene still had concerns about Alan's drinking, despite the prospect of his becoming a father, which was placing a further burden on their relationship. On 10 February 1999 she went into labour, and Irene called Dympna O'Kane down to Ice House to support her. Dympna arrived there shortly after 8 p.m. and, recalling what happened, she would later tell gardaí: 'As the night progressed [Irene] was aware that Alan was drinking and not doing what he was supposed to do. The nurses arrived and Alan was still drinking. During the time I was there Alan came up several times and asked us did we want a drink of whiskey. We declined, but he kept drinking, right through the night.' The following morning at 9 a.m. the couple's first child, Damhan White, was born at Ice House in a home delivery. The christening was held several months later but, as with the wedding, none of Irene's friends were invited. The only people present for the ceremony were Alan's family. Dympna would see less and less of her close friend as time went on, but they would stay in contact by phone, with Irene venting her annoyance at Alan while she was at home minding their baby.

A short time later Irene became pregnant again, but her husband's escapades continued. 'Irene was very unhappy because she knew what was facing her. He was acting like a single fella out drinking heavily,' one friend recalled. On 4 July 2000, Irene went into labour. Dympna O'Kane was on hand to help her once more, bringing her for a drive around Louth. While driving through the village of Blackrock, Irene's waters broke and they made their way back to Ice House. In a later statement, Dympna would say of Alan that night: 'He appeared at some stage as Irene was ringing him to get him out of the pub. Alan came back to the house. He continued drinking. When Irene and I came back from Blackrock it was about 7 p.m. The nurses didn't arrive until after 10 p.m. We were upstairs and he was downstairs drinking. You could see the disappointment and frustration on Irene about the way Alan was behaving.' That night their baby girl Dairine was born, the couple's second child, and Irene's third.

With a wife and three children to look after, Alan White was looking at other potential business opportunities to provide a comfortable life for his family. In the same month that Dairine was born, Alan's friend Niall Power set up a company called Premier Protection and Surveillance Security, which became known as PPS Security. Niall was from Jenkinstown, a small village outside Dundalk on the Cooley Peninsula in County Louth, and had worked with Alan at Classic Security before setting off to pursue his own business ventures. Ten years Alan's junior, Niall looked up to him as a mentor. He did have reservations about setting up the company, having only recently run into trouble with a trawler business that resulted in him owing a lot of money. However, on Alan's advice, Niall decided to proceed with setting up PPS Security, which carried out security work for a number of businesses around Dundalk, including providing door staff for bars in the busy town. One of their employees was Niall's housemate Gerry Ross, while a number of young men from the area were also employed to carry out the security work.

Over time Niall and Alan White became close friends and would socialise in the pubs around Dundalk, planning their business exploits into the early hours of the morning. Their partners would also be invited on occasion, and Irene got to know Niall's girlfriend, Ellen Johnson. From South Africa, Ellen met Niall while working in the Phoenix Bar in 2001, before they became serious and bought a house in the Garybawn area of the town. The romance eventually fizzled out, but Irene remained in contact with Ellen and they would become good friends.

While Alan White appeared to be no more than a casual employee of PPS Security, all indications were that he was the driving force behind Niall's successful business. The company used a room in Ice House as an office, and Irene was brought on board for a period to work as a receptionist. In October 2001 she turned 40 and decided she needed a weekend away to celebrate the milestone. She travelled with a friend to Galway, enjoying two nights respite from family life. It would, however, cost her when she returned home, with her friend later recalling: 'We had a great weekend. We came back and later on that week Irene told me that Alan had gone on a serious binge of drinking, and she said, "I'll not be going away again in a hurry, I paid dearly for my so-called 40th birthday weekend."' Life continued at Ice House.

Dundalk had its fair share of criminality at the turn of the millennium. It was a hotbed for dissident republican activity that had carried over from the Troubles, while organised crime, which was growing in Dublin, started spreading out from the capital into towns around the country, including Dundalk. People in the town also had to contend with day-to-day criminality. After one particularly violent assault in the area in 2002, Alan White decided to install an extensive alarm system at Ice House to provide extra security for his family.

The front door was covered by a camera that, if the doorbell was pressed, activated and relayed a live feed to a monitor inside, through which the family could communicate with any person at the door. Several panic buttons were also dotted around the house, one in each of the three front rooms, while an external security light operated at night. The systems had been installed by Alan's business associate Vincent Dullaghan, who was 14 years younger and from Mooretown in Dromiskin, a townland around 10 kilometres south of Dundalk. The two men had met while working together in Ardee in 1998, and in the intervening years Vincent had set up a security company with his fiancée, Donegal woman Cathy Wilson. The company, Superior Security, was operated from the couple's home in Lannett Cross, Killany, County Monaghan. Both had a close working relationship with Alan and Niall, regularly attending security conferences to familiarise themselves with the latest trends and developments in their business.

Irene and Alan's marriage continued to be strained, and in 2002 she suggested that they attend couples counselling to solve their problems. Irene believed that her husband's drinking was the main issue in the relationship, something which Alan always denied, but he nonetheless agreed to attend counselling. He went to seven appointments before deciding not to engage in the process any further, while Irene stayed for four more appointments on her own. That August, she realised that going to the couples sessions without Alan was pointless and so began seeing her own counsellor in Dundalk. Her mother, Maureen, also wanted to be closer to her daughter, and towards the end of 2002 she bought a mobile home for €3,500, which was moved into the large back garden at Ice House. The prospect of having his mother-in-law living close by wasn't met with any objections from Alan White. As part of this move, Maureen also signed over her house in Knocknagoran to Irene, on the condition that she would have residency rights there until her death.

The issues at Ice House persisted, and on 20 April 2003 gardaí were called to the family home. Irene had planned to travel to the nearby Carrickdale gym to go swimming with her daughter Dairine, but was prevented from leaving by Alan White. She walked to Dundalk garda station that afternoon, alleging that her husband was blocking her from driving out of the front gate of the home. Garda John Prunty and a colleague accompanied Irene back to Ice House and, as they arrived, Alan emerged from the property. Garda Prunty spoke to him about the allegation Irene was making, with her husband becoming angry when confronted with the accusation, explaining that he did not want their daughter leaving with Irene. As Alan spoke Garda Prunty noticed a strong smell of alcohol from him and thought that he was slightly incoherent too. While Alan acknowledged that he had been drinking, he said he was annoyed that gardaí had been called to his home.

Alan White became increasingly irate and made a scene, leaving the garda with no option but to direct him to desist and go back into the house. Having persisted momentarily, Alan was cautioned and told that he would be arrested under the Public Order Act if he didn't comply with the garda's direction. Having thought better of it, Alan calmed down and went back into his home. After her husband had gone, Irene told the garda that she would consider making a formal complaint. However, she eventually decided against it. Her reasoning for this, she would later inform the garda, was that the difficulties between the couple had eased.

While Ice House was her residence, Irene didn't have any legal entitlement to the property, and so on 9 October 2003 she registered her marriage against the house, which prevents a spouse from selling the family home without their partner's consent. The following month Irene once again called to Dundalk garda station to inform Garda Prunty that her husband had removed a substantial amount of money from their children's credit union accounts. The sums withdrawn included a total of €6,500 in May 2003 and €5,000 in January 2002. She had lodged the money into the accounts following the sale of her house in Ashbrook, and Irene told the garda that she only wanted to have the matter noted, as she believed she could retrieve the money. In truth, no crime had actually been committed, as Alan White's name was also on the accounts, and he was entitled to withdraw the money.

While in the station that afternoon, Irene also spoke with Garda Colin Dempsey, who was locally known as the 'domestic violence guard' in Dundalk. He had, up to that point, served with An Garda Síochána for 22 years and specialised in issues relating to gender-based violence. This was despite the fact that no such designated role existed in the force in the 2000s, with Garda Dempsey ahead of the curve in providing specialised help to countless women, and men, within the district who had come to him with complaints about domestic abuse. Irene would meet with Garda Dempsey on more than 10 separate occasions over the next year, in many instances chatting to him at domestic-violence seminars. During their conversations, Irene would outline her ongoing marital difficulties with Alan, revealing a pattern of verbal abuse and describing how she was constantly being put down by her husband. On some occasions, she alleged, he had been physically threatening to her to the extent that she was becoming very fearful of him.

In one meeting with the garda, Irene described Alan as a 'Jekyll and Hyde' personality – she didn't know from one minute to the next how he would be. Garda Dempsey informed her of her options under the Domestic Violence Act and strongly advised her to make a complaint, but she declined. The garda believed she was gathering the strength to seek help and support from other services. Over the months, the cycle of abuse being disclosed was growing much worse, with Irene alleging that her husband's behaviour was becoming increasingly unpredictable, while he was also constantly picking on her daughter Jennifer.

Despite regularly meeting with gardaí, Irene hadn't yet made a formal complaint over the allegations, in the hope that things would get better. Other unforeseen issues were to develop. Telecommunications company Eircom owned a yard directly beside Ice House and in the summer of 2003 started inquiring about the possibility of developing their land. Any expansion, however, would be difficult, given that their yard bordered the White family home. That November, an Eircom representative arrived at Ice House to speak with the home-owners. Would Alan White be interested, the Eircom official asked him, in selling the property to the telecommunications company? It was a meeting that would set off a chain reaction and lead to matters deteriorating within Ice House.

2

ICE HOUSE

The White family home was a modern two-storey flat-roofed house, located just outside of Dundalk town centre. The driveway at the front looked out onto Demesne Road, and a large garden at the rear of the property was used by Irene to grow organic vegetables and herbs. The seven-foot-high rear boundary wall backed onto Ice House Hill, a 12-acre public park which got its name from a double-vaulted chamber located on the grounds that had been used to store blocks of ice and food. It had once belonged to Dundalk House and the Earl of Clanbrassil, dating back to the 17th century, but had been left derelict until 1994, when restoration work was commissioned by the town council and funded by a local family.

The works carried out on Ice House Hill included the integration of the parkland perimeter with the surrounding neighbourhood, the burying of overhead cables underground, and the inclusion of gravel walkways that criss-crossed through the park. Four entrances were created for the green area: two at the O'Hanlon Park estate, one from Demesne Road, and one from the Pearse Park estate. The restoration work resulted in the park becoming a popular amenity for walkers and joggers, who used the mile-long pathway in the park. It would also prove a favoured location for local youths and drunkards to hang out. To the other side of Ice House was the large yard owned by Eircom, while a short walk up the road on Park Drive was Hynes Shop, run by Tony Hynes and his wife, Jennifer, who came to know the Whites who regularly used their store over the years.

Alan was interested in selling the house to Eircom, but while negotiations were still in their infancy, problems persisted within the marital home. In March 2004, Irene accused Alan of leaving the family without money to pay for heating oil over the course of two days. When she confronted him about this at the Phoenix Pub in Dundalk, he was said to have made a laugh out of her in front of other punters. The following month, with no signs of matters improving, Alan White drew up what he termed the 'Good Friday Agreement' – a deed of separation. The plan was for this to be put in place out of court, instead of the separation terms being decided by a judge. Among other things, it set out the division of any money derived from the sale of Ice House, advising that the couple each put away €35,000 from the sale for the children's education and upkeep. Ultimately, however, the couple couldn't agree on the terms of Alan's 'Good Friday Agreement'.

A month later there was trouble between Alan White and his stepdaughter. On 23 April 2004, she was treated by a local doctor for an injury to her eye. It was alleged that Alan pushed her and that when she went into the kitchen he followed her and hit her head against a kitchen press. While she received medical treatment from a local doctor for her injuries, no formal complaint was made to gardaí about the incident, which Alan denied happened. That May, Anne Delcassian had returned to Louth for a civil court hearing relating to another cottage in Omeath. The sisters hadn't spoken much since Maureen had willed the property Ceol to Irene, but they were always cordial. Anne met Irene on that visit home and would later recall how her sister 'seemed in good form' and 'never mentioned any difficulties she was having with Alan'.

Two months later, in July, Alan White had been at a funeral and returned home at around 7 a.m. the following morning. Irene went into Jennifer's room and picked up a radio, which had been borrowed from her friend Kerri Hynes, and brought it into her own room. Later recounting this incident to gardaí, Jennifer told them:

I was dozing off and Mam put the radio on and played some weird music fairly loud. This was because Alan had stayed out all night. Mam went downstairs and left the music blaring upstairs. Alan came stomping out of his room and into Mam's room, and he grabbed the radio. When I saw him, I ran into the room to try and stop Alan damaging the radio. Alan opened the window, and I was shouting at him not to throw it out because it wasn't mine. He threw the radio out the landing window and it ended up in the side garden. I think Alan went back to bed. After that I brought the radio back into the house and the tape cover was broken and one of the speaker covers was broken. I could still play the radio and the CD.

By this time Alan White had also purchased a cottage that he was renovating in Knockbridge, a rural village outside of Dundalk. He felt that his new property needed security, expressing concern to his friends about a particular individual potentially causing damage to the property. Alan decided to remove the extensive security system at Ice House, with plans to install it in the Knockbridge cottage, despite the fact that the family were still living in Ice House. That autumn, Irene decided enough was enough. The ill-treatment she was being subjected to by her husband, and his worsening behaviour towards her daughter, was something she could no longer take. In August she decided to initiate her own separation proceedings.

The plans to sell Ice House were still going ahead, to the point where a purchase price had been proposed by Eircom. They were offering Alan White €925,000 for the home, well above market value and the £66,000 (€72,000) mortgage that had been taken out on the property in 1995. As Irene also lived there with their children, Eircom insisted that she should be involved in the sale and that nothing would proceed without her. In late September, an Eircom representative met with Alan and Irene at the Fairways Hotel in Dundalk, where a lengthy discussion took place about the sale of Ice House. While progress had been made, there were concerns about timelines being met to complete the deal. The Eircom official would later say that they felt a price had been agreed, subject to terms and conditions.

Within the marital home the catalogue of incidents continued to build, and that October Irene alleged that her husband had purposely knocked a plate of food out of her hand. In another incident weeks later, it was claimed that Alan White had thrown another radio, which Jennifer had been listening to while doing homework, out of the back door. When Jennifer later spoke to gardaí about this incident, she told them: 'He started saying smart comments to me and he was winding me up and I was trying to wind him up as well. He said my boyfriend was a scumbag and I told him a woman beater was worse than that. He lifted the radio and threw it out the back door. I was a bit scared of this.' The boyfriend Alan White mentioned was Angelo O'Riordan, a local youth from Dundalk who had come to the attention of gardaí in the past. Jennifer had begun dating him that summer, and it was a relationship that her mother and stepfather didn't approve of.

On 4 November 2004, Eircom arranged a meeting with Irene and Alan, as well as their legal representatives, to push forward with the sale of Ice House. The meeting appeared productive, and all parties were of the belief that the sale was near completion, with a draft contract agreed in which Irene would be a co-signatory. This was also accepted by Eircom, who included a consent clause in the draft contract. While positive progress had been made in this respect, hostilities continued over the festive period that year. It was alleged that on 13 December Alan returned home under the influence of alcohol and, during an argument with Irene's daughter, took her mobile phone. Later describing this incident to gardaí, Jennifer recalled:

Myself and Mam were in the sitting room and Alan came in and took my phone and brought it upstairs. I went up after Alan and tried to get my phone back. I saw a phone that I thought was mine in Alan's pocket. I went to grab it and it fell on the floor. It was Alan's phone. I bent down to grab the phone and Alan jammed me against the door frame with his leg. He took his phone and when I got to get up Alan tried to push me down the stairs. I grabbed the first thing I saw, which was Alan's shirt pocket, and then I grabbed the banister. Mam came up the stairs and said she would get the phone back, but she didn't.

Jennifer also said that the following morning Alan came in to her and demanded €20 in compensation for the damage done to his shirt. If this was paid over, he told her, she would get her phone back, and he claimed that Jennifer had assaulted him. While gardaí initially believed that Jennifer would make a formal complaint about this incident, the phone was soon returned, and the matter ended there. Just two days later, Alan White left the family and went to live with his mother at her house in St Malachy's Villas. His departure was short-lived, and on the afternoon of 19 December, he returned to visit Damhan and Dairine at Ice House. Irene had gone out to drop off some plastics at a recycling facility and, when she returned, found Jennifer in a distressed state. Her daughter told her that Alan had caught her thumb in the handle of the radio, injuring it.

This time Jennifer decided to make a formal complaint against her stepfather, with gardaí investigating the incident. Alan White was charged with common assault of Jennifer and was subsequently found guilty of the offence the following year. He was spared a criminal conviction and instead received the Probation Act, an unofficial warning given by the courts to a first-time offender that spares them a criminal conviction or sentence.

That month, Irene once again met with Garda Colin Dempsey and outlined how she couldn't take much more of the abuse from her husband. She explained to the garda how Alan was becoming more and more threatening towards her, particularly in relation to the sale of Ice House, and that he was putting her under 'huge pressure' to agree to the sale so that they could go their separate ways. She confided in Garda Dempsey that on a number of occasions her husband had said he would kill her, but she declined to make any sort of a formal complaint. Garda Dempsey again gave her advice on the various mechanisms she could pursue under the Domestic Violence Act to protect herself.

While Ice House had once been fitted with an extensive security system, the safeguards at the home had decreased significantly in the previous 12 months. This was mainly due to the cameras being removed, but even the doors and gates had fallen into disrepair. Two solid timber gates at the side of the house, leading to the back garden, were broken and wouldn't close properly, and a locksmith had to be called to the house. Irene wanted the gates repaired to enable a security company to fix the electrics but, on inspecting the gates, the locksmith noticed that the control panel for the electrics had completely gone and wasn't working. He fitted a bolt to the gates so that Irene could lock them, and he noted that the back door of the house was also in bad condition, particularly one of the door panels. The locksmith placed a few screws in the panel and tightened it up, while also repairing some of the push bars on the top and bottom of the door.

In mid-January 2005, Irene once again met with Garda Dempsey to discuss the domestic issues that were plaguing her. During the meeting she directly told the garda 'he's going to kill me', referring to Alan White. When she was asked if Alan was capable of this, Irene told the garda that she believed he was, but that he would more than likely get someone else to do it. In a later statement, Garda Dempsey outlined this conversation with Irene, saying he once again advised her to seek a protection order from the courts, which would give her some level of security and peace of mind.

Progress on the sale of Ice House had also hit several obstacles. On 19 January Alan White's solicitor wrote to Irene's legal representative, asking why she wanted to be a co-signatory on the deal when she had no legal interest in the property. Alan White was also refusing to sign the contract, putting the sale in jeopardy. The following day, 20 January, Irene was granted an interim court protection order against her husband. After the hearing she rang Niall Power, asking him to pick up some of Alan's belongings from Ice House, and he arrived a short time later. Niall, though, had other things on his mind. As Irene accompanied him upstairs to get Alan's clothes, he turned to Maureen McBride, who was standing at the bottom of the stairs, and told her, 'We're going to the bedroom for a bit of fun.' Maureen wasn't impressed with the crude remark and reprimanded Niall, telling him not to talk like that.

It became clear that he wasn't interested in just collecting Alan White's clothes. While he was in the bedroom, he began rummaging behind a picture frame sitting on top of a bedside locker, where he found a sum of cash. Irene interrupted him and a row developed before she managed to take the money from him. Niall left the house empty-handed, apart from taking a phone charger belonging to Alan. The incident was reported to gardaí the following morning, but not by Irene. Her husband went into Dundalk garda station to report the incident as a theft, while his solicitor contacted Irene's legal representative, alleging that she was holding onto €1,800 belonging to their client.

On 8 February 2005, Irene decided it was finally time to make her own formal statement to gardaí. Sitting down with

Garda John Prunty in Dundalk garda station, she outlined a series of incidents that had allegedly occurred over the course of her marriage. Many of the allegations had already been relayed to gardaí on an informal basis, but they were now being put into a witness statement as part of a complaint that could be investigated. She told the garda about one specific threat in April 2003, when Alan was alleged to have blocked her from driving out of the front driveway. In her statement, Irene claimed: 'He said if things didn't go his way (meaning the separation), I wouldn't know the hour or the day. I think he said that I would be got and that he would have an alibi. This terrified me and had a major bearing on how I would deal with future incidents of this type with him. I was fearful in a lot of cases after that of involving the gardaí again.' This threat has always been denied by Alan.

She told Garda Prunty that life at home had deteriorated and that her husband's drinking had become unbearable. Irene also said that the sale of Ice House was virtually complete and all she had to do was sign the contracts. However, she also indicated that she wouldn't do so until Alan paid back the money he had withdrawn from their children's bank accounts. After making her statement, she met Garda Dempsey and told him that Alan had threatened her over the money, but she was adamant about standing her ground on the matter, believing it was the only way to recover the funds. According to a later statement made by Garda Dempsey, the last thing Irene said to him as she left the station was 'He would fucking kill me if I don't sign.'

On 10 February, Eircom wrote to both Alan and Irene, outlining how the company was willing to buy the site outright for €925,000 once the contracts were completed by 31 March.

'This date was just to speed things up,' an Eircom representative later explained. 'We were satisfied with the draft contract subject to the same conditions, one of which was the signature of Irene White.' He also said that when they began to investigate the purchase of Ice House as part of the negotiations, they requested a copy of the title of the house. 'We received this which clearly showed Alan White's name was on the title. There was no mention of Irene. Also, in order for us to lodge planning permission with the council we needed written permission from Alan and Irene, which we got on 23 September 2004.'

While separation proceedings were ongoing, Alan White would see his two children away from Ice House. On one occasion, he rang Irene to tell her that he needed a cardigan dropped off for their daughter. He arranged to meet Irene at the bus station in Dundalk and she agreed, but she later confided in a friend that she felt she was being watched by someone. Recalling this, her friend said: 'Irene told me that when she met him at the bus station, whatever he said to her, she had to go out of the car and walk around it, and she told me she got an eerie feeling as if someone was watching her. She told me that she realised when she got back to the house that Dairine did not need a cardigan.'

The couple's finances would also become a factor in the separation. That March, Alan inquired about the insurance policies the family had, including a life assurance policy Irene took out in 1999 valued at £142,000.

As the deadline grew closer for the sale contracts to be signed, Irene was becoming increasingly concerned that she wouldn't receive the half of the sale that she felt she was entitled to. A family friend, Larry O'Hagan, was out for a morning walk in mid-March 2005 when he bumped into Irene outside the Marist College secondary school. She told him about the sale of the house and that they were offered nearly a million euro for it. Irene also told him that she was going to make a will because she wanted the kids to be looked after. Mr O'Hagan would later tell gardaí of the encounter, saying:

I was surprised to hear her talking about making a will, because I thought she would be the one telling me I should have one made. I said with €500,000 each they would be well looked after. She laughed and said, 'I am not going to see any of this money.' I said, 'What do you mean?' She said Alan would make sure of this. I said don't be worrying, that's not going to happen. She always spoke well of Alan up to that point and never spoke of him having assaulted her at any time. I spoke with Irene for about two hours, and we arranged to sit down and talk at a later date. I didn't feel she was in danger.

Around this time, Alan White also wrote a letter to Irene, in which he asked her to set aside their differences and repair the marriage. Irene showed this letter to her daughter Jennifer, who later told gardaí: 'He wrote about his feelings and how much he loved Mam and asking could he come back. This letter was handwritten in Alan's writing. It was on one side of an A4 sheet. Mam kept this letter.'

The deadline of 31 March came and went, and the contracts for the sale of Ice House still hadn't been signed. Irene, though, was working on the basis that they would be and was planning for her future. She began viewing homes in the surrounding area for her and her children to move into. The properties she viewed were in Headfort, County Meath, Haggardstown near

Dundalk, and Mooreland House on the Armagh Road. While conversing with the realtor at Mooreland House, she spoke about how the deal with Eircom was almost finalised and vented about the terrible life she was living with her husband. Irene also said she was hopeful that the contracts would be signed by that weekend.

On 4 April, she viewed a property at Newtownbalregan and later another house on Lower Point Road in Dundalk that had a guide price of €400,000. She was expecting to receive half of the proceeds from the sale of Ice House, which would be more than enough to cover the cost of a new home. That same day her solicitors also contacted Alan's, asking that he sign the sale contract with no delay. Their offices had been closed over the Easter weekend, and her legal representatives were assured that the contracts would be signed. Irene also had a counselling session that afternoon and outlined how she was still in fear of her husband.

The following morning, 5 April, she looked at another house on Lower Point Road, with this property being advertised at a slightly lower price of €360,000. She also called in to her solicitors to collect a cheque for €17,866 that had been awarded to her following an accident claim. Irene had told her friend Diana McKevitt about the claim before collecting it that afternoon and said that, while Alan knew about the payout, she was adamant he 'wouldn't get any of it'.

Alan White had collected their youngest children from Réalt na Mara primary school that day, as per their usual weekly arrangement, and brought them back to his mother's house in St Malachy's Villas. Irene arrived at the house shortly after 6 p.m. to collect Dairine and Damhan and had a brief conversation with her estranged husband. 'I'll see you at the weekend,

Saturday,' he told her, with Irene replying, 'Eleven a.m., isn't that right?' She then guided the children into her car and made the short drive back home to Ice House. Unbeknown to Irene, events would unfold over the next 24 hours that would ensure she never made it to the weekend.

3

FINAL MOVEMENTS

The morning of 6 April 2005 began like any other weekday for Irene White, as she got up early to get her children ready for school. Four days earlier, Pope John Paul II had passed away in Vatican City, and many Irish households were following what was happening there on their televisions at home. Always well presented, Irene dressed for the cold and dry spring morning by putting on a white polo-neck jumper, blue jeans, and moccasin-style beige suede boots as she prepared herself for the day ahead. Shortly before 9 a.m. Irene ushered the younger children into her maroon Mazda, with Jennifer following them out not long after. Irene had become security conscious, and it was something that had been instilled in her children. As Jennifer came out, she closed the front door and waited until she heard the clicking sound to indicate that it was securely shut before getting into the front passenger seat of the car. Irene reversed her Mazda out of the driveway and turned onto Demesne Road, taking the right along the Long Walk and past the Carroll Village shopping centre.

The first drop-off point was the Marist College on St Mary's Road, where Irene pulled over to let her eldest daughter out. Jennifer said goodbye to her mother as she got out of the car, sure to see her again after school that evening. The next stop was Réalt na Mara primary school on Mill Street, where Damhan and Dairine were enrolled. Irene parked outside and went into the school building with the children to speak with teacher Marie Walters. They spoke about a book belonging to Dairine that appeared to have gone missing. Irene told Marie Walters that she hadn't heard her daughter's reading the previous night and said she would text Alan White to find out if he knew where the book was. As she walked out of the school building, she bumped into Yvonne Kennedy, the mother of another pupil. The two women became engrossed in conversation and talked about the sale of Ice House as well as the fact that Irene herself was looking for her own property. Yvonne Kennedy later told gardaí of the encounter: 'I was surprised. She knew by the look on my face that I did not know she was separated. She went on to explain that both her and Alan were separated before last Christmas. She told me that Alan was living with his mother. She was in good form. She said Alan was a bit of a drinker.'

They conversed for almost an hour, but it abruptly came to an end when bird droppings landed on Irene's hair. She used a tissue to clean herself up and remarked that she would have to go home and wash the droppings out. Irene then bid farewell to Yvonne Kennedy and got into her Mazda. Driving out onto Quay Street and on to the bypass, she then passed the Carroll Village shopping centre at 9.49 a.m. on her way back to Ice House, just around the corner. A minute later she had arrived home, with an Eircom employee noticing Irene in her front driveway standing beside her car at 9.50 a.m. She walked in through the front door of her house. Her hair had to be cleaned, and she then began washing the dishes left over from breakfast that morning. Up to this point, it was a normal day for Irene. As she stood over the kitchen sink, there was a loud knock on the back door.

*

At 12.30 p.m. Maureen McBride made her way up to Ice House as she did every day, exiting her mobile home and taking the short walk up the back garden. She knew Irene would be home by this stage so they could have their daily chat over a cup of tea. As Maureen reached the back door of the house, she noticed it was slightly ajar, which was unusual, while music was blaring from the kitchen. Maureen often had difficulty opening the lock on the heavy wooden door and thought to herself, 'Thank God she's here.' Holding a yellow mug in one hand, she gently pushed the door open with her other hand. Maureen walked through the utility room leading into the kitchen, expecting to see Irene inside, ready to greet her. Instead, what met her was a scene of horror.

She looked down and saw her youngest child lying motionless on her back. Irene's hair was disarranged and ruffled over her face, while her hands were laid out on top of her stomach. Shattered glass from a broken jug was scattered across the floor, two wooden chairs were knocked over, and the kitchen table was pushed up against the wall. It was clear Irene had been doing dishes before the chaos that unfolded in the kitchen: she was wearing orange gloves, a J-cloth was on the ground beside her, and the sink was full of water with a draining board placed beside it. A large pool of dark red liquid had formed around Irene, and as Maureen looked closer, she realised that her daughter was lying in a pool of her own blood. She walked over to check on her, but there was no response. Irene's body was cold and limp.

Maureen's throat went dry with the fright of what she was witnessing; she feared she was going to faint as she tried to comprehend the sight in front of her. 'I prayed to God I wouldn't collapse,' she later told gardaí about discovering Irene's body. She needed to raise the alarm but didn't have a phone, so she made her way outside to get help. Maureen had to unlock the front door to exit, and she hurried out of the house over to Tony Hynes's store. The shop owner was at the counter serving a customer as Maureen McBride came through entrance door in a fluster and exclaimed: 'Will you come down quick – Irene is lying dead on the floor.'

Tony Hynes, stunned by what he'd been told, asked his wife to mind the shop as he put his mobile phone into his pocket and rushed up the road to see for himself what was going on. He entered Ice House through the front door and walked up to the kitchen, where he saw a pair of legs sprawled out on the floor. Tony was hoping that Irene wasn't as badly injured as had been made out, expecting her to be sitting up in a daze. When he noticed her legs jutting out, though, he was alarmed that she was still on the floor. Tony took another step forward and now had a full view into the kitchen. He saw Irene's body lying stretched out on the ground at a slight angle, with her head pressed up against the dishwasher. Blood was visible at her mouth and more had formed around her body.

The shopkeeper walked out of the house and at 12.36 p.m. dialled 999 on the keypad on his mobile phone, informing the call taker of what he had just witnessed inside Ice

House. Sergeant Aidan Costello and Garda Mick Geraghty were on patrol in the area and rushed to the scene, arriving there within minutes of the call. They met Tony Hynes, who was standing in the front garden in a very distressed state. He told the gardaí that Irene was lying in the kitchen and that she looked like she had been attacked but that she might still be alive. The gardaí ran into the house and made their way towards the kitchen door. Garda Geraghty saw Irene lying on the ground in a large pool of blood, and also saw bloodstains on the handle of the back door. Irene's eyes were open and her pupils fixed. The garda carefully made his way over to the body, being sure not to interfere with any potential evidence in the kitchen. He lifted Irene's right hand and checked for a pulse, but there was no sign of life.

The radio in the kitchen was still loudly playing music, and he turned the volume down so he could contact the control room in Dundalk to request urgent assistance. Sergeant Costello had also entered the kitchen and looked down at the woman lying lifeless in front of him. He recognised her immediately, having known Irene White for over 20 years from his time stationed at Omeath garda station. The sergeant took charge and directed that the property be cordoned off, as it was now a crime scene, while Garda Geraghty searched through the rest of the house to make sure nobody else was inside. An ambulance had also been requested after the initial emergency call-out, but this was stood down. There was nothing they would be able to do for Irene.

A local priest, Fr Cathal Cumiskey, had been asked by gardaí to go to the scene as a matter of urgency and made his way to Ice House. When he arrived, gardaí told him there was a deceased woman inside, but he was not allowed to go into the kitchen. Fr Cumiskey walked up to the kitchen doorway and said a prayer. He then blessed the body before leaving and going to comfort Maureen McBride, who was still at Tony Hynes's shop. Gardaí also contacted the primary school where Irene's youngest children were still in class and instructed Sr Leonie Marron to keep Damhan and Dairine in their classrooms. Marist College was also notified of the discovery so the tragic news could be broken to Jennifer.

It was obvious that Irene was dead, but a doctor had to formally pronounce it, and within an hour Dr Grace Kenny had arrived at the house. Gardaí asked her if it was possible to declare death without going into the kitchen, so as not to disturb the crime scene. The doctor walked up to the kitchen doorway where she had a clear view of Irene White's body and, after observing her for three minutes, saw there was no sign of any respiratory movements. Irene White was formally pronounced dead at 1.35 p.m.

Word had spread quickly around Dundalk that a woman's body had been discovered in the town, and it didn't take long for local radio station LMFM to air the breaking news on their bulletin. That afternoon, Garda Pat Prendergast was working in the radio control room in Dundalk garda station when he answered the phone at 1.27 p.m. The man on the other end of the line was Irene's estranged husband, Alan White, who said his brother Derek had just phoned and informed him that there had been a murder at Ice House. The garda said that he could not confirm any information at this stage and asked him if he was in the area. When Alan said that he was at the Citywest Hotel in Dublin, Garda

Prendergast told him that he would get the senior investigating officer to call him back. He also noted that Alan White was calm and collected while on the phone to him.

It was obvious to emergency personnel at the scene that the mother-of-three had died violently. Her injuries weren't suffered accidentally or self-inflicted – there had to have been another party involved. A murder inquiry was launched and an incident room established at Dundalk garda station, from where a team of detectives and uniformed gardaí began working on the investigation. Detective Superintendent Jim Sheridan, who had responsibility for serious criminal investigations in the county, was appointed as the senior officer to oversee the murder probe.

Resources from across the garda organisation were drafted into the inquiry to help the local investigation team. Members of the Garda Technical Bureau were immediately dispatched from Dublin to the scene in Dundalk, while the garda's serious crime unit, the National Bureau of Criminal Investigation based in Dublin's Harcourt Square, were also notified of the murder. Local gardaí began carrying out door-to-door inquiries to establish if Irene's neighbours had noticed anything suspicious that morning, while the Office of the State Pathologist was contacted. Within an hour, the scale of what had happened at Ice House was realised and national media outlets began descending on Demesne Road. Press photographers lined up behind the garda cordon outside the property to take pictures of the garda forensic teams entering and exiting the house, while reporters began their own canvass of neighbours to find out what they could about the country's latest murder victim.

A short time after Alan White had called the garda

control room, Detective Superintendent Sheridan made contact with him. The senior investigator would have been appraised of the acrimony that existed in the marriage, and it was vital that they establish her estranged husband's whereabouts as soon as possible. Detective Superintendent Sheridan rang Alan White to inform him that Irene had been killed in a suspected homicide and asked him to make his way back to Dundalk. Within an hour Alan White appeared in the lobby of Dundalk garda station and was met by Detective Garda Michael O'Driscoll, who asked him to account for his movements earlier that day. Alan said that he had made prior arrangements to travel to a security exhibition taking place at the Citywest Hotel in Dublin. The plan was to travel there with his business associates Niall Power, Vincent Dullaghan, and Cathy Wilson.

He said Niall had called to his mother's house at St Malachy's Villas, where he was staying, at around 9.30 a.m. that morning, before Alan drove them in his grey Renault Laguna to Vincent's home in Lannett Cross, near Carrickmacross, County Monaghan. Alan explained that shortly after they arrived Niall received a phone call and said he had to return home. The two men then left, and he drove Niall back to St Malachy's Villas to collect his van. 'I returned to Vincent Dullaghan's home, I don't know what time it was,' he told the detective. 'I had coffee there while we waited for Vincent's fiancée Cathy to get ready. The three of us went straight to the expo in Citywest in my car. I was not there very long when I got a call from my brother Derek. I was about to have lunch at the time. Derek said to me "did you hear anything. Sister Leonie was on from the school and said the guards said no one was to take the kids from school."'

Alan said that after being informed of what had happened by Detective Superintendent Sheridan, he then made his way straight to Dundalk garda station.

The detective was aware that the couple were separated and asked Alan White when he was last at Ice House. He said it was on 20 January, the day of the court protection order. He acknowledged that there had been tensions between him and Irene over their separation but that, when he got access to the kids, there was no longer any friction between them. He told Detective Garda O'Driscoll of the plans to sell Ice House, adding that there was no agreement between him and Irene about the disposal of the property. 'I have a cottage at Knockbridge and I am doing it up, so I was in no hurry to sell at Demesne Road,' he said, also telling the detective: 'Jennifer has a boyfriend, Angelo O'Riordan, we did not approve of him and I did not have him in the house. I do not know him well and I did not wish to get to know him.' After taking the statement, Detective Garda O'Driscoll expressed his sympathies to Alan White and told him that gardaí would be in touch.

The investigation was already gathering pace, and gardaí wanted to verify Alan White's account. At 7 p.m. Detective Garda Tom Molloy contacted Niall Power, asking him to come in to the garda station to speak with them about his movements that day, as well as his interactions with Alan. A short time later Niall arrived and was asked to account for his whereabouts earlier. The previous night he had stayed at the home of his girlfriend, Jane McKenna, in Sliabh Foy, Muirhevnamore, and that morning dropped her child to school. Niall said he returned home briefly before making his way to St Malachy's Villas, with Alan then driving them out to Lannett Cross in his car. It was only after arriving there, Niall said, that he realised they would all be travelling in the same car to Dublin. 'When I heard this, I went out to the car and I put my phone up to my ear as if I was talking on it. I came back in and said to Alan, "Come on we have to go, my girlfriend is not well, she might have to go to hospital." I did this because I can't stand Cathy Wilson and couldn't spend the day in the car with her.'

Asked at what time he was dropped back to his van at St Malachy's Villas, Niall said it was between 10 a.m. and 10.15 a.m. He said he then collected Jane before they made their way to the credit union in the town and then travelled to Dundalk Institute of Technology (DKIT) on the Dublin Road. He said the reason for this stop was to meet one of his employees, Anthony Lambe, so he could pay him his wages. Niall added that he first heard about the murder when listening to a radio news bulletin, which incorrectly reported that a woman's body had been found at McSwiney Street, located beside Demesne Road. 'I didn't pass much remarks,' he said.

When I was coming onto the Ballymac Road from the roundabout Alan phoned me. He told me that either Sister Leonie or his brother Derek had phoned to say that the guards had told them to hold onto the kids at the school. He wanted to know if I knew what was going on. He told me he was in the café of the Citywest Hotel, or at least that's the impression I got. I went on home and my mother came home from a funeral in Omeath. She said 'did you hear anything about a body in McSwiney Street' or whatever LMFM had said. I got a second phone call from Alan, who told me he got a phone call from a guard to say that there had been an incident involving a woman and a doctor had been called, but it didn't look good. He broke up and lost the signal and I haven't been talking to him since.

Detective Garda Molloy also asked Niall Power what he knew of the relationship between Irene and Alan. Was it one of violence? Had his close friend confided in him about any troubles they had? Niall Power said that in the last two years or so there had been a breakdown in the marriage and, despite Irene having been murdered just hours earlier, he wasn't complimentary of her.

I was aware that their marriage was not going well over the last two years. [Alan] said that Irene was not contributing anything to the house at all. He spent a lot of time and money on it and after they got married Irene just let the garden go to ruin. Alan worked hard at his marriage, but nothing was ever good enough for Irene and in the last six months or so Alan had just given up. There was nobody else involved with either Alan or Irene. I never seen Alan raising a hand to her. Irene never wanted for anything, she always had a car, gas, clothes, food, etc. all paid for by Alan.

Speaking about the altercation in January when he tried to take money from Ice House, Niall claimed that Irene had verbally abused him.

I suddenly seen another person entirely, she was going ballistic. She was like a woman possessed, screaming at me so loud I couldn't make out what she was saying. I ended up not taking anything except the phone charger which was in my pocket. I actually walked down the stairs backwards until I got out the door. I went to Alan and told him what had happened. I reported it to the guards because I didn't know what I was going to be blamed for. I don't know what guard I was speaking to. Alan wasn't surprised when I told him this.

Niall said that he had last seen Irene on or before 21 March, when he was with Alan in the town centre. There was no cordial greeting or words exchanged between them. He was puzzled as to why anyone would want to murder Irene. He said:

I can't think of any reason why this has happened, and I don't know her to have had any enemies. The only dispute she had that I know of was with Jenny's boyfriend, Angelo. I was definitely not in Irene White's house since the night of the court protection order. I did not assault Irene White on that day, or any other day, and I don't know anyone who did. I am not in possession of any information, other than what I've given you today, relating to the attack on Irene White.

Before finishing, Detective Garda Molloy asked Niall what clothes he had been wearing earlier that day. 'I was wearing the same clothes I am wearing now which is a black pinstripe jacket, a black shirt, black stonewashed jeans and black slip-on shoes,' he replied. His statement was read back to him, and he agreed that it was an accurate account of what he had said. His shirt, trousers, and jacket were later seized to be forensically examined and to determine if any evidence linked to the murder could be recovered from the clothing.

Angelo O'Riordan's name had now been mentioned twice in the first statements taken as part of the murder investigation. Despite there not being an obvious motive for Angelo to murder his girlfriend's mother, he was a young man with a propensity for violence, and gardaí were keen to establish his whereabouts immediately. Detective Gardaí Enda Rice and James Kilgannon were dispatched to the O'Riordan family home in Bellurgan that night to locate him. They arrived at the house, and when they spoke with him, Angelo told the detectives that he had only woken up at around 2 p.m. that day, well over an hour after Irene's body had been discovered. He said that he got a call from a friend at 2.40 p.m. who inquired what the gardaí were doing at his girlfriend's house.

I said I don't know. I told him that I didn't have any credit and I told him to ring Jenny and ask her what's going on. I didn't hear anything back from him, so I started sending Jenny 'call me' messages by text because I had no credit. She rang me at 3 p.m., she was in an awful way. She just said her mam is dead and she didn't know what happened. She asked me to come into town to meet her.

Angelo O'Riordan said his mother dropped him into town at around 3.25 p.m. and he met his girlfriend at Tony Hynes's shop.

The gardaí asked him how he got on with Irene and Alan White, with Angelo saying that he didn't feel welcomed at the house by either.

Her mother never said anything to me to make me feel unwelcome, but I just knew. I only went into the house

when Jenny was there on her own. I never met her stepfather as such but there was one time I was at the door
and Jenny answered it. Her father couldn't see who was at
the door, so he went around the side and came in the front
door and pushed me aside as he passed by me. Jenny was
out here staying with us at Christmas after the stepfather
Alan had got rough with her.

The last time he was at Ice House was the previous afternoon, and when asked what clothes he had been wearing
earlier that day, Angelo said he was wearing a grey and navy
Adidas top, Umbro tracksuit bottoms, and white Nike runners.

*

The first murder case conference was held that night to delegate
jobs that needed to be done, with a full technical examination
of Ice House to be carried out in an effort to uncover any
evidence that could identify the killer. The house would be
sealed off for a further 10 days as gardaí carefully combed
through the property. The items recovered included a digital
safe containing €150, £6.84 in loose change, jewellery, credit
union books in Irene and the children's names, and passports.
The two cheques valued at almost €36,000 that had been issued
as part of the accident claims were also found in the safe,
having not been cashed. Irene's black handbag was found
hanging in the hallway, containing €130.73 along with her
driver's licence. Computer hard drives, memory sticks, and
three cameras were also seized, as well as Irene's diaries, telephone books, and other personal documentation. A shed used
by Alan White located in the back garden was also searched,

with gardaí seizing a computer and hard drive to have them examined.

That evening the state pathologist Professor Marie Cassidy arrived at the scene to carry out a preliminary examination of Irene's remains. Even from a cursory inspection of the body, it was apparent that Irene had suffered several stab wounds, and the pathologist ordered for the remains to be removed to the mortuary at Louth County Hospital for a full autopsy. Shortly after 8 p.m. a hearse carrying Irene White's body made the sombre journey to the morgue, accompanied by gardaí.

With the body removed, the scene could now be examined in detail by the Garda Technical Bureau. Detective Garda Shane Curran, a ballistics specialist, examined the blood splatter that had formed around Irene as she lay mortally wounded on the kitchen floor. Blood samples were also taken from her body and the rubber gloves she was wearing to compare with any samples retained during the investigation. In the middle of the floor, beside Irene's body and among the blood-splatter patterns, was a distinctive bloody footprint. It pointed in the direction of the back door, where gardaí noticed other similar footprints. The marks were followed out into the back garden and towards the rear wall, with a single footmark also being located in the soil among bushes on the other side of the wall in Ice House Hill park. Detective Garda Curran made footwear casts of the impressions as well as gel lifts to send to the Forensic Science Laboratory for analysis. It was estimated that the prints had been left by a person wearing Nike Air International Max runners with a shoe size of between 9 and 10.

All gardaí present at the scene were asked to hand over their footwear, which confirmed that they hadn't accidentally left the footprints, and an examination of the other shoes in the house didn't match them either. They were too large to belong to Irene or Maureen, and Tony Hynes hadn't entered the kitchen when he went to check the scene. The only person who could have left the large bloody footprint beside Irene White's lifeless body was the person who had stabbed her to death. The murder of a mother in her kitchen, by a killer who was now on the loose, was sure to cause concern in the area and lead to a media frenzy. The investigation team had to identify who the bloody footprints belonged to, and quickly. They also needed to know why an innocent housewife had become a target for such a vicious and cold killer.

4

34 STAB WOUNDS

As Professor Marie Cassidy carefully examined the body lying on the table in front of her at Louth County Hospital, the sheer barbarity of what Irene White had been subjected to became clear. Even for someone as experienced as the state pathologist, the level of violence used in the murder marked a savage and unwelcome new departure. There were multiple stab wounds around her neck, with one large cut-throat injury measuring 16 centimetres in length. More knife wounds were visible on the front of her body, as well as some small puncture wounds, with 14 of these injuries to her upper chest and another to the stomach. The cuts were deep and had been administered with force, as they penetrated Irene's lungs, heart, and liver. Professor Cassidy recorded a further 14 stab wounds to the back of the body, with all but one to the left upper back. There were also three stab wounds on her right arm, two on her left arm, and a short incised cut on the right index finger. There were no head injuries, apart from the cut-throat wound, while Irene had also been stabbed twice in the heart. Seven of the wounds had penetrated both of Irene's lungs. Irene White had been stabbed a total of 34 times.

In her report, Professor Cassidy concluded that death occurred following an assault with a knife, during which Irene suffered multiple wounds to her neck, front, back, and arms. She ruled that the penetrating chest injuries were the cause of death and that a narrow-bladed knife with a single sharp edge and blunt back was the likely murder weapon. Due to the irregularity of the surface injuries, she believed that the knife used may have had a serrated cutting edge. The state pathologist also concluded that, despite the appearance of numerous wounds, one knife would have been used to inflict all the injuries. She also said that the pattern of injuries indicated that Irene had moved, or had been moved, during the assault and that some of the wounds to her front were probably inflicted while she was lying defenceless on the floor.

One senior investigator says of the injuries Irene suffered:

The post-mortem revealed that Irene had been stabbed a total of 34 times. She never stood a chance. The level of violence used in the crime shocked even the most experienced detectives. Some gardaí who witnessed the scene and saw her body lying on the kitchen floor were deeply impacted by it. It was a cold and vicious crime and the person involved made sure that Irene wouldn't survive. There was the added possibility that Maureen McBride could have come across the killer in the kitchen. What would have happened if that was the case?

Establishing a motive for the murder would be crucial to identifying the killer, and the detective branch looked at the possibility that Irene was the victim of a random burglary that went tragically wrong. The hypothesis was unlikely, with professional burglars by their very nature being non-confrontational criminals. They prefer to target unoccupied homes, giving them time to go about their nefarious business undisturbed, and most would run when challenged. Gardaí found no signs of a break-in at the rear door or at any other access point to the house, and Irene was unlikely to have let a complete stranger into her home. Irene's handbag was still hanging in the hallway when gardaí arrived, beside the kitchen door, with over €100 in cash still in the bag. If a burglar had broken into her home, the handbag would have presented itself as an easy taking. Gardaí also reviewed a list of burglaries that had been carried out in the area in recent times to determine if any of these incidents had a similar modus operandi to the crime at Ice House. A look through the garda PULSE system showed that, in the month leading up to the murder, there had been 25 burglaries in the Dundalk district. While some were aggravated, with weapons being produced, none involved any significant levels of violence.

Gardaí were quickly satisfied that a burglary gone wrong could be ruled out as a possible reason for the murder. They also had to consider if the killing had some sort of sexual motive, with two rapes reported in Dundalk the previous month, one of which was a random attack. Again, though, the evidence at the scene as well as the post-mortem examination didn't support the possibility that the murder was sexually motivated. The level of violence inflicted on Irene could also shed some light on the reason for the murder. The 34 knife wounds were 'overkill', a term for a specific type of homicide where the number of injuries inflicted greatly surpasses the number necessary to prove fatal and indicate an impulsive, sadistic, or personal motive. Gardaí began looking at the latter of these as the reason for why Irene was murdered.

The mother-of-three had become the 49th woman to die violently in Ireland since the turn of the millennium. At the time of her murder, gardaí were continuing to hunt the man who'd murdered Rachel Callaly (30) at her home in Naul, County Dublin, the previous October. While unconnected, the crimes bore similarities, as both involved a housewife being targeted in their own home after dropping their children to school. Irene's murder had been the second case of femicide in the state in 2005, but it wouldn't be the last even that week. On 8 April, two days after Irene's murder, the charred remains of Emer O'Loughlin (23) were found in a caravan near Tubber on the Galway–Clare border and her death was later upgraded to a homicide inquiry. Less than two weeks later, on 22 April, Mary Hannon (59) was murdered at her home in Hampton Court, Inchicore, Dublin, stabbed 14 times by her husband Martin Kinneavy.

Femicide figures indicate that around nine in ten women who die violently are killed by a person known to them, with just over half of these killings carried out by a current or former partner. The investigation team had to identify and speak to the men Irene had been involved with. They had already taken an initial statement from Alan White, and the following day Irene's ex-partner George Bannister was requested to call in to Dundalk garda station and speak with members of the detective branch. He was asked about his relationship with Irene since things had been broken off, explaining that they had met on many occasions and were always polite and courteous to one another. The last time he'd spoken to her was the day before she died, when Irene phoned George, arranging to meet up with him and Jennifer. George told his ex-partner that he was sick but would meet her that Friday for a coffee.

Asked about his movements on the day of the murder, he said he was at home in Oaklawns, Dundalk, which his landlady later confirmed, and that he got a phone call at around 3 p.m. from his daughter's friend informing him of what had happened. 'She said that Jennifer's mother had been murdered. I could not believe it. I thought it was a late April Fool's trick. When I got there, the guards were there, and the house was taped off. I spoke to the guards there, but they would not confirm anything for me. I was directed to Hynes's shop and I made my way there. I met Jennifer and her grandmother. I spoke to Jennifer outside on the street, she was in a state of shock.' The gardaí knew that George Bannister wasn't a man of violence, and he also had an alibi, so they quickly ruled him out of their inquiries.

George Bannister was also asked about Irene's estranged husband, saying that the first time he'd encountered Alan White was at Jennifer's confirmation in St Patrick's Church a few years earlier. 'I remember meeting Alan that day and I was impressed with him, I was delighted that Irene had met what seemed a decent bloke, job, money.' However, he said that about 18 months before the murder, his daughter Jennifer called him and relayed how she was being tormented by Alan. 'She was not getting on with Alan. In fact, one time Jenny stayed with me about three or four months ago,' George told the gardaí.

Alan White was a person that gardaí needed to look at in greater detail. As well as the ongoing separation, there were serious disagreements around the sale of Ice House. Only three months earlier, Irene had also obtained a court protection order against him. His business partner, Niall Power, was visited again by gardaí on 7 April at his home in Jenkinstown. Their questions this time focused on what Alan White had been wearing the previous day. Niall explained that his friend would normally wear suit trousers and a shirt and tie, and was always well dressed, unless he was doing work in his garden or at the cottage in Knockbridge. 'Yesterday I think he had a suede jacket, light brown in colour, slacks, shirt and tie but I can't be 100 per cent sure,' Niall told gardaí. He had never known Alan to wear a tracksuit and, when specifically asked about what footwear he would use, said he doubted that Alan even owned a pair of runners.

Gardaí later seized some of Alan White's clothing, including a tie, shirt, trousers, underwear, a belt, and socks. Nothing of evidential value was discovered, though, with the Forensic Science Laboratory confirming that no blood was present on any of the clothing. Alan's grey Renault Laguna was also forensically examined, but gardaí found no signs of a recent clean-up or anything untoward in the car. An electronic sweep was carried out of Ice House, to see if any devices had been placed around the home to surreptitiously monitor Irene. In a report on their examination, gardaí noted that no unexpected devices were found, but that a significant amount of installed wiring was found that 'would be surplus to what would be expected in a standard alarm system'.

In a follow-up statement in the days after the murder, Alan White was asked about the removal of the security system at his family home. He said that they weren't in the habit of using the alarm, apart from when they went on holidays or if they were all away at the same time, and that it was in working order when he had left the home. He said:

At one time Ice House was well covered by security cameras. I had cameras covering the external area around the house, I would have had eight or nine cameras. The system was recording and was viewable from inside. I had this installed around the time the wee child was attacked and raped on the Castletown Road in Dundalk. This system was removed because of the impending sale of the property to Eircom and part of it is now being installed in the cottage at Knockbridge. This system was removed about last summer and maybe later.

While Alan White's movements up to 10 a.m. on 6 April had been corroborated by Niall Power, gardaí needed to speak with those who could verify his account for the rest of the day, specifically at the time of the murder. Two members of the detective branch were dispatched to Lannett Cross to speak with Vincent Dullaghan and Cathy Wilson. Sitting down in one room with Detective Garda James Kilgannon, Vincent explained that he was planning on setting up a camera-monitoring company with Alan and Niall and that a premises had been arranged for the business. 'Basically, it would mean that Alan would be able to monitor the cameras that I had on a given secure premises,' he explained. They needed to look at monitoring stations to use for their new business and had arranged to go to the security exhibition taking place at the Citywest Hotel in Dublin.

Recalling 6 April, Vincent said he looked at the clock that morning with the time showing 9.25 a.m. A short time later Alan and Niall arrived, but he said that Niall got a phone call not long after and the two men left. Vincent was 'almost certain' that Alan returned to Lannett Cross at 10.10 a.m. 'As soon as Alan came back, we left for Dublin because we were supposed to have a meeting at 12 noon in Dublin. Myself and Cathy went with Alan in his car. I don't know what time we arrived at the Citywest Hotel, but I do know we were on the Red Cow Roundabout at 12.15 p.m. because we were late for our meeting, and I looked at the clock in the car.' Vincent said they had just sat down to eat shortly after arriving at the expo when their meal was interrupted.

> We didn't even get to have lunch because Alan's brother Derek called him, but he could not hear him with all the noise so Alan said 'it sounds like he is in a fluster, I better phone him back'. Alan phoned Derek back, but he could not tell him much, only that something had happened at Ice House. So, then Alan rang Dundalk garda station but the garda on the desk did not know much. So, then a few minutes later [Detective Superintendent] Jim Sheridan rang Alan back and then we knew something was wrong in Dundalk and we left to come back. Alan drove myself and Cathy back to Dundalk and we came down the motorway, the M1, and we went through both toll bridges. We went straight to Dundalk garda station.

Vincent Dullaghan said he'd last met Irene in March 2004 when she came into the Phoenix Pub in Dundalk to confront Alan about their home having no heating. 'Basically, I stopped calling to Irene because I did not want to hear her giving out about Alan. I have never heard Alan give out about Irene. He often said that she had told lies in court in relation to other problems they had but that was it. The only reason Alan took the cameras from the house was to put them up on his house in Knockbridge because he was afraid somebody might put a skip on fire on him, and the cameras were there to prevent this.'

In another room of the house, Detective Garda Enda Rice took a statement from Cathy Wilson, who had known for some time that the Whites' marriage wasn't going well. 'She wanted Alan out of her life and especially when Eircom made the offer on their home,' Cathy explained. She said that on 6 April, Alan and Niall arrived at her home but left immediately after Niall had received a phone call. Alan rang their landline around 15 minutes later to say he was on his way back. Cathy believed he returned sometime between 10.20 a.m. and 10.25 a.m. 'We left the house at around 10.30 a.m. or 10.45 a.m. and headed. Alan was relaxed and I asked him about Irene and the kids, and he seemed happy enough. He said that she was throwing the kids at him with regards to access and it was great. He said that he would have them for two weeks in the summer and was wondering where to take them.'

Cathy told the detective that the trio signed in to the Citywest Hotel expo at around midday and, shortly after arriving, her companions complained that they were hungry. They decided to sit down for lunch but Alan then received a phone call informing him that something serious had happened at Ice House. 'He was getting agitated because he didn't know what was going on and the kids were involved. I suggested he ring the guards and Vincent agreed with me.' Cathy said they made their way straight back to Dundalk and described Alan as being 'annoyed' on the way home because he didn't know what had happened and whether Irene was dead or alive.

The accounts needed to be verified, and members of the crime branch travelled to the Citywest Hotel. They looked over registration slips for the event, which showed that Alan,

Vincent, and Cathy had indeed all signed in at 12.39 p.m. CCTV footage from the venue corroborated their presence there, while a garda based in Monaghan, who was at the expo, also confirmed that he had met all three that afternoon. There were some slight discrepancies in the accounts provided by Vincent and Cathy. He placed Alan as being back in Lannett Cross at 10.10 a.m., while she put this time close to 10.25 a.m. Alan's mother, Florence, was also spoken to and recalled seeing Niall Power's van driving away from her house at around 10 a.m. Test drives were later carried out by gardaí to determine the time it would take to drive from St Malachy's Villas to Lannett Cross at that hour of the morning. If Alan White had left his mother's home immediately after dropping Niall off, then he would have returned to Lannett Cross by 10.20 a.m.

Alan's phone records were also reviewed, which showed that he had received two calls on the morning of the murder: one from Vincent Dullaghan at 9.50 a.m. and one from Niall Power at 11.36 a.m., while Alan was on the way to Dublin. He had also made two calls, one to a painter carrying out work at the Knockbridge cottage and another to the landline in Lannett Cross at 10.31 a.m. That meant that Alan White couldn't have returned to Vincent Dullaghan's home any earlier. However, even though there were slight anomalies in the times, it was impossible for Alan White to have dropped Niall off, travelled to Ice House, and then made his way back to Lannett Cross in such a short space of time. There was also nothing in Vincent's and Cathy's statements to indicate that Alan had been involved in any sort of violent altercation or that he changed his clothes. Irene's estranged husband had a solid alibi for the time of her death, as he had allegedly predicted.

*

Three days after she was murdered in her home, Irene White was laid to rest amid heartbreaking scenes of grief in Dundalk. The funeral service took place at St Patrick's Church, where Irene had married Alan seven years earlier. Alan, Jennifer, and the McBride family accompanied Irene's coffin into the church, with a white floral tribute with the word MUM spelt out in pink flowers adorning the casket, to signify Irene's main devotion in life. Students from Réalt na Mara and Marist College formed a poignant guard of honour as Irene's remains were slowly carried into the church. Chief celebrant Father Mark O'Hagan told the shocked congregation on that grey Saturday morning that the community was in mourning and that Irene's family were left with the feeling they had been robbed. 'They are left to take in Irene's death. They are left alone and bewildered. They are feeling a deep loss of a future without hope,' he told the hundreds of mourners who had turned out to pay their respects. Fr O'Hagan told the congregation that Irene's death had left her family in darkness. 'We have all experienced an electrical blackout. There is no television, no cooker and worst of all no lights. We are all plunged into darkness, leaving us all feeling lost, helpless, and frightened. A tragic death like that of Irene is a little like a blackout. One minute she was here full of life, and the next there is nothing, only darkness.' He said that now was the time to look back on memories of Irene and find refuge 'in the little things – in the things that you thought about her'. After the service, Irene's remains were taken for burial to Omeath, where she was laid to rest in the village cemetery with prayers led by local parish priest Fr Jim Carroll.

The following day, a Sunday newspaper led with a story on their front page titled 'Rachel Copy Cat Murder'. The story outlined how gardaí believed the murder of Irene White bore 'chilling similarities' to the killing of Rachel Callaly the previous October. Retired Detective Inspector Pat Marry was at that time the senior investigator overseeing the Callaly murder inquiry. Discussing both cases now, he says that while they were similar crimes, they were completely separate investigations – although the man who would later be convicted of Rachel Callaly's murder did discuss Irene's killing with him.

When Irene White was murdered, I was a detective sergeant in Balbriggan, and even though it was in north Dublin, it was then part of the Louth/Meath policing division. Once a major crime occurred in the division, such as a murder, all detective units took stock, as they could be called in to assist in the initial stages of the investigation. We were not required, however, as the incident room in Dundalk was well manned by experienced local detectives.

Irene's murder was a vicious affair, and the scene indicated the actions of a deranged killer. The previous October we had our own murder, that of Rachel Callaly in Naul. Rachel was bludgeoned to death in her own home after leaving her children to school, as Irene White also had. Both women were alone in the house when their attackers struck and, by coincidence, both were working as Avon reps. They were the only connections between the murders.

I remember talking to Rachel's husband, Joe O'Reilly, about her murder, and he specifically referred to the unsolved murder of Irene White. I often thought in those early stages, if I caught Rachel's killer, would it be the same person that murdered Irene. This is the way one would think in the early stages, but as we know, the evidence and pattern of the investigation led to Joe O'Reilly, who was later convicted of his wife's murder, and he had nothing to do with Irene White's death.

While not being initially required in the Dundalk case, in time Pat Marry would become centrally involved in the Irene White murder investigation.

With his wife now deceased, Alan White could proceed with the sale of Ice House to Eircom, but there would be legal efforts to stop this. On 13 April, a week after the murder, Maureen and Jennifer McBride applied to the High Court for an injunction to prevent the property from being sold. Justice Joseph Finnegan was told that Irene had been murdered in the family home and that a murder investigation was being carried out by gardaí.

Counsel for Maureen McBride said her client believed that Irene and Alan had agreed to sell their family home at Ice House to Eircom for the purchase price of €925,000, and that the proceeds of the sale were to be divided equally between the parties. Maureen was concerned that, unless restrained by the court, Alan would dissipate or transfer the monies received from the sale of the family home, and Irene's estate, out of the jurisdiction. The request was granted, and under the court injunction, Alan White and all persons who had notice of the order were restrained from completing the sale of the house until the following week, when the case was due to return before the court. Alan was also restrained from entering the property at Knocknagoran in Omeath, which was in Irene's name, and from interfering in any way with any assets forming part of Irene's estate.

On the day that the High Court injunction was granted, Detective Sergeant Bill Piper met Alan White at St Malachy's Villas to take another statement from him as part of the investigation. Discussing his marriage, Alan said that they had got on 'very well for a couple that were separating', and added: 'I want to put it on record that I never had a relationship with a woman outside my marriage to Irene and I'm still not involved with anybody. I don't really suspect that Irene was involved with another man while she was married to me.' By all accounts, Irene White was a respectable woman in the community who was liked by most people she encountered. She wasn't known to be in dispute with anyone, save for her husband, and didn't approach life in an adversarial way that would have made her a target for anyone. But gardaí had to speak to those closest to Irene to be sure that she didn't have any enemies that they didn't know about. Only one name featured time and time again.

5

LIVING IN FEAR

As gardaí interviewed Irene White's family in the days after her murder, they soon realised that she had been confiding in a lot of people about fears she had for her own safety. While recalling finding her daughter's body, Maureen was asked if Irene had fallen out with anyone recently. Irene was a 'very honest' person, her mother said, and she was shocked at the thought that anybody would want to harm her. 'We got on very well and she didn't deserve that. I don't think Irene had any enemies apart from Alan,' she told gardaí.

Irene's friends also painted a similar picture to detectives when spoken to about the months and years leading up to her death. Rosemary Jones had met Irene when she was co-opted onto the Omeath Development Committee, and the two struck up a friendship, growing closer as the years went on. She recalled Irene visiting her house one day and crying as she spoke about her relationship with Alan. 'She did say that she thought that there was a department within the gardaí that she could go to for professional help and advice,' Rosemary said in her statement.

Before she left, I advised her to go and get help and advice, and that she should go and talk to that person in the gardaí. She asked me to say a prayer for her and asked me for a hug. She was so upset leaving here that I rang her every day to check that she was okay. At some stage I began to be careful what I said on the phone because Irene became fearful that the phones were bugged. Irene said that Alan suggested that instead of them splitting up that they would live separately in the house.

Rosemary told gardaí that Irene had only found out about the planned sale of Ice House through her solicitor, after developers began looking at the site. 'I think it was then she realised that was why Alan didn't want a separation, that he wanted to stay in the house.' Her friend became concerned for Irene's wellbeing when she began regularly asking Rosemary to say a prayer and light a candle for her. 'I repeatedly asked her "are you safe?" She said, "I think so." Irene was a very good friend and I will miss her very much. She certainly didn't deserve what happened to her. She said that she confronted Niall and took the money from him. She was very distrustful and afraid of Niall,' Rosemary added.

Irene had also confided on multiple occasions in one of her closest friends, Dympna O'Kane, about her issues with Alan. 'She said that when he was drinking, he came out with vile and abusive talk,' Dympna said in one statement to gardaí. 'She called it the stinking thinking. She told me that he called her a whore, a slut, a tramp and vile filth. She told me about his mood swings, at times he wouldn't talk to her and then when he did it was all vile. She said he sometimes drank all night and when she got up to get the kids out for school the vile abuse would start from Alan.'

The previous November, Irene had rung Dympna, saying she wanted to speak with her. 'Irene said that she needed to tell me things in the event of anything happening to her. At this stage Irene's relationship with Alan had completely gone,' Dympna told gardaí. 'She repeated the words Alan said to her and they were "you'll not see it coming, you'll not know the day or the hour, and I'll have an alibi". Irene was fearful that something was going to happen to her. She wanted me to know about this.' The last time Dympna spoke to Irene was four days before the murder, telling gardaí that her friend had a 'load of things' she wanted to discuss. She said Irene had been speaking to Ellen Johnson, Niall Power's ex-girlfriend, who had told her things that concerned her. Dympna was mourning the death of her father a week earlier, and the two women agreed to meet that Wednesday night to talk. However, hours before their planned catch-up, Dympna got the phone call saying that her friend was dead.

Aine McCourt, who had known Irene from their school days, also spoke to gardaí and said her friend relayed similar concerns to her. 'While I found Alan okay, I have no reason to doubt what Irene told me. Through my work in social welfare, I have often come across people who appear to be nice on the outside but are someone very different underneath. For all the years I know Irene, we have never had a falling-out, and I have never heard her bad-mouthing anyone. Irene was always trying to keep the best side out and look on the bright side of things.' Tony Hynes had come to know Irene over the years from her visits to his shop, and he told gardaí that he didn't know Irene to have any enemies. 'She was very likeable and could even pass herself with Angelo O'Riordan even though she didn't approve of him. I was aware that the house was for sale. I heard from Alan himself that the house was being sold for €1 million and I knew that Irene was out looking at houses with auctioneers.'

Tony's wife, Jennifer, initially made a brief statement outlining her recollection of events on the day of the murder, but later contacted gardaí again saying there were more things she wanted to reveal. 'Recently she told me of an incident that happened about four to six months ago on a Sunday morning. Alan was making scrambled eggs in the kitchen. Irene told me that she asked him for some, and he said no. When he moved away from the cooker she put some of the egg on a plate for herself. She told me that Alan then came up behind her and tipped her plate knocking the egg all over the floor. He said, "when I say no I mean no", this is the way Irene explained it to me.' In another conversation the previous Christmas, Irene had told Jennifer Hynes about the alleged alibi threat made by her husband, which she had also disclosed to Dympna O'Kane and reported to Garda Prunty. Gardaí also discovered that the alleged alibi threat had been raised in court by Irene when she'd sought the court protection order against Alan.

Other people spoken to by gardaí, in particular Alan White's family, rubbished any suggestion that he was capable of violence. Their statements also revealed their indifferent attitude towards Irene. Florence White told Detective Garda Mick O'Driscoll that her son was 'very good' to Irene and that he would 'give her anything' she wanted. 'She seldom came to our house; she only came up to me around Christmas or at birthdays. I never had a bad word with her, but we did just not get on well. They got an offer for the house and that seemed to change Irene in a big way. She seemed to want the money, that's all she was interested in, money. Alan was only interested in the children. I don't know who would do that to Irene, it must be a crazy person, or maybe a woman. I don't know why I think that. I even thought that Mo [Maureen McBride] did it, or maybe someone on drugs. Irene was always fond of her body, she thought she had a beautiful body. Alan would always stay an odd night with me over the years, but Irene would know where he was.'

She told gardaí that in recent times her son 'was getting soft towards Irene again' but she had hoped they wouldn't reconcile. Florence White described how Alan was 'very broken up over the way Irene died, you would not wish that on your worst enemy'. Gardaí also spoke to Alan White's siblings to establish what they knew about his marriage. One sister, Patricia, said she didn't think Irene was the right person for her brother. 'Alan was always madly in love with her, and he would always go along with her wishes. I never fell out with Alan over Irene; it was his life. I don't know why anyone would want to kill Irene. I don't know of anyone who would want to do that to her. I have been racking my brain over her death and I have thought about who could have done it. Irene had a circle of friends, and they were all either separated or separating and maybe one of their husbands had enough. Irene would not let anyone into the house unless she knew them very well.'

Another sister, Valerie, said Irene tried to influence Alan to give up the security business, and that she had 'odd ideas' that they did not need to work all the time. 'I never went out socially with Alan and Irene, she was only in my house once. Alan knew how I felt about her, and he would not take her out to our house, she would hardly look at me if she met me in Dundalk.' She said:

When Alan and Irene got married, we were all shocked, I could not believe that he would agree to such a wedding. Not to invite his mother and sisters, we were devastated, it was not like Alan, he was always a quiet lad, would not have liked a big fuss. But if it was up to him, he could at least have invited his mother and sisters. I felt it was because of Irene's wishes that they got married in this way. Alan was a very deep person and did not confide in me during the marriage. He was very good to Irene; he would buy her expensive presents. I have no idea who would have caused the death of Irene, I do feel sorry for her and for Alan. I have their two young children with me since, Damhan and Dairine, they have settled in very well with us, they know their mammy is dead and in heaven. Alan would not bite back or run down Irene at any time.

Irene's friend Helen Conway told gardaí that the deceased wasn't herself lately and that it was evident something was going on. 'Since things started going really bad with Irene and Alan, she told me that he had threatened her. She said he would get her when she wasn't expecting it and that nobody would ever know it was him. I remember saying to her not to pass any remarks on him that he was only trying to scare her,' Helen told gardaí. Another friend, Carmel Lynn, made a statement saying Irene told her she had been offered €200,000 by Alan White from proceeds of the sale of Ice House, so that she could buy a property for herself and the children. 'She said he asked her to sign a document which would give him control of the sale of the house, but she refused to sign. On 28 March 2005, I collected Irene from Dympna O'Kane's father's wake, she showed me a letter from Alan referring to what happened in the past and that he wanted to get back with Irene. She said she couldn't understand how Alan could write a letter like that, and she was going to tell me what happened the previous week. Her main interest in life was the welfare of her children.' Carmel also told gardaí of the time Irene had dropped a cardigan to Alan for their daughter and felt she was being watched. The last time she had seen Irene was four days before the murder, when she seemed 'her normal, happy self'.

It was also important for gardaí to interview the counsellors that Irene had spoken with, to determine if she had revealed any fears within the confidential setting. Her first appointment had been on 8 August 2002, and she last spoke with her counsellor two days before her murder. The investigation team soon established that over the course of 48 sessions Irene had expressed concerns about her husband's apparent anger and aggression. Within the confines of the counselling room, Irene discussed how Alan was abusive to both her and Jennifer and that she kept a record in her diary of instances when this happened. 'I took it from her that a lot of events had happened and that she wanted to keep track of it for future reference,' one counsellor told gardaí. A record from one meeting, in February 2005, noted that Irene felt 'Alan is going to fight her all the way and is capable of anything to get his own way'. In notes from another meeting in November 2003, it was recorded by her counsellor that Irene described Alan as 'devious, cold and callous'. Just two days before her murder, Irene told her counsellor that she was in fear of Alan and what he could be capable of.

The diaries kept by Irene were also reviewed by the garda investigation team and covered some of the alleged abuse she had outlined to her friends. On 21 April 2003, Irene wrote that Alan had threatened her, saying he would have her 'done' but that he would have an alibi. Three months later she made a diary entry about how, while she was washing Alan's jeans, she found a photocopy of her documents including credit cards and shopping cards. In December 2004, she wrote that Alan was showing aggressive behaviour to both her and Jennifer. She alleged he used a lot of verbal abuse and that he would tell the younger children that Jennifer was not part of their family. That same month Irene wrote: 'Alan has said he can't wait to get rid of Jenny and I', that she had no rights to the house, and that she was a failure as a mother.

It was evident that there was animosity from Alan White towards his wife, but another person also appeared to have a grievance against her. Within days of the murder, gardaí spoke to Ellen Johnson, and she had an interesting story to tell. She said that Alan White disclosed 'every aspect' of his personal and professional life to Niall, who in turn relayed the information to her in confidence. 'Niall told me that Alan grew to hate Irene. He despised her. He felt that she was after his money and that was all she was interested in. She was very independent, and this seemed to upset Alan. Once Alan and Niall were planning to set up Irene, the plan was that Niall was going to seduce Irene at Ice House Hill, the seduction was to be taped or recorded by hidden cameras which they both had installed in the house. Alan was going to use this evidence as grounds for separation/custody of his two kids.' In her witness statement, taken on the day of Irene's funeral, Ellen told gardaí that the plan didn't go ahead and that she herself had informed Irene about it the previous Easter Sunday. 'Irene was shocked, she commented: "I would never go to bed with that baldy bastard Niall."' Ellen also informed gardaí that her ex-partner had an illegal firearm and alleged that he had contemplated using it in a murder, but decided against it.

> Niall and Irene relayed to me on separate occasions [that] Alan said: 'You won't know the time or the place, but I will come back and get you and will have a damn good alibi.' Irene also asked would I give evidence about the planned seduction with Niall and herself if required. I told her that I would. Niall told me that he was also involved in the IRA. I don't have any evidence of this. I would imagine if you were involved with the IRA, you would not be mouthing.

She also felt that Niall's character had changed, he had become more aggressive and seemed under the control of Alan. Ellen then went on to make a bombshell claim about her now ex-partner:

> Niall told me once that he was involved in a murder at the border, somewhere north. It was an RUC [Royal Ulster Constabulary] man. This used to give him nightmares. He would often wake up during the night having nightmares and cold sweats. He was consumed with guilt even though this happened years ago, even though this happened in his early 20s. Niall also told me that at times he considered confessing his involvement in this incident to the gardaí. If Niall was abusive to me, I used this knowledge as power of control over him. As far as I know Niall keeps a weapon or firearm under the passenger seat of his van.

The comments made by Ellen about her ex-boyfriend meant that Niall Power was now also a person of significant interest to the investigation team. While he was with Alan White until about 10 a.m., they hadn't yet spoken to anyone who could corroborate his whereabouts for the rest of that morning. St Malachy's Villas, where he had collected his van, was also conveniently located less than a kilometre from Ice House. The two people he claimed to have been with now had to be interviewed by gardaí. When they spoke with his girlfriend, Jane McKenna told detectives that she believed he had returned home at around 11 a.m. that morning. 'I asked him "what are you doing back?" and he said he couldn't be bothered, he said "they were all going in one car and there's enough of them",' referring to his decision not to attend the security expo. Jane said her partner had given the excuse that she was sick. 'I didn't pay much heed to him. I then got ready, and we left the house in Niall's van. It would've been shortly before 12 p.m. Some time that morning Niall got a phone call from one of the lads that works part-time for him called Anthony. This fellow was looking for money, his wages. I know him and the girlfriend were heading away that weekend.' Jane said they travelled to the grounds of DKIT, with Anthony Lambe arriving at around 1 p.m. 'Anthony and Niall got out of the cars and both me and Anthony's girlfriend stayed in the cars [separately]. Anthony and Niall chatted for about 10 or 15 minutes and then Anthony left. We headed back into town.'

Jane McKenna went on to say that her boyfriend received a phone call from Alan White at around 2 p.m. 'He told me Alan was in a state, that he'd received calls, from whom I'm not sure, to say the police were at Ice House and the kids were to be picked up. Alan had said to him there was a murder at Ice House. Niall said "what the hell does he mean by murder? What are the guards doing there", and I was trying to calm him down. I was saying maybe it's just a row, something simple. I was trying to be positive, and Niall was saying, "I hope you're right."'

PPS Security employed five people at that time, among them Anthony Lambe, a 22-year-old student studying civil engineering in DKIT. On 21 April, Detective Garda Mick Sheridan invited the part-time security worker down to Dundalk garda station to give his own account of meeting Niall Power on the day of the murder. Explaining how he began working for Niall, Anthony told the detective: 'One Thursday there was a band playing in the college and I met a man who was doing the door there. I now know him as Niall Power. He asked me that day to give him a hand and he subsequently offered me a bit of part-time security work. I took it on as I was paying back for a car I bought. I would normally work two 12-hour shifts on a Saturday and Sunday night from 2 p.m. to 2 a.m. at Belfry Park in Dundalk. I would normally get paid on a Thursday when my wages would be paid directly into my bank account.'

He stated that on the afternoon of 6 April he travelled to England, as his girlfriend, Annie Kane, was graduating from a college in London. The couple and her parents had flown to Stansted Airport, departing at around 2.30 p.m. Asked to give an account of his earlier movements that morning, Anthony said he drove up to DKIT at 9 a.m. and ate breakfast in the canteen, before leaving at 9.45 a.m. and driving home to Castleblayney. He said he got home around half an hour later, showered and shaved, before leaving again at 11 a.m. 'I forgot to mention that when I was about halfway home to

Castleblayney that morning I rang Niall Power on his mobile. It would've been around 10 a.m. I asked him could I get my pay a day early, that I needed a few pound to go to England. He said he was going to Dublin that morning over some security thing, but he said he would meet me at the college at around 12 p.m.'

Anthony collected his girlfriend from her house in Castleblayney and the couple went shopping in the town before speaking to Niall once again. 'It would've been about 11.40 a.m., I was ringing to tell him that I didn't think that I would make it for 12 p.m. but it would be close to it. When we left Castleblayney it would've been about 11.50 a.m.' He said they drove up to the college shortly after midday and entered through the main gate, where his boss was waiting for him. 'Niall gave me €400 in cash. Niall was dressed up, he had a jacket and a shirt on. I got the money from Niall. He was congratulating Annie for her graduation from nursing college in England. We then headed for the airport,' he said. At the end of his statement, Anthony made it clear to the detective that he didn't have any information that could assist the investigation. 'I only heard about the murder of Irene White on the Friday when I came back. I did not know Irene White. I never met her before,' he said.

There was nothing in the statements given by Anthony Lambe or Jane McKenna to suggest that Niall Power had recently been involved in a violent altercation, although suspicions remained over his decision to abruptly call off the trip to the security exhibition. Irene White only had one clear enemy: her estranged husband, whom she had expressed serious fears about to her friends, but he could not have been the killer. There was also no evidence to indicate that Alan White's business partner and confidant, Niall, could have carried out the murder. The investigation team had to begin identifying anyone else who could have, for some unknown reason, murdered Irene. They had a number of men in mind who they wanted to speak with.

6

THE USUAL SUSPECTS

The mysterious killer's footprints had led from the kitchen of Ice House, into the garden, and over the back wall. It was obvious that he had escaped through Ice House Hill, a busy park surrounded by two housing estates. The investigation team were sure that someone had spotted the elusive figure running away from the crime scene. Homeowners were canvassed and media appeals were made for anyone who had been in the park that morning to contact Dundalk garda station. Mobile-phone data analysis was also becoming a growing trend in serious criminal investigations, and gardaí wanted to establish if the killer had used a phone in the area around the time of the murder. All service providers were asked to hand over call records as part of a cell site dump for the time of the murder, and it showed that more than 1,600 people had made phone calls using masts in Dundalk between 8.30 a.m. and 12.30 p.m. on 6 April. Over the course of the investigation gardaí would track down nearly every person on the list, to establish what they were doing in the area that day, in what became a particularly lengthy and protracted process.

Ultimately, nothing of evidential value relating to a suspect was unearthed, but gardaí did identify a substantial number of people who had been in the vicinity of Ice House. In total gardaí spoke to 60 people who were in the area at the time of the murder and, while most hadn't witnessed anything out of the ordinary, some did report seeing a man acting suspiciously around the time Irene was attacked. Alison Ryan was walking in the park that morning and saw a man wearing a dark-coloured zip-up jacket turning down the hill near the rear wall of Ice House. He appeared to be 'fairly tall with dark hair', she said. Alison Ryan recalled bidding him a 'good morning' as she walked by him, but the man didn't respond to her. She said the stranger even turned away from her as she spoke to him, and she thought that the man's ignorant behaviour was odd. The last she saw of him was when he ran towards the gate at the Pearse Park entrance before he disappeared.

Deirdre Smith told gardaí that she saw a man who was between 5 feet 5 inches and 5 feet 8 inches in height in the park at around 9.25 a.m. He was wearing a three-quarter-length green jacket with a hood and a black scarf around his face and appeared to be looking over his shoulder. 'He was walking from the pond towards the Eircom building,' she added. Gardaí thought this could possibly have been Irene's killer loitering in the park as he waited for Irene to return home from the school run. Brenda O'Reilly was walking through Ice House Hill at around 10.10 a.m. when she noticed a figure moving across the green area towards the gate at the O'Hanlon Park entrance. She described the man as 'not running but moving quickly' and said he seemed to be wearing a grey top with the hood up.

A canvass of homes in the area yielded few results, but one local woman, Colleen McGregor, told gardaí that she had noticed some unusual behaviour at O'Hanlon Park that morning. She was waiting for a taxi to arrive and had just got off the phone to the driver when she looked up and saw a man running across the hill towards the gate. 'He looked like he was running from something,' she told detectives, describing the man as 'not young' but possibly aged between 30 and 40. He was wearing a waist-length jacket with no hood, and possibly a baseball cap on his head. Colleen McGregor said a dark-coloured car was parked on the street, but she wasn't sure if the man got into it or not. Asked to describe the man's physique, she said he was stocky but not fat and of medium build. The witness later checked her phone records after speaking to gardaí and confirmed that she rang the taxi driver at 10.09 a.m., the exact time at which she saw the man running through the park.

Gardaí also spoke to another witness who had been in the area before the murder. Sam Ellison was helping his son with his courier business that morning and had travelled to the Eircom building to deliver a package. It wasn't open so he put the post to the back of the bundle, returning at around 8.40 a.m. He drove up McSwiney Street and onto Demesne Road, passing Ice House. 'When I approached Eircom I did not see Irene White's car at the front of the house,' Sam Ellison said. 'I did not know her car at that time but I know now since the murder. I seen a small dark hatchback car like a Peugeot parked on the right-hand corner of the driveway at the front of the house at Ice House Hill. I knew this house to be Alan White's because I used to mail deliveries to him for his security business. I drove into Eircom, but I cannot say if the wooden gates at the side of [Ice House] were open or not,' he told gardaí.

In her statement, Jennifer McBride also recalled noticing a suspicious man in the rear garden of their home a number of weeks before the murder. 'He was scruffy-looking, about 25–30 years of age, he was about 5 feet 9 inches tall. He was stout and had a big belly, he was wearing a puffy jacket, either blue or navy, and had a black beard,' she told gardaí. It was a description that bore some similarities to the witness sightings of the man seen running through Ice House Hill park after the murder, and gardaí wondered if this could have been the killer carrying out reconnaissance of Irene in the lead-up to the murder.

Gardaí utilised the media to make several public appeals, and on 26 April the *Crimecall* programme on RTÉ featured details of the case along with a reconstruction of the murder. A €10,000 reward was now also on offer for anyone willing to come forward and provide information that would lead to the prosecution and conviction of the person involved in Irene's killing. The appeal resulted in a number of calls being made to the *Crimecall* offices. A 14-year-old boy made contact with the tipline and said he'd seen 'a fellow hanging around Ice House Hill park' that morning. This suspicious man was wearing a black hooded top and white Nike runners, the teenager said, and had a black bag in the shape of a weapon. The statement was of potential significance as the Nike runners described by the witness matched the footwear the killer had more than likely worn. After reviewing all of the statements from witnesses who were in the area at the time, gardaí were confident that the unidentified man who was seen running through the park at 10.09 a.m. was the murderer.

With no other obvious suspects, gardaí began to draw up a list of local criminals who were living in the area at the time and could potentially have been involved in the murder. It included serial burglars, men of violence, and some linked to dissident republican groups, as well as others who were rumoured locally to have had an involvement in Irene's murder. During house-to-house inquiries on McSwiney Street, gardaí also became aware that a number of foreign nationals were living in the area. They were spoken to, and contact was made with Interpol to determine if any of the men had a violent past as part of routine inquiries. However, there was nothing to suggest any of these men were involved in the crime and gardaí quickly moved on to others.

Detective Garda Tom Molloy was tasked with compiling the list of known offenders from the nearby area – the usual suspects. A detective who had by this stage served in Dundalk for three decades, he had plenty of experience with the local criminal fraternity. The detective drew up a 10-man list of people who gardaí wanted to speak to about the murder. One of these was Jennifer McBride's boyfriend, Angelo O'Riordan, who had already given a witness statement in the hours after Irene's body was found. The rationale for putting him on the list was that just over two months before the murder, on 30 January, he was arrested in possession of a hunting knife and a screwdriver on Church Street in Dundalk. Given that Angelo O'Riordan was also considered a violent offender and wasn't well regarded by the murder victim, detectives had to definitively rule him in or out of their inquiries.

His brother was interviewed and told gardaí that he had returned home at around 2 p.m. on the day of the murder, but made no reference to Angelo being at their home in Bellurgan. Investigators then interviewed their mother, Bernadette, who provided an alibi for her son at the time of the murder. She said she had returned to the family home in Bellurgan at around 9 p.m. the previous night and that Angelo was there. She went about her routine at home the next day, saying that her son was still in bed until around 2 p.m. Angelo O'Riordan's phone records were also examined, and they didn't reveal any suspicious activity. The friend who rang Angelo and told him about the crime was interviewed too and confirmed his story.

Gardaí also looked at the possibility that an associate of Angelo's may have had some involvement in the murder. This man was known for carrying out burglaries in the town, having been linked to 13 break-ins around Dundalk in the previous months. One of these was an aggravated burglary during which he entered a house with a knife and other weapons, demanding money and jewellery from the occupants. Other properties he was alleged to have targeted were sheds, marine buildings, pubs, warehouses, shops, and an office. He had also gained entry to two homes through the back door.

This man was interviewed by the investigation team and said that he was in his girlfriend's house the night before the murder. 'I stayed there all night. I don't go out during the week at all because I have to get up early for work. I stayed there all night. I got up at about 10 a.m. the next morning as I was in court in Dundalk,' he said, with his appearance in court confirmed and clearing him of having any involvement. Another close associate of Angelo O'Riordan's was also looked at, with gardaí compiling a report on this potential suspect as part of their inquiries. The report noted that this man 'is liable to become involved in any type of activity that might be of financial benefit to him' but that he is 'unlikely to be the brains behind any major criminal activity'. Ultimately, there was nothing to suggest that Angelo or any of his associates had anything to do with the murder of Irene White, and all had alibis that eliminated them from the inquiry.

Another man on the suspects list was Robert 'Robbie' Maguire, a settled Traveller who lived in Dundalk with his mother and 16 siblings. He had been included on the list because rumours had been spread locally that he had some involvement. Alan White had even mentioned this to gardaí, telling them in the days after the murder: 'I heard there was a Maguire fella arrested for questioning.' Gardaí originally spoke to Robbie Maguire informally on 12 April while he was being detained at Dundalk garda station on foot of outstanding warrants. He told gardaí that he was staying with a friend at the time and that at 10.30 a.m. on the morning of the murder he had made his way to another acquaintance's house, located on Clanbrassil Street, not far from Ice House. He said he stayed at this friend's house until around 1 p.m., a critical time for the murder inquiry.

He had heard he was being blamed in the locality for committing the murder 'with one of the O'Riordans'. In a memo of the meeting, gardaí noted that Robbie 'didn't know the deceased or daughter, or where the house is. He did drink in Ice House Hill but hasn't been there in about three months'. Writing down a description of Robbie Maguire, the gardaí who spoke to him noted that he was around 5 feet 10 inches with short hair and that he had a baseball cap. The profile bore similarities to one of the witness descriptions of the suspicious male seen running through Ice House Hill park after the murder.

Efforts were made to confirm his alibi, but this would lead to further suspicions being cast over him. One of the men he professed to have been with told gardaí: 'Robbie Maguire was not in my house that morning before I left to go. He had no idea where I lived. He was never in my house prior to the murder. He certainly wasn't in my house on the morning of the murder.' Another friend whom Maguire used as an alibi said he 'didn't see or speak' to him that day. To add to the garda interest in Robbie Maguire as a potential suspect, when he was taken into garda custody in relation to a bench warrant, he was wearing a white Nike sports jacket that had bloodstains. The clothing was seized and sent to the Forensic Science Laboratory to compare it with DNA samples taken from the murder scene at Ice House. It didn't take long for the items to be tested given the gravity of what was being investigated. In a report, the forensic examiner stated: 'Blood was found on the collar and lower front of Robert Maguire's white jacket. I grouped the blood from the collar of the jacket and found it did not match Irene White's blood.'

Gardaí searched another property that Robbie Maguire had stayed at around the time of the murder, and a dark blue jacket belonging to him was seized. Again, nothing of evidential value was recovered from the clothing, with no blood at all found on the jacket. It wasn't until that June that gardaí would get to the bottom of Robbie's whereabouts on the day of the murder. Two detectives visited him in prison, where he was being held in custody on other matters. Robbie told the investigators that he had had to leave his mother's house after she complained about the gardaí constantly knocking on their door looking for him, and he went to stay with his friend who lived at a halting site in the town.

Explaining the inconsistencies in his original account, Robbie Maguire told gardaí: 'I know the day I was talking to you, I told you where I was on the day the woman was murdered, but that is where I was the day before I was arrested. I was on heroin at that time, I hadn't a clue what day it was or what was going on.' He said several people told him that he was being blamed for the murder, but denied knowing where Irene White lived or even who she was. 'I know the O'Riordans but I never palled about with them. I don't know Jennifer McBride or that she is going with one of the O'Riordans. The only thing I heard about the murder was that O'Riordan and me were supposed to have done it. My brother Thomas told me that people were going around saying that I did it. I know I was down around Muirhevnamore the whole time because the guards were looking for me'.

He couldn't remember what he'd done on 6 April but was sure that he had nothing to do with Irene's death. 'I can remember that I didn't do any murder. I don't carry a knife at any time. I didn't murder Irene White or help anybody else to murder her. I know nothing about the murder or who done it. Anything about me being involved in the murder is all lies.' The two men he was actually with that day later confirmed his whereabouts, telling gardaí that they were all playing cards when they'd heard over the radio that a woman had been killed. 'There is no doubt it was a Wednesday. Robert was in the site all day. I know he had nothing to do with the murder,' one of the men stated. He also told gardaí that he had heard the rumours about Maguire's involvement but was certain they weren't true. Explaining how the claims began circulating, the man said that the home of a woman known to Maguire had been searched in the days after Irene was killed.

The guards ransacked [the] house and took away blood from the shower. News got out about the search. I heard the guards were looking for Robbie about the murder. I knew Robbie was running from the guards about fines and warrants. All the sisters and brothers knew the guards were looking for him. I met Robbie on the sites, and I told him that there was a rumour going around about him in relation to the murder. I told him to go up the guards and tell them the truth. He wouldn't go up because there were warrants out against him.

With an alibi and no evidence tying him to the murder, Robbie Maguire was also ruled out of having any involvement. Other names were crossed off one by one, as there was no evidence connecting them to the crime. One of the last men on the list that gardaí had to follow up on was a dangerous criminal with links to subversive groups. Thomas Murray, who was 32 years old at the time of the murder, was well known to both local gardaí and the Special Detective Unit, which investigates dissident republican groups. He had a long list of previous convictions and had associations to the Irish National Liberation Army (INLA), a dissident terror group responsible for a wave of violence both during the Northern Ireland conflict and in the post-Troubles era.

In 1996 he was part of an INLA gang who were hired to carry out an attack on an innocent woman's home after she had spurned the sexual advances of a Dublin businessman. Murray and two other men were armed with a lump hammer as they entered her house in Castleknock in Dublin and threatened her. Unfortunately for the gang, members of the Special Detective Unit had received a tip-off that the INLA were planning 'a job' in the capital that night and were watching their every move. Thomas Murray was later convicted of intimidation relating to the incident at the non-jury Special Criminal Court. He had told gardaí in his statements that the gang were to be paid £100 each for the job and that he wouldn't have used the lump hammer 'unless I had to'.

In 1998 he was back before the Special Criminal Court after firing shots through a neighbour's window, and in 2003 he received a suspended sentence for violent disorder. In September 2004, just six months before Irene's murder, he had broken into a house in Aisling Park, Dundalk, armed with a knife in the early hours of the morning. The homeowner was lying in bed and was attacked and stabbed by Murray, leaving him with lacerations to his throat and ear. Murray was later charged over the attack and granted bail, with gardaí recording his movements around Dundalk in the weeks before and after the murder.

Given Murray's healthy criminal record, his recent alleged involvement in a violent home invasion, and that he had previously been hired to carry out a 'job', gardaí took a keen interest in him. When he was interviewed about the murder, however, Murray said that he had stayed in his sister's home in Rostrevor, County Down, from 5 April until 8 April, with this account later confirmed by his sibling. There was also nothing concrete to connect him to the murder or suggest he was involved in any way, and thus gardaí ruled another person out of their inquiries. The investigation team were quickly running out of possible suspects.

The legal battle over the future of Ice House dragged on as the murder probe continued, and on 9 May the case was back before the High Court in Dublin. Alan White got a reprieve that day, as the order restraining him from selling Ice House was lifted. However, separate court orders preventing him from entering the Omeath cottage in Irene's name and interfering with his dead wife's assets were continued. Detectives had by this stage built a clear picture of Irene's personal circumstances in the lead-up to her murder but continued gathering as much information as possible. On 17 May, Anne Delcassian and her husband, Kenneth, travelled to Ireland from the UK. They sat down with Detective Sergeant Brian Mohan in Dundalk garda station to outline what they knew of Irene's marriage and their thoughts on her estranged husband. Anne said she'd first met Alan White in or around 1997 and found him 'quiet and uncommunicative'. On this trip back to her home county she was informed of her sister's marital plans.

> She told me she was getting married and was doing the same as me which was a quiet wedding with only witnesses present. I knew that Irene was getting married to Alan White and that she was pregnant to him. I feel that if she hadn't been pregnant, she wouldn't have married Alan White at all. I feel this because I was aware that Irene and her daughter Jenny, which she had to George Bannister in 1988, had been living in with Alan at Ice House before they were married, and Irene phoned me one morning to tell me that Alan had put her and Jennifer out of Ice House as he wanted a break. Irene was very upset with this, and she went back out to live with my mother for a while. I didn't feel that this was a normal thing in a relationship, and I told Irene that.

Anne described how she visited her sister on a number of occasions but always felt she was being watched in Ice House. The last time they'd spoken was nearly a year before Irene's murder, in May 2004, during a civil court hearing relating to another cottage in Omeath, which had been willed to Maureen by her mother Ellen. Anne said her sister seemed to be in good form and didn't allude to any difficulties she was having. 'It is only since I came home that I have learned the extent of the problem between Irene and Alan. I did not realise that things were so bad,' she told Detective Sergeant Mohan. Kenneth Delcassian also disclosed how he was wary of Alan White shortly after being introduced to him for the first time.

I never felt comfortable in his house with all the cameras there. The whole thing only led to the feeling of uncomfortableness in his house – that you were being watched all the time. I also noticed that Alan couldn't hold a conversation with me unless he had a few Bush whiskeys in him. He was always on about the qualities of Black Bush as against ordinary Bush. I would describe Alan as antisocial unless he had drink. He was a sulky person and I seen him arguing with Irene about his drinking. We came over for the case in May 2004 and I met Irene and Maureen in Omeath and later in the solicitor's office in Dundalk and also in the court. I thanked Irene for being willing to go on Anne's behalf. That was the last time that I saw or spoke with Irene. I was not aware that things were as bad as they were. I asked Maureen why she hadn't told us that things were as bad as they were, and she told me that she was in fear for her life. I haven't spoken to anybody associated with the White family and I have no wish to since this happened.

By this stage, over 100 gardaí made up of local, regional, and national units were working on the murder inquiry, but there was still no breakthrough in identifying the killer. The process of gathering and reviewing hundreds of hours of CCTV footage from around Dundalk was ongoing, while witnesses who had previously been spoken to were followed up with in the hope of further key information coming to light. In time, these two aspects of the investigation would raise serious questions over the actions of one man in particular on the day Irene was murdered.

7

DEEP SUSPICIONS

I t was unusual for Niall Power to miss what seemed like a business meeting of huge importance. Plans had long been put in place for him to go to Citywest, but suddenly he wasn't enthusiastic about sitting in the same car as Cathy Wilson for the three-hour round trip. Gardaí had to establish if the visit to the security expo wasn't as essential as had been made out, or if something of greater importance had kept him in Dundalk on 6 April 2005.

While the people he had met that day had already been spoken to, gardaí decided to reinterview them in case any important information had been omitted when giving their statements. From the outset of the murder, detectives from the National Bureau of Criminal Investigation had been assisting the local investigation team with the high-profile inquiry and were well versed in the details of the case. As they are specially trained in interview techniques and taking comprehensive statements, it was decided that detectives from the serious crime unit should follow up with a number of witnesses to see if they could shed any further light on the day of the murder itself. They were also interested to know more about the camera-monitoring business being discussed.

On 2 May, Detective Sergeant Maura Walsh met with Cathy Wilson in Carrickmacross, in the hope of recording a more detailed account from her. Sitting down to give her second witness statement, Cathy was specifically asked what she made of Niall Power's decision not to travel to the security conference with them. Cathy said it was 'unthinkable' that he wouldn't go as it was 'absolutely vital' to their business. 'Niall and Alan knew how important it was to us and for them to attend for their new business venture,' she told Detective Sergeant Walsh. Cathy explained that they would have known about the conference some months in advance and that she personally spoke with Niall to remind him to go. 'I was the driving force behind bringing the three of them to the show with me. Niall told me personally he was going to go with us because at the end of the day he was the man that was going to be working the machinery,' she said of his planned role within the monitoring company. 'It was essential, I cannot stress enough how important it was for him to be there, because they were going to see what they needed for their business, he wouldn't get another opportunity like this for another 12 months.'

When asked to think back to the moment Niall left her home that morning, Cathy recalled him being on the phone for about 30 seconds before he turned to Alan White and said 'have to go – problems'. She also described Niall as being 'in a tizzy' when he left. Later that morning when Alan returned, he explained to her that Niall was having 'woman problems'. While Niall Power told gardaí that he didn't want to go to the conference as he couldn't stand Cathy Wilson, she painted an altogether different picture of their friendship and how they got on. 'One time when I was going through a rough patch with Vincent, Niall knew this and told me he was always there if I needed him. I would confide in him as much as he would confide in me. I would consider that Niall would consider me a close friend.'

Three days later, Vincent Dullaghan met with Detective Sergeant Walsh and was also asked more specific questions about the day of the murder and his business plans. 'Both myself and Alan discussed the possibility of setting up a new monitoring station, in fact, the one who was pushing it in the recent past was Niall, after all it was in his interest.' He added that, while Alan was technically sound, he would depend on Vincent for advice on such matters. Niall, on the other hand, wouldn't have much knowledge of the technical aspects involved, he said. 'The monitoring station was going to be run by PPS Security and my connection was purely to secure the building and get the commission from supplying my customers with the monitor. I would get an annual commission. In an effort to gain a better understanding of the latest technology, it was essential that both Alan and Niall attended the various technical exhibitions.' It was apparent that the proposed monitoring business was an advanced concept, well ahead of its time, presenting a potentially lucrative enterprise for all involved. The security expo was important, but despite this, Vincent Dullaghan had formed the impression that Niall Power didn't want to go at all, judging by the clothes he was wearing that morning. 'During the week you'd see Niall dressed in a suit and I felt he was underdressed, if he was going to Citywest.'

He recalled Alan White getting a phone call from Niall as they were in the car on their way to Dublin and that there was a comment about Jane McKenna being sick. 'We were on the

M50 when he rang, and he was still talking about the hospital, he hadn't been there yet. I thought this was suspicious. Niall is a funny guy, you wouldn't know what was in his head. If it was a story, I couldn't figure out why he'd waste half an hour coming out here. In fact, when I rang Alan from the house I suggested to him to turn around, come back and we could all go together and save time,' Vincent recalled. 'But, Alan said he was in Ballykelly and Niall was panicky. Niall doesn't normally panic, and I thought this was strange. I felt like calling the whole thing off because I was annoyed, but I knew Alan really wanted to go and see this monitoring station because it was the only place where we could view one. The chance was not going to come again until next year.' The sales manager they were due to meet in Citywest was also spoken to by gardaí and confirmed the importance of the planned meeting, believing they would 'clinch the deal that day for the monitoring station'.

While he had told his friends that his girlfriend rang him that morning, Niall Power's phone records showed that this wasn't the case. He was, however, in phone contact with Anthony Lambe that day. Gardaí again spoke to the part-time PPS Security worker on 16 June 2005 to see if his employer had mentioned anything unusual over the phone. In a brief statement, Anthony recalled making one call after 10 a.m. when Niall was either on the way to Dublin or getting ready to travel to the Citywest Hotel. 'I know at that stage I was looking for my money from him. I can recall him asking if I could leave it until next week, and I told him I needed the money that day as I was going on holidays. He said "alright", and that he would get back to me on it,' Anthony explained. 'I know after that there was a couple of broken calls that didn't get through. I eventually arranged to meet him at the college. It was only when I arrived at the college that Niall told me that he wasn't going to bother going to Dublin, I think he said he wasn't too pushed to go in the first place,' he added.

The fresh statements from Cathy Wilson, Vincent Dullaghan, and Anthony Lambe raised further questions about Niall Power's suspicious behaviour that morning. His business partners agreed that the meeting at the Citywest security conference was important, with Cathy saying it was 'unthinkable' that he would miss it.

However, Vincent said Niall was underdressed for the occasion, while Anthony Lambe believed his boss never had any intention of travelling to Dublin at all. Four days after speaking with Anthony Lambe, gardaí visited Alan White at his home. No formal statement was taken but Detective Sergeant Piper and Detective Garda O'Driscoll took down contemporaneous notes of the encounter. During the conversation, Alan asked the detectives if there was truth in the rumour that his wife's throat had been cut. When told they couldn't divulge specifics of the case, Alan speculated about the potential involvement of his mother-in-law and wondered if Maureen McBride had seen more than she had said.

In their notes of the meeting, the detectives recorded that Alan said he did not believe that Maureen would have cut Irene's throat, but all of his family believe she could have been involved. He said that he felt sorry for his stepdaughter Jennifer at times, while adding: 'but basically she has accused me of murder'. Alan then circled back to his baseless theory about Maureen, saying he 'could well imagine' a row between her and Irene, but if Irene's throat had been cut, he could not accept that possibility. Over a week later, members of the detective branch visited Niall Power's parents, Pat and Mary, but they were less than impressed with the arrival of gardaí at their door. They refused to make a statement, saying that certain gardaí had made derogatory remarks about their son when speaking to people as part of their inquiries. During the somewhat hostile encounter, of which gardaí took detailed notes, his mother did give some background to the security company and how it was set up.

'Mary Power admitted that she was asked by her son Niall to be a director of PPS Security when he was setting up the company and she agreed to let her name be used,' gardaí noted. 'She can't put a date on this but said it was the same time as the company first started. She had her name taken off the company register about 12 months ago, but she didn't, or says she couldn't, give any reason why it was taken off. She stated that the house at Jenkinstown was being used as a base and that post still was coming to the house for PPS Security.'

Niall's mother also told the detectives that the very fact they were at her home questioning her 'smacked of the McBrearty case in Donegal', referring to the businessman who sued the state for €2.5 million in damages as a result of garda harassment. Mary Power told the gardaí that they were not to be trusted and demanded to know if they had tapped her home phone. 'She stated that they started having problems with the phone from 2.30 p.m. on the day of the murder,' gardaí noted. 'She reported it to Eircom who sent a man out to check it and he couldn't find anything wrong with it. Her husband Pat stated that he had a direct line to McDowell's office [a reference to then Justice Minister Michael McDowell] and he intended to use it as he also thought that our investigation was a repeat of the McBrearty case.' Towards the end of the conversation, Pat Power again insisted that his son's reputation had been seriously damaged by the alleged remarks made by certain gardaí to witnesses and that they were intent on seeking redress. Despite Niall Power's parents' accusations of harassment and professing their son's innocence, the investigation team were firmly of the view that he knew a lot more than he was letting on.

Niall's phone usage for the day of the murder was looked at in more detail, and it showed a flurry of contact with Anthony Lambe. The first call was made by Anthony at 8.30 a.m., with the men speaking for just over two minutes, before two successive calls at 9.44 a.m., the second of which was Niall returning a call to Anthony, which lasted for 39 seconds. There was another call from Anthony to Niall at 10.13 a.m. for 24 seconds and again a minute later for 3 seconds. The businessman then rang his employee back at 10.15 a.m., speaking with him for 45 seconds, before another call at 10.19 a.m. that lasted 25 seconds. Their final call that day was at 11.39 a.m., when Anthony Lambe rang his boss and spoke to him for 59 seconds. The large amount of activity was of interest to gardaí, and they decided that a third statement should be taken from the student and part-time security worker to find out if all the calls were about organising a meeting to pay his wages.

On 15 September, Detective Sergeant Walsh met Anthony Lambe by appointment at Dundalk garda station to go over his recollection of the days surrounding Irene's murder in more detail. The night before, he had gone drinking in a pub in Dundalk where he met a woman called Noelle and, despite having a girlfriend, spent the night with her. 'The following morning was 6 April and early that morning I thought I may have text Niall Power telling him about the girl I met, the night before. I have been told that records show that I made a phone call at 8.30 am. I don't recall it, but I may have rung him instead of texting him,' Anthony said. 'I'm not sure of my times that morning. I do remember driving from her home to the college. I drove up the back way in my own car, a black Peugeot. I probably arrived about 20 minutes after leaving the house which was probably about 9.05 a.m.,' he said. Anthony Lambe again repeated what he'd mentioned in his previous statements, saying that he travelled to DKIT for breakfast and then drove towards his home. He interrupted himself when recalling his day, saying:

> I have just remembered having thought about the two-minute phone call at 8.30 a.m., and as far as I can recollect Niall Power had told me that he was going to Dublin, and I probably wouldn't be getting my €400 which he had said he'd give me a week beforehand. We probably would have ended the conversation by him saying 'he'd see what he could do for me'. That's probably why I hung around Dundalk. After breakfast as I said I went towards home. I rang him on a number of occasions, I couldn't say how many, and I couldn't say how many I got through to him and spoke to him. In the final conversation we agreed to meet at DKIT about 12 p.m., roughly.

The student added that he bought a pair of trousers in Castleblayney that morning, ringing his boss for a final time to say he would be running late. 'I want to say that I had arrived home to my parents' house at about 10 a.m. or maybe 10.30 a.m. and I met my mother in the house. She asked me to go out and give silage to the cattle. After buying the trousers myself and Annie drove in my car to DKIT, and we arrived there at about 12.05 p.m. Niall was already there. I had a brief conversation with him, he seemed in good form, and he congratulated Annie as she was being conferred the following day in England.'

Going through the events of the Friday after the murder, he told the detective sergeant that he called into DKIT and met a barman working there. The murder of Irene White had been the talk of the town over the previous two days, and Anthony said he had only been informed on his return from England of what had happened. 'It didn't really affect me because I didn't know the woman – Irene White – and I'd only met Alan White once, several weeks prior. I've never been to Ice House before. I was in Ice House Hill within the last year, but it would have been months before 6 April. I was just nosing around the park on my own. I would have entered it near where those little houses are, there's two entrances there. I went in one of those near the railway,' he told Detective Sergeant Walsh. For someone who had been speaking with Niall Power throughout the morning, Anthony didn't reveal anything untoward or suspicious on the part of his boss. The accounts in his three statements appeared consistent, and the story of plaguing his employer with phone calls to urgently get paid before travelling abroad seemed genuine.

*

There was further tragedy for Irene's family that autumn. On 21 October Maureen McBride, who had never recovered from finding her daughter lying fatally injured on her kitchen floor, collapsed beside her bed at home. The 79-year-old woman was rushed to Louth County Hospital but sadly passed away the following afternoon from natural causes. It was a tragic and cruel irony that Maureen died on her late daughter's birthday, 22 October, the day Irene would have turned 44. Anne Declassian had now lost both her mother and sister just months apart. The death of her father when she was a teenager, and her brother when they were children, meant that she was the only surviving member of her immediate family. Anne was determined to ensure that Irene would get justice and set about organising an intense and dignified campaign to keep her sister's case in the public consciousness and the pressure on gardaí to catch the killer.

In one of her first media interviews, she described how the person who had murdered her sister had also killed her mother, who 'died inside' the day she found Irene's body. 'My mother never got over Irene's murder and the sight of her beloved daughter lying in a pool of blood on her kitchen floor never left her to her dying day,' she said. Anne said that Maureen desperately wanted justice for Irene, and the fact that she died on her birthday 'says it all'. Anne continued making public appeals in both the local and national media, pleading for anyone with information to contact gardaí.

The inquest into Irene White's death was opened before a jury by Louth County Coroner Ronan Maguire BL on 12 December 2005, but it was adjourned at the request of gardaí because of the ongoing investigation. A brief summary of evidence was given of statements taken by gardaí who'd arrived at the scene and the pathologist's report by Professor Marie Cassidy. Adjourning the inquest, the coroner said that Irene had suffered a dreadful death that shocked the town, and he expressed his sympathies to her family. 'Words are deeply inadequate for the pain the family must feel. They have suffered much more than anyone deserves.' As families celebrated Christmas and rang in the New Year, it was a sombre festive season for Irene's family.

In a media interview in January 2006, Anne described how Christmas would normally be a time of year where the word 'family' would have a special meaning. 'This year, however, my family has been decimated by the savage murder of my sister Irene – a sweet, gentle lady. I have already made a plea to the people of Dundalk and I do so again. Please ask yourselves do individuals responsible for this murder deserve to be allowed to walk free through your town, among you and among your children – literally getting away with murder.'

That same month, Dympna O'Kane made a further statement to gardaí, providing more information about the difficulties that existed in Irene's marriage. She told Detective Garda Charlie Geoghegan that the alleged threatening behaviour from Alan White was 'constant' and that Irene said he would regularly square up to her. 'Before Christmas 2004 Irene told me that he had offered her €200,000 to leave the house. I'm sure Irene wouldn't have known the sale of the house was taking place with Eircom. I told Irene what you would get for that. Irene was disgusted with the offer.'

As the first anniversary of Irene's death approached, some media reports focused on the fact that the murderer was still at large a year on. On 6 April 2006, the *Evening Herald* newspaper led with the front-page headline 'Irene's killer still loose a year later'. Alan White himself vented his frustration at how the case had been portrayed in the media in his first public comments since the murder of his wife. Speaking with journalist Eoin Reynolds, he was quoted as saying: 'Yes, obviously I want the killer to come forward. I didn't like how the story was covered in the media, and I have been advised not to comment any further. I have thought about it a lot. I'd love to give my side, but I can't.' The newspaper also reported how Ice House had sold, since the injunction preventing him from selling the property had been lifted, for around €1.1 million. His mother, Florence, spoke to the journalist too, saying: 'Alan is just trying to get on with his life. He wants to keep the kids away from what happened. Every day we listen and hope we will hear they got someone.' She added that her son took little interest in the investigation, preferring to leave that to the gardaí and Irene's sister, Anne.

The lack of significant progress in the inquiry was frustrating not just for Irene's family, but also for the garda investigation team. The laborious task of tracking and tracing CCTV footage from individual businesses and homes across Dundalk had been ongoing for several months. A team of gardaí had to identify dozens of cameras scattered around the town, request the footage, and then meticulously review it to ensure that nothing of importance was missed. They began by tracking Irene's movements that morning, watching her maroon Mazda, which was easily identifiable from the hubcap missing on the front wheel on the right-hand side. There was nothing to suggest that any vehicle had been following Irene that morning or that she was under surveillance.

They also traced Niall Power's movements that morning and, clip by clip, viewed the footage to see if there were any discrepancies in his account. The gardaí tracked his white Ford Fiesta van, with a distinctive orange stripe on the side, driving through Dundalk that morning. At 9.32 a.m., his van was seen driving onto Stapleton Place, heading in the direction of St Malachy's Villas where Alan White was staying. Later he was captured on footage from Ann Street at 10.29 a.m. and along Clanbrassil Street, where he had gone to the Permanent TSB to withdraw a sum of money. The Ford Fiesta was later traced as it began travelling around the town again after he collected his girlfriend, heading to Cuchulainn credit union, where he stayed briefly before leaving at 11.40 a.m. Nothing was out of the ordinary so far, and Niall appeared to be telling the truth about what he'd done that morning.

Niall's van was next picked up on CCTV footage at the Carroll Village shopping centre on the Long Walk at 11.48 a.m., before being sighted on cameras at Hill Street three minutes later. This struck the gardaí as peculiar as they viewed the footage. The route he had taken would have led him onto Demesne Road and directly past Ice House at a time when Irene's body still lay in the kitchen, yet to be found. Despite giving a number of statements to gardaí over the course of several months, Niall Power never disclosed that he had driven by the scene of the murder that day, and at such a critical time. The fact that he been so close to the scene at all, along with the calculated decision to keep this from the detective branch, was highly suspect. Over a year after Irene was murdered, the investigation decided it was finally time to move on their only suspects.

8

'IRENE HAD NOTHING TO FEAR FROM ME'

The judge listened carefully as Detective Superintendent Jim Sheridan outlined the reason why he needed two search warrants as part of the Irene White murder investigation. Following a long and protracted inquiry, the senior investigator believed that a substantial amount of money had been paid to Irene's killer. In sworn evidence, he told the judge at Carrickmacross District Court it was his belief that evidence of financial transactions, call records, and mobile phones could be found at Alan White's cottage in Knockbridge, along with further evidence connected to the crime. Applying for a warrant to search Niall's home in Muirhevnamore, Detective Superintendent Sheridan affirmed that, from inquiries carried out, he also believed that Niall was involved in planning the murder and that relevant evidence connected to the crime could be found at his home. The judge, satisfied with the information he'd received, signed both warrants on 26 May 2006, permitting gardaí to search the properties.

The following morning at 6.50 a.m. a team led by Detective Sergeant Tom Duffy arrived at Alan White's cottage in

Knockbridge. Alan answered the door and was informed of the reason for their visit, before being told that he was being arrested on suspicion of withholding information relating to his wife's murder. The house was searched and gardaí seized a laptop, desktop computer, and some documents that were shown to Alan White before he was walked out to a garda car. His two children, who were living with him by this stage, having spent time with their aunt after the murder, were also in the house at the time, and his sister arrived to care for them. In Muirhevnamore, a simultaneous operation took place at the residence of Niall Power, who was arrested for the same offence by Detective Sergeant Bill Piper. Gardaí recovered documents from the home that were taken away to be analysed as part of the inquiry.

The Garda Press Office issued a media release about the arrests, only confirming that two men, aged in their 30s and 40s, were arrested on suspicion of withholding information in relation to Irene White's murder. It didn't take long for word to reach crime reporters that Alan White was one of those arrested. While he wasn't named, newspaper articles referred to a person 'well known' to Irene as being one of the men in custody.

The arrests had been planned for several weeks, with gardaí carefully devising an interview strategy they hoped would yield results. All relevant documentation and statements were compiled for the interrogation, and a number of key areas were identified that the teams of detectives wanted to quiz Alan and Niall about. This included their movements on the day of the murder, Alan's marriage to Irene and the history of alleged violence, the threats he was said to have made against her, and evidence recovered during the search of Ice House. They also wanted to ask both men about the alleged plot to seduce Irene, their phone contacts on 6 April 2005, and the fact that Niall Power's van was spotted near the scene after the murder.

They were taken to Kells garda station in County Meath and detained under Section 30 of the Offences Against the State Act, 1939, meaning they could be held for up to 72 hours. Both men were fingerprinted and provided DNA samples before being photographed, with two teams of detectives then beginning the interview process. As Detective Sergeant Duffy and Detective Garda Errol Boyle sat down with Alan White, he told them that he would not answer any questions on the advice of his solicitor and that he was going to exercise his right to silence. When they informed Alan that there may be allegations put to him during the course of his interviews that he might like to refute, he told them: 'So would I, but I have to go with his professionalism, I do understand where you are coming from, but he has advised me this way.' They began questioning him about his business relationship with Niall Power. Why, they asked, was he only working for Niall, when it was known that he was the brains behind PPS Security? 'Thanks for the compliment, no comment,' Alan replied.

He also responded 'no comment' after being asked to give the detectives a rundown of his movements on the day of the murder. When they put a series of allegations to him about domestic abuse during his marriage to Irene, as well as attending counselling to try and save the relationship, he told them: 'I have no comment to make in relation to any of the rubbish that has been said.' He denied that he had attempted to block Irene from leaving their home or that he threatened her after gardaí were called to Ice House in April 2003. Detective Sergeant Duffy remarked: 'If someone said to me that if something does not go right for me out in the street, and that

I would be got, I would look on that remark totally different in the future, and Irene did look at things in a different light after that.' Again, Alan White said he would not comment on the matter put to him, only adding: 'Irene had nothing to fear from me.'

The garda interviewers then became more direct in their approach. 'You kicked in her two doors, you called her a tramp and a traitor and you told her if things did not go well for you in the separation, she would be got and that you would have an alibi, and then you say "Irene had nothing to fear from me", would you get off the stage, what do you mean she would have nothing to fear from you, and we didn't even get near the violence you gave to Jennifer, banging her head off the wall.' Again, Alan White had no comment to make. It was a response he stuck to over the next number of hours, including when gardaí asked him what he meant when he allegedly told Irene 'she would not know the hour nor the day'.

'From reading you, Alan, I have no doubt what was in your head, and that you meant it,' the detective said. Alan was told there were statements from both Irene and Niall about this, while several other people had come forward to tell gardaí that Irene was terrified of him. Detective Sergeant Duffy put it to Alan that he had warned his wife he would have an alibi when she died, and so it proved at the time of her murder. 'No comment,' Alan replied. The first interview ended, and when gardaí asked him to sign the memo of interview, he refused.

The next round of interrogation was taken up by Detective Gardaí Gerard Murray and Charlie Geoghegan. From the outset, Alan told them that he was paying his solicitor for his advice and that it would be pointless paying him if he didn't heed that advice. Detective Garda Murray then began homing in on the close relationship between Alan and Niall. Alan replied 'no comment' to a series of questions, including whether it was fair to say that he would tell his business associate everything he did, and if there was a plan to record an alleged seduction plot of Irene in their house. Alan said he had a licensed firearm a long time ago for hunting, and when asked if he ever saw Niall with a firearm, again responded 'no comment'.

Detective Garda Murray put it to Alan that Ellen Johnson said she had been told on separate occasions that he had said to Irene, 'you won't know the time or the place, but I will come back and get you and I will have a good alibi'. He didn't respond to the question, but the gardaí pressed him further. 'Why would this girl come and tell the gardaí that she was concerned about this, and she had heard it from two people, from Irene and Niall? Why would she say such a thing?' Detective Garda Murray asked, with Alan replying that he didn't know.

When the interviewers asked him about the extensive monitoring system that had been in place at Ice House, Alan White bluntly said that this was 'for security'. He didn't comment when asked if he ever had the house phones bugged or monitored or if he used the cameras to keep an eye on Irene's movements. The interview then shifted towards the violence he inflicted on Irene's daughter, with Detective Garda Murray asking Alan if he denied what had happened. 'It was not an assault,' he replied, saying that he wasn't convicted but instead got the Probation Act. Alan eventually accepted that the judge who presided over the case found the facts proven as outlined by Jennifer. When the detective put it to Alan that he was in denial about the assaults and violence, he replied: 'I appreciate your opinion.'

The interview then circled back to the alleged alibi threat made against Irene. Alan replied that the 'alleged threats, they never happened' and said he didn't know why his wife would mention the word 'alibi' if she was making it up. 'Sounds better, does it not?' he added. The gardaí remarked how it was strange that Irene made a complaint in which she said her husband threatened her that he would have an alibi when she was murdered, which was ultimately what transpired. 'It is even stranger to think that I am responsible for her murder, even though she made these allegations in an open court,' Alan White replied.

In the other interview room, Detective Sergeant Piper and Detective Garda O'Driscoll were quizzing Niall Power about his knowledge of the murder. Niall said the 'dogs in the street knew' that Alan and Irene had marital difficulties, but that he didn't want to talk about it. When gardaí asked him about his movements on the day of the murder, he repeatedly said that they already had his statements in which he gave his account. 'You know all of this, this is madness,' Niall told them. Asked how much it would cost to set up a new remote monitoring business, he believed around €40,000, on top of the cost of getting a premises for the monitoring equipment. Questioned on his reaction when he heard about the murder, he said: 'The first thing I thought, was holy Jesus, what did he do, I know Alan so well and I thought hold it, no. I trust Alan so much and if he did something like this, I would be devastated. Alan and Irene were very good to me when I had my own rough time. Irene was a saint to me, you don't forget things like that.' Niall also denied being anywhere near Ice House on the day of the murder, saying his visit to the garda station that evening was as close as he got to the crime scene.

His next interview was taken up by Detective Gardaí Tom Molloy (TM) and Adrian Donohoe (who was later murdered in the line of duty while on a cash escort at Lordship Credit Union in 2013). The interviewers focused on whether Niall Power (NP) ever intended going to the security exhibition in Citywest at all that day.

TM: Did you feel it was casual clothing for you to be wearing to this exhibition?

NP: No.

TM: Vincent Dullaghan feels you were dressed casually on this occasion – normally you dress in a suit.

NP: I don't normally wear a shirt and tie or suit. Only when I have meetings with clients. The suit jacket was valued at €220, the jeans were brand new costing €80, the shirt cost €120 and shoes €70. So that doesn't sound too casual to me.

TM: You can have expensive casual clothes, but Vincent feels you were unusually casually dressed, normally you would wear a suit?

NP: What can I say to that – I apologise to Vincent for letting his dress standard down.

TM: He felt that you didn't want to go?

NP: I don't understand that.

TM: I put it to you that you had no notion of going to the conference in Citywest that day.

NP: I disagree with you.

TM: You set up this excuse about your girlfriend Jane to get out of it.

NP: Yes, I said that from day one.

TM: Are they all the reasons why you didn't go to Dublin?

NP: Yes, I think I have covered everything to the best of my recollection.

Niall went on to explain that he didn't go to the security expo because he had to be back by 2 p.m. to be at a site in Dundalk. He also had to pay Anthony Lambe an advance on his wages before his employee boarded a flight to the UK. He told the gardaí: 'You are making me feel guilty now – you are pointing the finger at me. I don't feel guilty. You are going around and around in circles. Me coming back to Dundalk that day was my decision. It was done for my reasons and that's it. I have explained my reasons and if there is a problem with it I'm sorry, I have no more to say on that subject.' The detectives put to him that his ex-girlfriend, Ellen Johnson, said in her statement that he and Alan planned a plot by which he would seduce Irene on camera to use it as evidence in any future separation case. 'You are kidding me,' he responded. 'Absolutely rubbish – what more do you want to say to that.'

TM: At the same time this is a specific allegation about you seducing Irene. I put it to you that she is telling the truth.

NP: Without being discourteous to you, I am telling you the truth. 99 per cent of people that talk about me would have good things to say. She had it in for me, it is a good opportunity for her to mouth off about me. That's it, Tom.

TM: She also states that you said that Alan said to Irene 'you won't know the time or the place, but I will come back and get you and I will have a good alibi'.

NP: Absolutely not, in the name of the good Lord, definitely not.

TM: You mentioned yourself, Ellen said, about you killing an RUC man and it used to give you nightmares.

NP: Absolutely not.

When asked if he was withholding information as to the identity of the killer, Niall said that on his solicitor's advice, he would not be answering any further questions.

Gardaí repeatedly told him that they didn't believe he was revealing everything he knew. They said that surely if he had no involvement in the murder he would have made inquiries to try and find out what had happened. 'I told you everything I know,' Niall replied. 'I told you where I was on the day. I have been compliant with you and helpful in every way. I can't help any more, and my solicitor has advised me to answer no more questions. I am sorry I can't help you any more. If I hear something, I'll tell you. I have my own life. I am worried about my own business. I am not a bad boy, and I wasn't brought up that way.' The detectives then asked if he was withholding information about the murder out of long-term loyalty to Alan White? The suspect didn't address the question, only answering: 'no comment'.

As the evening wore on, gardaí in the other interview room continued to grill Alan White about the murder of his wife, as well as their marriage in the lead-up to her death. He denied inflicting violence or mental torture on her and said he never hit Irene or grabbed her by the throat. Alan again denied making the alleged alibi threat, saying the first he had heard of it was when it was brought up in a court hearing. 'These were wild allegations – if it was based on truth and Irene said it in court, it would be suicidal on my part to follow it through with a violent act against her,' he said. When the gardaí pointed out that he never mentioned these allegations to them before, he replied: 'But there weren't any incidents – that should be easy to check out. Again, when I try to explain these allegations, I'm going against what the solicitor told me.' He slowly started to deviate from his 'no comment' approach and began interacting more with his garda interviewers. The detective put it to Alan that there was a lot of evidence indicating that he and Niall planned Irene's murder. Alan replied that there were only statements from others alleging that he'd said he would get Irene and that he would have an alibi. 'A threat is a threat,' the detective told him, going on to ask if he had ever grabbed Irene by the throat. This was denied by Alan, who said he had never struck or hit Irene, and that if he did anything to his wife, she would have documented it. He said that he was one the one who organized the family counselling sessions, and that they went to the majority of them in the best of form.

He claimed that Irene would change once she was in the counselling session, and suggested that she 'tried to portray the image of playing the victim but only to selective people'. Alan told the detectives that other people who knew him, including his family, wouldn't agree with Irene's allegations. When it was put to him that Irene would say they all hated her, Alan replied that his family felt they weren't encouraged to visit, although some did. 'After all that, did you set up her death?' the detectives asked him. 'No,' Alan simply replied.

At the end of his fourth interview, Alan White said there were no bad feelings between the couple over the separation and that he was offering her 50 per cent of the net sale from the house. 'I wasn't seeing the kids and I thought if I sold, I would never see them. I decided to pull out of the sale. Eircom put a deadline on the deal. I purposely didn't reply for the children's sake. I am amazed that I am being accused of withholding information, and yet nobody approached me for ages for information.' When the gardaí put it to him that he offered Irene €200,000 from the profits of the sale of the house, as had been claimed by one of Irene's friends, he said he couldn't remember this.

Alan acknowledged there were difficult times in the relationship, but said they were quite minor, and that the idea that there is 'war at home' when people are going through a separation isn't true. He denied pulling out of the house sale deal when he realized that Irene was going to get half of the proceeds, saying he offered her 50 per cent.

The detectives put it to him that money and greed were at the heart of the issue, and that they believed he was keeping back information about the murder of his wife because of his greed. 'I have never been accused of greed by anybody,' Alan retorted. 'I have helped out numerous people.' The detectives replied that they wanted him to tell them the truth. Alan said he had been telling the truth and that, no matter where Irene was to end up living, it would have to be suitable for their children. The detectives pressed on, telling him that, from their inquiries, they believed he had information about Irene's murder that he was not telling them. 'I have no information,' he replied.

Across the hall in Niall Power's fourth interview, which began at 8.51 p.m., the gardaí probed him on his knowledge of Irene living in fear before her death, and if he was sure he had given a truthful account of his movements on the day of the murder. Time and time again, Niall Power replied, 'My solicitor has advised me to answer no more questions.' The interrogation was beginning to wear him down, though, and he asked if he could go for a cigarette. 'You are not entitled to a break yet,' the detectives informed him. When they asked if he was tired, Niall whined, 'I am knackered.'

A short time later the interviews finished for the day, and both Alan White and Niall Power agreed for the questioning to be suspended so they could avail of their rest periods. Both men slept in the custody suites of Kells garda station that night, a far cry from the comfort of their own beds. Neither had revealed anything incriminating during the interview process, and gardaí felt that more time was needed to interrogate the suspects, with their periods of detention extended that night. More intense questioning awaited Alan and Niall the following day.

9

'NO COMMENT'

The next morning, at 8.48 a.m., Alan White once again sat down in the interview room to face a further barrage of questions about his wife's murder. Gardaí began by asking him why he hadn't mentioned anything about the alleged violence towards Irene and Jennifer, with Alan replying: 'In each of the four statements, I answered any questions that were put to me and gave other background information at the time, if the gardaí required any further clarification there would have been no hesitation on my part. The gardaí have not spoken to me in almost a year and they know where and how to contact me. I have no further comment.'

Detective Garda Tom Molloy put it to him that he revealed the minimum and was drip-feeding information as he wanted to on any given day. 'The reason being, you set the thing up, and why wouldn't you hold back on it. I do believe that you set up that murder,' the detective told Alan White.

'No comment.'

He also put it to Alan that he was at breaking point at the time of the murder: his relationship was in ruins, he was potentially losing access to his children, and he was going to hand over half of everything to a woman he detested.

'No comment.'

When the detective told him that, with Irene out of the picture, it would make things an awful lot easier, he said: 'A simplistic view, no comment.'

The detective read out a statement made by Garda John Prunty, who had responded to the disturbance at Ice House in April 2003. Alan White denied the details contained in the garda's account, which described him as being angry at the scene.

The detective told him that Garda Prunty wasn't going to make a statement containing false facts, and put it to Alan that he got irate because the guards were called to his home. This was denied by Alan, who recalled being informed he would be charged with obstruction and so took his daughter from the car and went into his house. When the statements of Dympna O'Kane, in which she said Irene was in fear of Alan, were put to him he questioned if she had actually witnessed any of this. When the detective said that she was a reasonable person who wasn't going to make up stories, Alan replied that he didn't have much respect for her. Detective Garda Molloy tried to get Alan to expand on this, who only responded by saying that he had no further comment to make.

Niall Power was continuing to exercise his right to silence in the next room, refusing to answer many of the detectives' questions. When asked what he and Alan had talked about after the murder, he said he couldn't remember. The gardaí then began taking him through CCTV stills tracking his van on the morning of 6 April 2005, and his refusal to comment gradually began to change with each image that was laid out in front of him. He agreed that it was him driving the white Ford Fiesta van in the stills, before Detective Garda Adrian Donohoe (AD) showed him an image of his van passing the Carroll Village shopping centre.

AD: Where were you going?

NP: I haven't a clue, honest to God. If this is the case, I must have turned left past the house. In hindsight it's strange – that morning when I woke up, I didn't think it was important to remember every little route I took. I drove past Ice House at 11.48 a.m., so what does that prove?

AD: I will tell you in a minute. I put it to you that you went around to check out the house to see what was happening?

NP: In two minutes?

AD: I do find it strange that you were specific about most of your movements on that morning, but that you don't recall driving past the murder scene after the event happened, the murder.

NP: What are you saying? That is a strange question, I am not answering it. It's you here talking – you twist everything.

AD: Were you checking to see if the guards were there?

NP: No.

AD: Do you remember going past Ice House?

NP: I don't remember, I have said that already.

Niall repeated that his travelling past Ice House in the hours after the murder, before Irene's body was found, 'proves nothing'.

AD: Did curiosity get the better of you when you went around by Ice House?

NP: My solicitor told me not to answer any more questions.

AD: Were you checking to see if the job was done?

NP: My solicitor told me not to answer any more questions. I think it is ridiculous – that's if I even drove past the house. I may have turned right at the junction. I may have turned into Superquinn.

AD: No, you didn't. We would have picked it up.

NP: I don't think it proves anything – it doesn't point the finger at me.

AD: I put it to you that the reason you didn't travel to Dublin was that you stayed around Dundalk to keep an eye on things, and you went up by Ice House to check things out at 11.48 a.m. What have you to say to that?

NP: My solicitor told me not to answer any other questions. All you have is hindsight.

Niall accused the gardaí of trying to draw him out, and he claimed to have forgotten passing Ice House when he was making his original statement. 'It was an ordinary run-of-the-mill day for me. I know loads of houses around Dundalk. You are just getting into an argument with me. There were a few wee things

I got wrong. I made a mistake that I went up Dublin Street. I didn't know what was going on at that time. I don't know what you are talking about. My solicitor said not to answer any more questions. I'm saying no more to you,' he moaned.

In the next interview, Detective Sergeant Piper went through Niall's phone records with him and asked him about the call he made to Alan at 11.36 a.m. The men spoke for one minute and ten seconds in what gardaí felt was a 'crucial time' relating to the murder of Irene. 'Given that you had just left Alan White less than an hour and a half beforehand, what was the purpose of that call, what was said?' the detective sergeant asked.

Niall was becoming worn down by the intense questioning and needed a break. He asked for the tape to be stopped and said: 'You talk to Adrian Donohoe now, bring him in for a few minutes, please, if possible.' The interview was briefly halted but continued at 7.15 p.m., with Niall again asked about his movements close to the scene that day.

'No comment.'

Niall disagreed that Alan White was responsible for Irene's murder and said he wasn't aware of any physical or mental abuse in the marriage.

Detective Molloy didn't believe he was telling the truth. He told Niall that he made an excuse not to go to Dublin, that he drove to Ice House when he had no reason to be there, and that he used Jane as an alibi. This was at the very least suspicious, the detective commented.

'My solicitor has told me not to answer any further questions,' Niall replied.

The investigators put it to him that he was being loyal to Alan White and wouldn't discuss what he had to say about the break-up of Alan's marriage, but that he had lots to say about Irene. When Niall accused the interviewers of 'over-exaggerating', as he had only said a paragraph at most about Irene, Detective Garda Donohoe fired back: 'That's one more paragraph than you said against Alan.'

AD: Seeing as Irene was such a close friend of yours, do you know anyone other than Alan that would want her dead or would gain anything from her death?

NP: My solicitor told me to answer no more questions.

AD: Do you know who killed Irene White?

NP: No.

AD: Were you asked by Alan or anyone else to assist in any way in this murder?

NP: Definitely not.

AD: Is it possible he got someone to murder Irene unbeknownst to you?

NP: I doubt it, but everything is a possibility.

AD: Have you any information that could assist us in bringing this murder to a conclusion?

NP: I've told you everything.

The other team of detectives interrogating Alan White again brought up the alleged alibi threat, but he refused to comment on it. Asked about Irene seeking professional help to save their relationship, he told them: 'Irene went for counselling over the death of her father. Irene went to counselling for everything.'

Did he plan the murder, gardaí asked, once he started removing the cameras from Ice House, when he knew he was going to lose his children and give over half of the money from the house sale?

'No comment.'

Despite Alan White's firm stance, the detectives continued to prod at him. 'I am putting it to you that you set up and planned this from the minute you saw that you were going to lose the kids and half of your estate. The mistake you made was that you told Power and he went home and told the woman, and she told it back to Irene. What have you to say to that, Alan?'

He responded once more, 'No comment.'

The gardaí then took out several photographs recovered from electronic devices seized at Ice House. One of the pictures showed Irene in a distressed state at home early one morning in August 2004. He replied 'no comment' when asked if he had taken the photographs, only agreeing that the memory stick on which the images were saved looked like his. The detectives then produced the letters and diaries kept by Irene in which she documented threats allegedly made by Alan. Her estranged husband again had nothing to say. The questioning wore on, and shortly after 11 p.m. gardaí were about to conclude their interrogation. At the end of this final interview, Detective Sergeant Duffy brought up Niall's movements that day, and in particular that he drove past Ice House over an hour after Irene's murder.

'I am putting it to you now, Alan, that you had him in Dundalk for that period of time to keep an eye on developments, and that's why he didn't go to Dublin with you that day. That this was the final part of your plan to see Irene off. What have you to say to that?'

At this stage Alan White had been in Kells garda station for over 36 hours, in which time he had sat down to be interrogated on 12 separate occasions. At the end of his final interview, Alan repeated the phrase he had uttered 303 times over the past two days. 'No comment.' A short time later he was released without charge and walked out of the garda station, with Niall Power following him out a few minutes later.

Despite the gardaí's deep suspicions about both men knowing more than they had let on, nothing of evidential value that would prove incriminating was revealed during their interviews. They suspected that both men had conspired with the unidentified killer to murder Irene, but a decision was made not to submit an investigative file to the Director of Public Prosecutions (DPP) to consider criminal charges at this stage of the inquiry. With no evidence against Alan White or Niall Power, and the identity of the killer remaining a mystery, the investigation had run into the sand.

*

It wasn't long before Alan White was approached by the media following his arrest and asked for his thoughts on the garda investigation. In his first interview since being released from custody, he spoke with Eoin Reynolds of the *Evening Herald* newspaper and criticised the garda investigation. Alan said that 'millions of questions' remained and vented his frustration that gardaí wouldn't tell him how their investigation was progressing. He also denied being unfaithful to Irene or that he had been in another relationship since her murder, adding, 'I always loved her.' There was no mention of the fact that he had been questioned over the course of two days on suspicion of withholding information about his wife's murder.

Alan White told the journalist that he believed a mystery man was staying in Ice House in the weeks before Irene's death. 'A lot of things just looked out of place. A lot of it just wasn't right. It suggested to me that somebody else was sleeping there,' he said. Separately, he also stated that items from the property, including bank cards, were missing, which suggested to him that Irene may have disturbed a burglar. The newspaper also quoted him as saying that Irene's bank cards were discovered in the grounds of a nearby building seven months after her death and that a man was seen driving Irene's car the day before she was killed. In relation to the burglary motive, Alan White queried: 'How can they assume nothing was taken on the day? How do they know if they didn't ask me what was there in the first place?' By this stage, gardaí had definitively ruled out burglary as a motive for the murder, while there was nothing to suggest that an unknown man had been staying at Ice House. A week later in an interview with a local newspaper, Alan White acknowledged that he had been arrested on suspicion of withholding information, expressing surprise at his detention and saying he had voluntarily spoken to gardaí on a number of occasions after his wife's murder.

He was also approached at his home by crime journalist Ken Foy, of the *Star on Sunday* newspaper, and spoke about his arrest, while denying he had any involvement in Irene's death. 'I did not kill my wife,' Alan told the journalist. 'I know I am a suspect in this case, but when someone's wife is murdered, the husband is normally blamed for it. I had not been living with Irene for five months before she was murdered, and I was completely shocked when I was told about it – and I am still shocked now.' He added that he 'loved Irene' and 'had not been with another woman since. I still cannot understand why they arrested me. I don't know whether it was some kind of publicity stunt or not. The fact is that ever since this happened, I have always been on very civil terms with the gardaí.'

He went on to describe his interactions with the investigators. 'We would sit down, and I always answered all the questions they asked me, so it was very frustrating to get arrested. I spent two days in Kells garda station. It was so weird. When I was being brought to the station and brought home, the gardaí were talking and joking with me, but it was a different story in the station.' He said that he felt 'inclined to answer their questions' because 'if I was not answering what they asked, it would have seemed I had something to hide – and I have nothing to hide'.

Gardaí would have a further interaction with Alan later that year, but it was unconnected to the murder investigation. Shortly after midday on Saturday, 23 September 2006, he called into Omeath garda station to inform the guard on duty that he intended to board up broken windows at the cottage in Knocknagoran that had been willed to his dead wife by her mother. He went to the property with two workmen, a father and son, to carry out the repairs. Within ten minutes, the father and son arrived at the station to inform gardaí that there was a row at the property. Garda Michael Kermath was on duty and made his way to the cottage, where he found Kenneth Delcassian seated on top of Alan White, restraining him.

Garda Kermath separated the men and then took statements from everyone present to establish what exactly had happened. Kenneth said that he and his wife, Anne, had intended to stay at the cottage while visiting Louth, and when he arrived there that afternoon, he saw Alan in the kitchen. In a statement, he told gardaí: 'Alan White was walking towards me with a steel grinder in his hand. I think at that point I said, "you're in some fucking trouble now" and I screamed as loud as I could, "Anne, get the guards. Phone the guards." Alan was advancing towards me, and I withdrew from him. I believe he said, "Fuck off." He still had the steel grinder in his hand and I was aware of it. I said, "The guards will be here in a minute and you'll be in some shit, boy."' He then said that Alan lifted the steel grinder and, fearing he was about to be hit, Kenneth grabbed an antler ornament and struck Alan on the shoulder and leg to defend himself.

'I shouted at him again to stay back, the guards would be here any second,' Kenneth told the garda. 'Alan straightened himself up again and as he screamed, "You fucking bastard, I'll kill you", he raised the circular saw once again swinging it over his head in preparation for bringing it down on mine. Just as his arm began to move towards me once more, I swung the antler at his leg in the same position once again.' The two men then became involved in a tussle, he said, at which point the garda arrived.

Anne Delcassian also gave a similar account of the incident, saying Alan White tried to assault her husband. At the time she was looking for visitation rights to see her sister's children and had nominated the cottage as the place where the visits would occur. 'I believe that by trying to board up the house, he believed it would prevent me from bringing the children here and thus interfere with my access application,' Anne said in her statement about Alan being at the property.

In his version of events, Alan White claimed that Kenneth wouldn't allow him to open the door to leave.

The scene was sealed off by gardaí for a forensic examination, with both parties making allegations of assault against one another. In his report on the matter, Garda Kermath said he was aware legal proceedings were ongoing to decide ownership of the property, and that Anne Delcassian told him there was a court order preventing Alan White from entering the cottage. In the end, nothing came of the assault complaints.

In April 2007, on the second anniversary of Irene's murder, her sister organised a vigil in memory of every woman who had died violently in Ireland over the previous decade. The poignant service at Ice House was attended by families of some of the 126 women who had been killed in the Irish state over the previous 10 years. They included Rose and Jim Callaly, whose daughter Rachel had been murdered by her husband, Joe O'Reilly, at their home in Naul, County Dublin, on 4 October 2004. Also at the vigil were the parents and sister of Siobhan Kearney, the 38-year-old mother-of-one who was killed in her South Dublin home on 28 February 2006. It was another case in which a woman had died violently at the hands of her partner; her husband, Brian Kearney, would later be convicted of her murder. He had used a flex from a vacuum cleaner to strangle Siobhan, before pulling over the door of the en suite in their bedroom to try to make her death look like a suicide. Anne Delcassian addressed the large crowd, with some of her comments aimed directly at those involved in her sister's murder.

I know who you are. I know why you had my sister killed and I ask any of your family to have the guts to come forward with information. I know in my heart who did it, and there has to be someone out there who has a conscience and who will come forward to the gardaí. We are very, very hopeful we could identify the people who committed this crime against my sister.

Irene's daughter Jennifer was also in the crowd and listened as her aunt spoke passionately about the case, saying she was confident that gardaí would be in a position to make further arrests soon. Confirming that a €10,000 reward remained for anyone who provided information leading to the successful prosecution of those involved, Anne added: 'I won't stop until the last one of those who conspired against my sister are convicted.' Unfortunately, breaking the circle of silence would prove far more difficult than expected.

*

While the inquiry had stalled, one witness made contact with gardaí out of the blue the following year.

On 2 October 2007, Cathy Wilson requested a meeting with members of the crime branch, saying she was living in Donegal, having broken up with Vincent Dullaghan. Cathy was frightened about being seen speaking to investigators anywhere near Dundalk, and she asked that they would travel to her home. That afternoon, Detective Sergeant Brian Mohan and Detective Garda Charlie Geoghegan made the journey north, arriving at Cathy's home at 2 p.m. and speaking with her over the course of six hours. She declined to make a statement but wanted to speak to gardaí about Irene's murder. Because of her apprehensiveness, gardaí didn't take notes during the meeting, but did later make a contemporaneous record. They described Cathy as frightened of a particular individual because of their political connections and links to people involved in illegal organisations. She relayed how Niall Power was getting married to Jane McKenna in the coming months at Darver Castle in Louth and that Alan White had recently sold Ice House to a property developer. She also revealed how Niall and Alan had come to Lannett Cross after their release from garda custody in April 2006 and that both men were joking and 'treating the whole thing as a big laugh'. While she didn't make a new statement, gardaí decided to keep in contact with her in case her mind changed.

Another witness contacted investigators in September 2008, saying something had been preying on his mind ever since the murder. John Flaherty didn't initially think it was important, but then he'd heard mention of a dark car being connected to the murder in a recent newspaper report. 'I remember that day three years ago,' he told gardaí in a statement.

I left my house, and I got a bus from the Quay area. It was before 10 a.m. I was going to visit [a friend] in Cox's Demesne. She has passed away now. I think I got off the bus somewhere around the Magnet Road. I walked along what I know as the Magnet Road. I remember walking past Ice House. It was some time around 10.10 a.m. or 10.15 a.m. and I turned on to O'Hanlon Park. I walked on the footpath on the left-hand side. I noticed a car parked on the same side as the park. This car was facing down O'Hanlon Park. I walked past it. I saw a man in the driver's seat of this car. I thought that he looked like he was waiting on somebody. This fellow was rough-looking. He had a stubble. He had dark-coloured hair. He was well-built-looking. I can't say his size because he was sitting down. He looked tanned or brownish. He wasn't foreign, he just looked tanned. I crossed the street in front of the car, and I did get a good look at this man. I have no idea what type of car. I was never into cars. I didn't even look at the number. I just looked at your man because he looked at me. This car was parked next to the park which I thought was strange. It was not parked near houses. I went on about my business and headed for Cox's. I heard about the murder the next day.

The witness said he didn't initially come forward with the information because he didn't think it was relevant and feared he could wrongly implicate an innocent man. However, as the years went on, John Flaherty believed the sighting was more significant than first thought. His observations, and the timing, matched some of the descriptions given by witnesses who had seen a man running through Ice House Hill park at around 10.10 a.m. that day and approaching a car. Despite his best efforts, he wasn't able to identify the car's make or model, making it difficult for gardaí to progress this line of inquiry.

While the garda investigation had effectively ground to a halt, Anne Delcassian continued her persistent campaign. She set up a website named 'Good Night Irene', which was dedicated to her sister's memory while also posting updates on the investigation and appeals for information. Dozens of photographs of Irene were uploaded onto the website, depicting a picture montage of her life growing up in Omeath with her family and her later years in Dundalk with her children. It showed Irene enjoying happier, normal times, in stark contrast to the violent death she suffered.

On 26 April 2009, the murder of Irene White featured on RTÉ's *Crimecall* programme once again, with Anne making an emotional call for information and to keep her sister's case alive. 'I'd like to appeal to women to put themselves in my position – think of their sister on the kitchen floor, brutally murdered, bleeding when their mother would walk in and find them,' she told the programme. 'How would they feel? Just think of her. Think of a mother of three gorgeous children that will never see them again. I'll never see my sister again. I urge you just if you have the information please come forward.' Once again, however, her pleas for those with information to step forward and bring those involved to justice fell on deaf ears. With no real progress in the investigation for over three years, it seemed that Irene's case had reached a dead end, and the file was set to gather dust in an office. Anne's determination, however, would soon ensure that a newly formed team of specialist detectives reviewing cases that had gone cold would be brought in to try and solve Irene's murder.

10

THE COLD CASE UNIT

The years passed by in Dundalk and life went on, as did the violence in the town. Over time, the detectives working on the Irene White murder case were assigned to newer criminal investigations, while others were promoted, transferred, or retired. In 2010, Pat Marry was appointed as the detective inspector for the Louth policing division. A qualified senior investigating officer, he would now oversee all serious criminal investigations in the division, which included the busy towns of Drogheda and Dundalk as well as the smaller villages that stretched along the border and presented their own unique challenges. Speaking about being appointed to the new role, Detective Inspector Marry says:

It was a small division covering a small county, but an area full of all types of violent crime including murder. It had more crimes reported than any other division in the northern region, which included counties Cavan, Monaghan, Sligo, Leitrim, and Donegal. Over 50 per cent of crime recorded in the northern region occurred in Louth at that time. I was proud, full of gusto, and ready for any challenge. On my first day as detective inspector, I was faced with my first murder, that of Niall Dorr, a young man who was the victim of a vicious assault. During that investigation I was also landed with the murder of Mohammad Arif in Drogheda, another challenging inquiry into what was the first honour killing in Ireland.

Balancing these investigations was difficult, but as I have always said, the teams of detectives in Drogheda, Dundalk, and Ardee were second to none, and without them, I would have been at sea. I realised early on that the structure of a team is paramount to solving any crime. As the man in charge, I had to identify each detective's skill set and their capabilities, how best to assign tasks and manage and control each job to its maximum outcome. This strategy worked both ways. As time passed my detectives became very aware of what I stood for, what I expected from them, and knew that they could rely on me to have their backs. It was a strategy of mine that I believed in, and it worked.

As detective inspector, my new role was off to an interesting start, with two murders in a short space of time. What I was not prepared for was the workload, the willing donkey syndrome, as I was also appointed as senior investigating officer to legacy cases within the division. A box arrived at my office, and written on it was the name 'Ciara Breen', a 17-year-old girl who had disappeared from Dundalk in February 1997 and was presumed murdered.

Another box arrived in relation to the historic sexual abuse allegations against Dr Michael Shine at Our Lady of Lourdes Hospital in Drogheda. Yet another was marked 'Irene White'. I remember looking at these boxes in my office on several occasions and wondering, 'Where will I start?' If there was not enough already to push me to the limit, the legacy cases certainly did. I put these boxes on top of my filing cabinet in my office. You could not get away from the fact they were real cases and I had to investigate them at some stage. I set about getting up to date with the Michael Shine investigation, which was ongoing and, in my mind, a dragged-out affair, eventually taking two files to the DPP, resulting in his conviction in 2019.

Meanwhile, the file on the unsolved murder of Irene White remained in a box in my office. I would regularly take it down and look through the documents to see if I could make sense of the case, and to see what was done by the previous investigation team to solve it. I always remember studying the crime scene photographs, and looking at Irene's body covered in blood with her head propped against the dishwasher, and evidence of the culprit's runner footprint in blood as he left the scene. I often thought to myself, 'Who was that person in those runners – could I catch him?' You reflect on who could have done this and think of how senseless the whole thing was.

By the time Detective Inspector Marry took up the murder investigation, a new and unique unit within the garda organisation was in operation. Made up of a team of detectives looking at so-called 'cold cases', the Serious Crime Review Team would become the focus of Anne's unwavering resolve. The unit had been formed in 2007 and gave the state a specialist tool with which to bring historical cases to a successful conclusion. Its purview was to focus on serious criminal investigations that had gone unsolved, but which could be progressed through modern investigative techniques, advances in forensic science, or simply reviewing an inquiry from a fresh perspective. Given the nature of their work, they became colloquially known as the 'cold case unit'.

The man tasked with setting up the new unit was Detective Superintendent Christy Mangan. A highly experienced and respected criminal investigator, he had previously served as a detective in the Crumlin garda district and the Garda National Drugs Unit, and was later appointed detective inspector for Fitzgibbon Street garda station. While stationed in Dublin's north inner city he oversaw the high-profile investigation into the 2005 murder of Farah Swaleh Noor, whose body was dismembered and scattered across different parts of the capital. Charlotte and Linda Mulhall, the daughters of Noor's lover, would later be convicted of his murder and manslaughter respectively and were given the moniker 'The Scissor Sisters' by the media.

Detective Superintendent Mangan's small team began examining files of over 200 homicides that had occurred in Ireland since 1980, assessing and prioritising cases where there was a realistic chance of advancing the investigation. The team were brought in under the umbrella of the Garda National Bureau of Criminal Investigation and operated out of their offices in Harcourt Square. The idea of a cold case unit had been popularised in the United States and was a growing phenomenon in the UK. While such a unit was a relatively new concept in Ireland, it wasn't completely alien either. A decade earlier, a special task force working under Operation Trace had been set up to investigate the disappearances of several women in the Leinster area to determine if the unsolved cases were connected and if a sole perpetrator was responsible.

Having received specialist training in cold case review techniques in the UK, Detective Superintendent Mangan set about meeting with senior detectives across the country to brief them on the assistance his unit could provide. While the prospect of a separate team of gardaí poring over every decision made in a case could cause apprehension among the original investigation team, the unit received praise for its unbiased approach. Detective Inspector Marry says of this:

> I knew how solid the review team were and they could bring the case to a successful conclusion. They were highly respected within the organisation. Detective Superintendent Christopher Mangan had set up the review team, which he built into a very professional outfit, with a method of review that is second to none.

In its early stages the unit showed how significant advancements could be made in an investigation by looking at it through a fresh lens, while some cases also highlighted how they were in a constant battle against the passage of time. One of their first reviews was the murder of Rita Ponsford, a 45-year-old woman found dead in her Limerick home in January 1985. A post-mortem examination established that she had been strangled with a man's necktie and that she had died up to two months before her body was discovered. Her husband, Martin, had disappeared before his wife's remains were found, and despite extensive garda inquiries at the time, he had never been located. The Serious Crime Review Team began looking at the original case file and eventually managed to trace Martin Ponsford's movements.

He had initially travelled to the United States and onto Mexico, before flying to Spain. The garda inquiries established that he was staying at a sheltered accommodation in the English county of Lancashire by 2007. The investigation team's review pointed to Martin Ponsford as the only suspect in his wife's murder, and they started making arrangements to fly over to the UK and interview him. However, fate intervened, and as gardaí set about contacting the Lancashire constabulary to put the final plans in place, Martin Ponsford passed away suddenly. The only suspect in the murder had died, robbing Rita Ponsford, her family, and the gardaí of bringing the killer to justice. It was, though, an early indication of the progress that could be achieved with a dedicated cold case unit.

Another case that the Serious Crime Review Team focused on in its formative years was the murder of 43-year-old Bernard 'Brian' McGrath. McGrath had been last seen in 1987, but human remains were recovered near his home in Longford in 1993 following a tip-off, and examinations revealed that he had been beaten to death before his body was dismembered, burned, and later buried. It wasn't until 2008 that advancements in forensic science established beyond doubt that the remains were those of Brian McGrath. The cold case unit travelled to the UK to interview witnesses, which resulted in a breakthrough in the investigation. His wife, Vera, and his daughter's fiancé, Colin Pinder, were later charged with the murder. Pinder was subsequently found guilty of manslaughter, while Vera McGrath was convicted of her husband's murder. However, she successfully appealed the conviction, and the murder charge was quashed. Vera McGrath later pleaded guilty to a lesser charge of being an accessory after the fact in helping Pinder dispose of her husband's remains.

The unit instilled fresh hope in Anne Delcassian, and she began canvassing Detective Superintendent Mangan to take up the investigation into her sister's murder. She remained in regular contact with the senior detective, showing up at his office at Harcourt Square unannounced, armed with scones, to have an impromptu meeting with him about Irene's murder. Anne's tenacity paid off, and in November 2010 the unit requested an 85-page briefing document from Dundalk garda station that detailed the circumstances of Irene's murder and outlined where the investigation stood. Two months later, on 9 January 2011, Detective Superintendent Mangan was formally appointed to undertake a review into the murder of Irene White. The news was met with relief by Detective Inspector Marry.

Anne Delcassian was a formidable force and she fought relentlessly for justice and for her sister's killer to be brought to book. When I was appointed as the senior investigating officer of Irene's murder it wasn't long before she made contact. I was told 'Your heart will be broken with her contacting you and wanting to know what you are doing.' I respected her approach, and it was her resilience that led to the cold case review team taking a look at the case. I remember thinking to myself, 'Happy days – I don't have to do anything until their review is complete.'

I was to hand over all material that had been accumulated as a result of the investigation by Dundalk gardaí to the review team. I knew if I was to get the case back again, they would have evaluated and recommended actions to be taken on certain aspects of the case. I saw this handing over the file as a win-win for me at that time. I was relieved that I didn't have to get started into the case, as I already had a busy workload. After documenting every item, I handed over the file to the review team in early February 2011. I honestly thought at that stage that this would be the last I would see or hear of the Irene White murder. How wrong was I.

*

To start the process, the Serious Crime Review Team served terms of reference on Dundalk gardaí which included the strategy that would be implemented to try and solve the murder. Detective Garda Frank O'Neill was appointed to lead the review and got to work with his colleagues. Senior garda management had set an ambitious target for the task to be completed, and a letter sent to the Dundalk investigation team stated that the review would be finalised by 1 June 2011. As the inquiry progressed, it became clear that there was a significant workload to undertake and the deadline wouldn't be met. They started examining the status of all suspects and evaluated their connection to the crime with an aim of implicating or eliminating every single person. A similar approach was taken with witnesses and persons of interest, while all phone data and CCTV footage recovered during the original investigation was also re-examined. While the crime had occurred in 2005, the retention of evidence would have to meet the standards of any criminal trial in the present day, and it was of paramount importance that all CCTV material retained during the investigation could be tracked from the original source to its current location. While the unit would set out its list of recommendations in a final report, 'fast-track' recommendations would also be made while the review was live for the crime branch in Dundalk to follow up on immediately.

In the initial stages of their work, the cold case team familiarised themselves with the details of the case, which included not only the murder itself, but also Irene's background and her marriage to Alan. They began looking at all possible motives for the crime, including whether Irene was murdered in a burglary gone wrong or if there was sexual intent behind the killing. Again, though, there was nothing to support these theories, and the cold case unit agreed with the original investigation team's findings: that Irene White had been murdered as a result of a number of people working in concert to have her killed.

Family liaison officers had been appointed during the original investigation to Anne Delcassian and Alan White, to keep them informed of developments in the case as well as providing ongoing support. But one liaison garda had by now retired and the other had been promoted, and no new officers had been appointed to formally communicate with the family. It was one of the first aspects of the case that needed to be addressed. It was clear that the original murder inquiry had covered a significant amount of ground but lost momentum after Alan White and Niall Power were released without charge in May 2006. Documentation showed that the last case conference was held in the days before the two men were arrested, and there

Irene White (née McBride) with her estranged
husband, Alan White.

Louth businessman Niall Power: the 'middleman' in orchestrating the murder.

© Ciara Wilkinson

Former student and security worker Anthony Lambe,
hired to carry out the murder.

The crime scene at Ice House on Demesne Road, Dundalk, Co Louth, on April 6, 2005.

An aerial photograph of Ice House and the surrounding area. The markings show the route Anthony Lambe took through the adjacent park to get to and from the murder.

The back door of Ice House, where Anthony Lambe launched his fatal attack on Irene White.

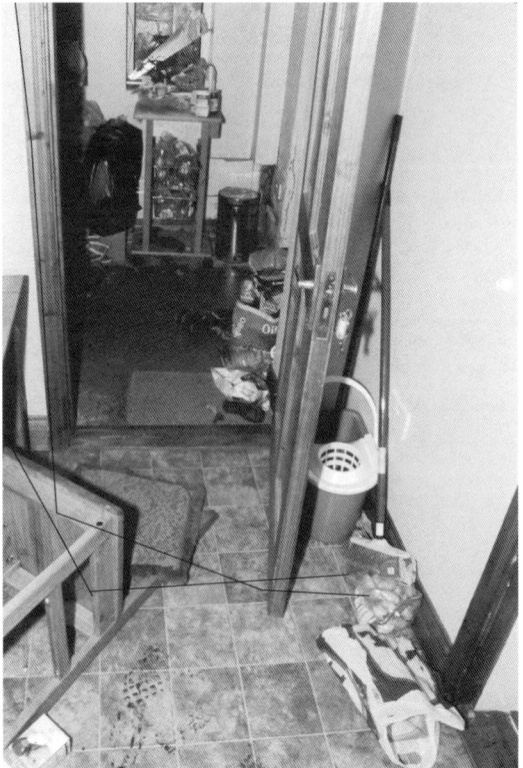

The kitchen in Ice House where Irene White's body was discovered by her mother Maureen.

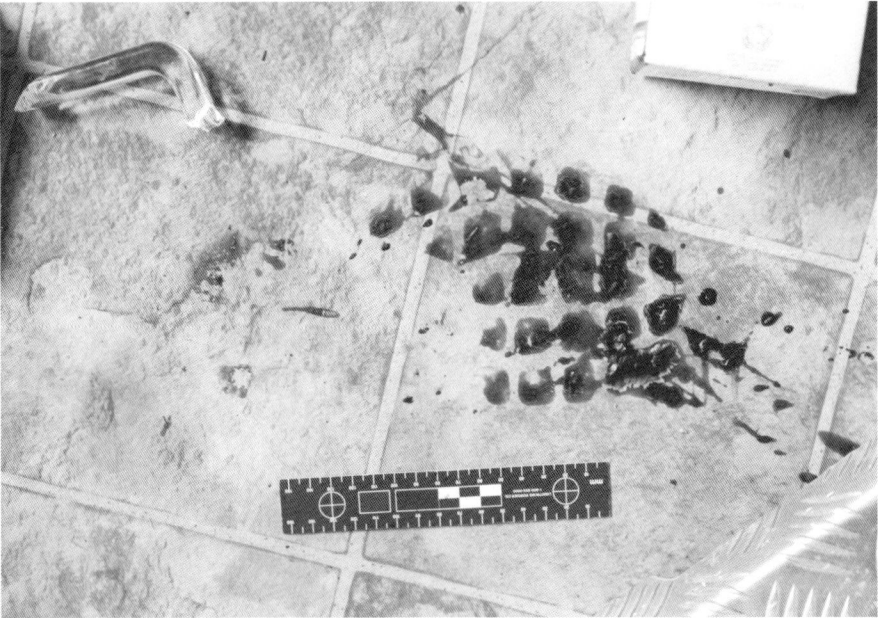

A bloodied runner print left at the scene by Anthony Lambe.

A runner cast discovered in Ice House Hill park, near the murder scene, which was left by Anthony Lambe.

Niall Power's Ford Fiesta work van, with a distinctive orange stripe, captured on CCTV footage driving around Dundalk shortly after the murder.

Niall Power's Ford Fiesta work van captured on CCTV travelling towards Ice House shortly after he was informed of the murder.

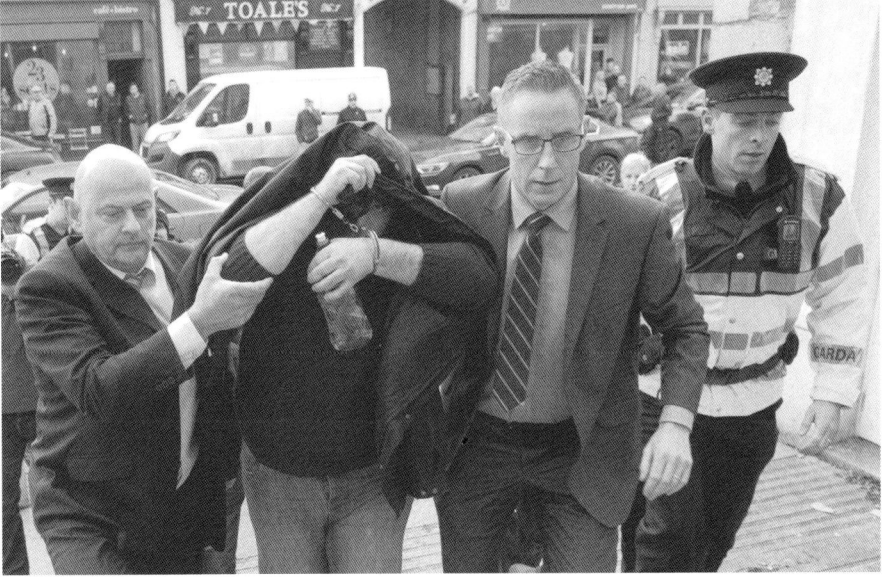

© Ciara Wilkinson

Detective Inspector Pat Marry (l) and Detective Sergeant Mick Sheridan (r) escorting Anthony Lambe, with his face covered, to Dundalk court.

© Collins Photo Agency

Anne Delcassian, who relentlessly led a dignified campaign to ensure her sister got justice, speaking to the media outside the Criminal Courts of Justice on Parkgate Street, Dublin.

© Collins Photo Agency

Irene White's eldest daughter Jennifer leaving court following Anthony Lambe's sentencing hearing.

© Collins Photo Agency

Alan White, the estranged husband of Irene White, who has always denied any involvement in her murder.

was no record of any further briefings taking place over the course of nearly five years. The review team could also only find records of three jobs that had been generated since 2006, relating to witnesses that were followed up on, showing that the original investigation had exhausted all avenues available to them.

New lines of inquiry were looked at, one of which related to the footprints left by the killer at the scene. The forensic scientist involved in examining the plaster casts of the runner marks still had the exhibits in his possession, and no statement had been taken from him about his findings. The casts could prove vital in identifying any suspects, or at least narrowing down the pool of potential killers, and had to be investigated further.

While the Serious Crime Review Team were issued with a detailed covering report, it didn't formally specify who was considered a suspect in the case. Two handwritten lists were located among the files, one with ten names and the other with five, referred to as persons of interest. The ten names were referred to as the 'suspects list', which included the likes of Angelo O'Riordan and Robbie Maguire, who had been interviewed as part of the initial investigation and ruled out. The five persons of interest were thought to possibly have had some knowledge of the crime but were also eliminated from inquiries. The review team, though, were approaching the matter with a clean slate and believed further inquiries should be carried out into every person on the suspect lists. This included comparing their shoe sizes to the footmarks left at the scene and locating pictures of the men from 2005 in order to compare their likenesses with the suspicious male seen near Ice House on the morning of the murder.

On review, they saw that Angelo O'Riordan had an alibi

and there was no motive for him to murder his girlfriend's mother, while they found that Robbie Maguire had only come into the investigation because a local woman had heard a rumour that he was involved, after he was allegedly seen cleaning blood off himself sometime after the murder. The cold case detectives realised that a statement had never even been taken from this woman, and they suggested that she should be interviewed in a station on camera. Once this process was complete, they recommended that the senior investigating officer should consider conclusively eliminating Robbie Maguire from garda inquiries. As the review progressed, the cold case team also came to believe that none of the men on the lists had any involvement in the crime.

Given that both Alan White and Niall Power had been arrested during the investigation, the Serious Crime Review Team considered both suspects in the case, and they too had to either be implicated or eliminated from the inquiry as time went on.

As well as looking at how the investigation had been carried out, the review team evaluated organisational issues that could be improved to help not just the Irene White investigation but also future cases. The only marks left by the killer at the scene were the bloody shoeprints, but when gardaí examined the PULSE database, they found there was no facility on the system to search for individuals based on their shoe size. This was a potentially important factor to help narrow down a list of suspects, and they recommended that a new field be made available on the PULSE system to accommodate a search based on footwear size.

The review also raised questions about how details were recorded on the garda database. One man on the suspects list had four different profiles and was linked to hundreds of incidents including a sexual assault. However, his four PULSE profiles each contained contradictory information. He had different dates of birth recorded on two profiles, while his height varied from 5 foot to 5 feet 10 inches tall. Another suspect on the list had a common first name and surname, and a search of the system showed that 23 people with the same full name lived in the Dundalk area. The review team noted it was 'vitally important' to establish which individual was the suspect referred to on the list, as they were 'not in a position to identify which [suspect] is being referred to and therefore cannot offer advice on this person'. In its later report, the Serious Crime Review Team also stated that sparse backgrounds were compiled on many of the suspects.

From looking at the documents and statements provided to them, the cold case unit believed that close contact should be kept with several witnesses interviewed during the original investigation, to see if they had any further information to offer. This included Vincent Dullaghan and Cathy Wilson as well as Niall Power's ex-girlfriend Ellen Johnson. They also advised that Ellen should be 'reinterviewed regarding her knowledge of the relationship between Irene and Alan, as well as other information which Niall Power may have relayed to her regarding an alleged plan to get rid of Irene White'. The fact that she stated Niall had admitted to murdering an RUC member was also of interest to the review team.

A study of the investigation files showed that 'Job 341' had been generated to examine any links Niall Power had to the IRA or the murder of an RUC member in Northern Ireland. The review team found a note contained within the original jobs book that stated: 'No intelligence to suggest this is true.

No record by gardaí.' For the cold case unit, however, it wasn't clear whether this referred to the IRA connection or the RUC murder, and there was no indication of what inquiries had been carried out into the claims. They believed it was important to speak with Ellen Johnson again about Niall Power's alleged admission of murdering an RUC member and that any relevant information should be passed on to the Police Service of Northern Ireland (PSNI), which replaced the RUC in 2001.

The cold case detectives also reviewed each statement provided by the 60 people who were in or near Ice House Hill park on the morning of 6 April 2005. From reviewing these witness statements, which contained sightings of other people in the park, they believed that a further 92 potential witnesses were never identified or spoken to. However, they did acknowledge that many reports of people seeing an unidentified person could have been multiple sightings of the one individual. The review team were also cognisant that there would be ongoing concerns in the locality that a killer was still at large. In one report they noted: 'In order to allay any fear in the community, the murder of Irene White must be solved. This crime remains unresolved almost ten years on. Therefore, it may be perceived that a murderer may be living in the Dundalk community or surrounding communities. In today's digital and social media society, a multitude of communication channels are available to An Garda Síochána enabling them to reach people throughout the world.'

As with most serious criminal investigations, press clippings covering Irene White's murder were gathered during the original inquiry. These were reviewed, and in some instances there wasn't any evidence to corroborate claims made in certain media reports. In one newspaper article, reference was made to gardaí recovering DNA at the crime scene from a man who 'has long been the chief suspect' in the murder. However, the Serious Crime Review Team found no documentation within the case files to support this report and recommended that gardaí should establish 'if the facts behind the aforementioned articles have been researched'.

One media report of interest was the interview Alan White did with the *Evening Herald* newspaper in July 2006, in which he claimed a mystery man may have been sleeping in his wife's house and that items, including bank cards, had been missing from the property. Detectives found several bank cards belonging to Irene White stored within the exhibits, but there was no indication of when and where they were found or at what time they were last used. It was important to establish if the cards were recovered from the house or elsewhere after the murder, as the cold case unit noted: 'These cards may have been stolen by Irene White's killer on the day of the murder, or stolen in advance by a person known to Irene White or a person who had access to her cards, and used as a red herring for the investigation team.'

As news spread of the cold case unit's involvement in the Irene White murder investigation, potentially significant information was coming to light. Through confidential informants and new witnesses, they were about to follow different paths leading them to IRA members, gangsters, and a man whose partner believed he had carried out the murder. The review team's work was only beginning.

11

INFORMANTS AND TIP-OFFS

The correspondence that arrived at Dundalk garda station clearly contained sensitive information, with the word 'SECRET' marked in bold letters across the front page. The file had been sent from Crime and Security, the clandestine garda section that oversees intelligence relating to serious crime and national security. It contained potentially significant information about the murder of Irene White that needed to be looked into. As the case was still being reviewed by the cold case unit, the correspondence was forwarded on to their offices at Harcourt Square.

When members of the Serious Crime Review Team looked at the document, they saw that it contained intelligence naming two men alleged to have been responsible for Irene's murder. Both were known to gardaí for their involvement in IRA activity, but they had never appeared in the murder investigation before now. A confidential informant had claimed that one IRA member was paid €60,000 by a person known to Irene White to have her killed, and that the actual murder was carried out by a younger member of the dissident republican group. Gardaí carried out inquiries into the explosive claim and established that the IRA man alleged to have organised the killing lived in close proximity to Lannett Cross in Monaghan, where Alan White and Niall Power were on the morning of 6 April 2005.

The IRA man, who was 33 years old at the time of the murder, was no stranger to authorities on both sides of the border. He had come to the attention of gardaí on no less than 74 occasions, including for firearm-related crimes, aggravated burglary, and brothel keeping. He had also been investigated for his suspected involvement in an armed robbery during which a gang dressed as gardaí stole hundreds of thousands of euros worth of cigarettes. The man had also been arrested on several occasions for membership of an illegal organisation. The most serious crime he had been investigated for was the murder of David McGuinness, a security worker who was 35 years old when he was shot dead at the front door of his Tallaght home in 2003. The IRA man now being linked to the Irene White murder had also been the target of violence himself in the past, when he was the victim of a shooting. He had also once been issued with a Garda Information Message (GIM) form – a formal document served on a person where gardaí have information that there is a credible threat to their life.

The details contained in the intelligence, referring to a specific amount of €60,000 being paid to Irene's killers, led gardaí to believe that there could be substance to the claims. There was an early setback, though, when investigators carried out inquiries into the IRA man and it became clear that he couldn't have been at the murder scene on 6 April 2005. That morning, in an unrelated investigation into firearms offences, he had been arrested at his home shortly after 7 a.m. The man was detained at Drogheda garda station for two days and only released from garda custody shortly before midnight on 8 April 2005. The cold case team concluded that he therefore could not have been directly involved, although it was possible that he solicited another person to carry out the murder. Inquiries by the Garda Bureau of Fraud Investigation showed that no large sums of money had been lodged into any of the man's bank accounts.

The other person named in the garda intelligence, aged 32 at the time of Irene's murder, was a violent criminal with dissident republican links, and gardaí looked at the possibility that he could have carried out the actual killing. He had come to garda attention on multiple occasions for crimes including aggravated burglary, firearms offences, issuing death threats, and robbery. The man had also been investigated previously over a rape, with the matter proceeding to the Central Criminal Court until the injured party withdrew her original statement, resulting in the case collapsing. This line of inquiry would also lead to a dead end for the cold case unit, as it emerged that this man had been in custody in Portlaoise Prison at the time of Irene's murder for firearms offences. Financial checks also showed that no large sums of money were lodged into his bank account.

While the information from the informant was clearly incorrect, the cold case unit couldn't eliminate the men from their inquiries completely. In a report on the suspects, the review team said it couldn't be discounted that those who conspired to murder Irene White requested the man serving a custodial sentence in Portlaoise Prison 'to assist in the murder', adding that the investigation team should consider identifying everyone who visited the criminal while he was serving his custodial sentence. It was the first of many tip-offs that would have to be carefully scrutinised.

On 10 October 2011, a woman rang Dundalk garda station asking to speak to a detective about the murder of Irene White. The caller said she had information which may be relevant to the investigation team, and four days later Detective Sergeant Piper met the woman to take a witness statement from her. She had concerns about her former partner, who had made strange comments to her a number of years earlier. His remarks led her to believe that he could have been the man who attacked Irene White. She recalled how in or around 2008 her partner, who had a history of psychiatric problems, spoke about wanting to die, that he had done 'something terrible' in the past, and that he had said, 'I killed the bitch.' When the woman asked him who he was referring to, he responded: 'That bitch who rejected me, the one in Ice House.'

The woman also revealed how a year earlier, in 2007, she had been passing Ice House with her partner when he stated that a woman had been killed at the property. He was also sure to emphasise that the gardaí never caught the killer. The witness had been informed by her boyfriend that he had gone to school with Irene and had a crush on her, but that she had rejected him, leaving him devastated. The core of the woman's information was that she suspected her former partner may have had something to do with Irene's death, given his unusual and pointed remarks. Unfortunately, the man had taken his own life in 2009, having on multiple occasions said that he had done something awful in the past and didn't deserve to live. The review team made several fast-track recommendations, which were forwarded to the investigation to follow up on. With the man now deceased, though, it would be a difficult task to pursue.

Other avenues of investigation came to the attention of gardaí through the local community. On 6 April 2012, the seventh anniversary of Irene's murder, her brother-in-law Kenneth Delcassian was attending the annual vigil at Ice House. He met local woman Dinah McKevitt, who informed him that her friend 'had observed a male running from the park on the morning of the murder'. Kenneth relayed the information to his wife, Anne, who in turn spoke to Dinah, saying she would check with her friend to ensure that the information was accurate. Gardaí were also informed of what had been said. However, the account changed, and the friend said that she had heard about a man running from the park on the morning of the murder, rather than witnessing it herself.

A review of witness statements showed that the friend had not previously spoken to gardaí, and Dinah was approached by members of the cold case team who told her they needed to confirm exactly what was heard and by whom to determine if it could assist their investigation. She said her friend was pregnant at the time and she wanted to speak to her first, out of fear that she would get a shock if gardaí arrived at her door unannounced. Detective Garda Frank O'Neill subsequently met with the friend at her home in Dundalk. She informed him that she had not observed a man in Ice House Hill park on the day of the murder or heard anything about it and that Dinah McKevitt had been mistaken.

*

The unsolved murder was still gathering media interest even seven years on, and on the evening of 31 July 2012, the *Cracking Crime* documentary series on RTÉ aired an episode featuring the killing of Irene White. The programme included a reconstruction of the murder, as well as Irene's final days, and focused on a number of specific strands that the investigation team were keen to follow up on. Detective Sergeant Brian Mohan spoke on the programme and said that gardaí had interviewed some 2,500 people since the investigation began, but three people spotted in Ice House Hill park on the morning of the murder hadn't yet been accounted for. The investigator said that gardaí were anxious to speak to these people, one of whom was seen crossing the park in the direction of Ice House at around 9.25 a.m., wearing a three-quarter-length green coat and a black scarf. The second person, dressed in a grey hoodie with the hood up, was seen going in the opposite direction from Ice House, towards the O'Hanlon Park entrance. The third person they sought was described as wearing a waist-length jacket and possibly a baseball cap. He was witnessed running through the park and getting into a dark-coloured car at the O'Hanlon Park entrance.

Detective Superintendent Mangan also spoke on the documentary and explained to viewers that gardaí were trying to implicate or eliminate these people from their inquiries. He added that if the third person 'got into a car driven by someone else, then there are at least one if not a number of people who are in possession of information'. Appealing for anyone with knowledge of these people to come forward, he said: 'What we have seen before is that, over time, people want to impart the information. They don't know how to deal with it in their mind, especially if they have lived with this for years.' He described the murder as a 'very vicious, very violent attack', with the killer leaving 'little or no opportunity for Irene to defend herself'. Detective Superintendent Mangan continued:

'I have no doubt that for the person who entered the house and assaulted Irene, their intention was to kill her.' The senior investigator said he understood that there may be an element of fear for people around going to the gardaí about what they know, but added: 'We will certainly look at the reasons why they could not or did not come forward at the time.'

Speaking on the same programme, Anne Delcassian described the devastating sight that had greeted her elderly mother as she came across the body. 'Irene had lost eight pints of blood – it was a horrific scene for our poor mother, who died six months later on the day of Irene's birthday. Irene was in fear for her life at this point. She was a very clever lady, she knew she had to tell people. Was she thinking, "Am I going to be murdered today or tomorrow?"' The investigators who spoke on the programme said that the killer may have been wearing bloodstained clothing fleeing the scene. 'We are anxious to find out what happened to these clothes. Were they discarded? Were they washed?' Detective Superintendent Mangan said. He urged people to consider if anyone they knew was acting strangely or suspiciously before the date of Irene's murder, on the day of it, or afterwards. The programme also informed the public that a €34,000 reward was now in place for information that would lead to the arrests and convictions of the people responsible. The gardaí and Anne Delcassian hoped that the documentary would result in someone coming forward with more information. It didn't take long after the end credits began to roll for people to get in touch.

Shortly after the programme aired, a woman rang into the RTÉ offices but there was no answer. She immediately phoned back at 10.47 p.m. and still couldn't get through to anyone who had worked on the programme. The woman, clearly annoyed that her phone calls had gone unanswered, left a voicemail on the answering machine.

> Hi, I'm just ringing in relation to the television documentary tonight. There's not one person to answer the phone to me in regard to this documentary so whatever I was giving at the minute, you're not going to know it now anyway. Alright, bye.

When producers listened back to the message they immediately notified gardaí, who were intrigued by the phone call. Clearly the woman felt she had information that could help the investigation, but she hadn't left her name or any details of how to contact her. An application was subsequently made to the Crime and Security branch to identify the caller through the name registered to the phone number. It turned out that the woman was well known to the investigation team. The anonymous caller was Cathy Wilson.

She had already made two statements to gardaí and also spoken to them informally in recent years, but the voicemail suggested she had more to say. By chance, Cathy had encountered a garda while at a sporting event in Dublin on 5 August, five days after the *Cracking Crime* documentary aired. She inquired if the garda had seen the programme and informed him that a lot of the information in it was incorrect. She also said that she was in the process of a civil court action and, once this was completed, she would sort out the matter of making a new witness statement. On the back of the phone call and these comments, the investigation team looked at Cathy Wilson from a different perspective and began making arrangements to speak with her.

In the meantime, another person called the *Crimecall* line wishing to get something off his chest. Shortly before 6 p.m. on 7 August 2012, a phoneline operator answered a call from a man speaking with a Louth accent. At first it sounded like the caller was muttering to himself, or speaking to someone beside him. 'Eh ... what do I do? ... Hello ... Hello...' he said before hanging up. The man immediately rang back from the same number, telling the call taker:

> I'd like to report from the Irene White murder ... eh ... I want to remain anonymous on this ... that morning of that murder I was coming to work. I saw a man coming out of the park, Ice House Hill park. He was about 5 feet 9 inches, well dressed, blood on his shirt, and got into an Audi A4, a light green Audi A4 ... and it had tinted-out windows. He got in by the Echo Road and that's the last I seen of it. I wish to remain anonymous with this information ... just it has annoyed me that I never gave it sooner ... Thank you very much, bye-bye.

The recording and phone number used to make the call were sent on to Dundalk gardaí, who soon identified the source of the strange phone call. The man who had called in was from Dundalk and had been in his late teens at the time Irene White was murdered. On 18 November 2012, Detective Sergeant Mohan and Detective Garda O'Neill called to the man's home, and he agreed to tell gardaí what he had seen on the day of the murder. While he declined to make a formal statement, the detectives took a memorandum of the conversation. The witness said he had spoken to his sister on the day of the murder and told her what he had seen, but seven years on, he was struggling to recall the exact events. His sister, who was present as gardaí spoke to her brother, interjected and said he had seen a suspicious man in the park that morning. At the time, she had told her brother to keep quiet and not to tell anyone what he had witnessed, as she feared for his safety if he got involved in the case.

Asked to think back and describe the mysterious figure getting into the car, the man said he was about 5 feet 9 inches, clean-shaven with a tight haircut.

> I couldn't tell you what colour the hair was, it was that tight. I'd put him in his early to mid-40s. He wasn't well built; I'd say medium build. He was wearing a white shirt, black trousers, black shoes, and a black jacket which came down to his knees. The shirt was closed up but the top button was open. He was dressed like a doorman basically. When I first saw him he was walking with his hands down by his side, but he was pacing along, walking fast. The jacket was open, that's how I copped the blood on his shirt. The blood was on the left side of his shirt, kind of by his side. He put his head down and paced past, closing his coat over and going towards the Echo Road, heading under the railway bridge.

The witness said he was cycling past the man, who got into an old-style Audi A4 with tinted windows.

The cold case unit began reviewing CCTV footage available to them from the surrounding area but, much to their frustration, some of the camera footage seized during the original investigation had degraded and was no longer viewable. In one fast-track recommendation to Dundalk gardaí, the unit said that investigators should travel the route outlined by the witness 'in order to accurately map the route taken by him on the way to work and in particular the precise location where he saw the man exiting Ice House Hill park'. They also said that the investigation team should establish if the witness had told any other family members or friends about what he had seen. One final fast-track recommendation made was to consider asking the witness 'to view a montage of photographs containing images of the persons of interest (as they were at the time of the murder), who have come to the attention of the investigation team, with a view to identifying the man he saw exiting Ice House Hill park on 6 April 2005'.

Eventually the cold case unit's inquiries identified a similar green Audi belonging to a female associate of Patrick 'Mooch' Blair, a notorious member of the Provisional IRA. In 2002 he had been named in the UK House of Commons as the man who built the bomb that caused the Omagh massacre, the largest single atrocity of the Northern Ireland conflict, claiming 29 lives. It was an allegation he strenuously denied. In later years Blair was also described as the leader of a splinter dissident republican group, the Continuity IRA. He was also listed in garda intelligence as a close associate of the IRA man named by the confidential informant as receiving €60,000 to murder Irene White. Following a number of inquiries, the cold case unit nominated Blair as a person of interest in the murder of Irene White, given the sighting of a man with blood getting into an Audi similar to the one Blair had access to. They made some 10 fast-track recommendations that should be conducted in respect of Blair. As with other persons of interest, this included confirming his shoe size and comparing images of him from 2005 to sightings of the man seen running through

Ice House Hill shortly after the murder. Ultimately, though, this line of inquiry came to nothing, and Blair was ruled out of having any connection to the crime. Speaking about how this played out, Detective Inspector Marry says:

Sometimes some recommendations are futile and lead to nothing, like when the cold case team were contacted by a man who alleged he saw a green Audi parked near Ice House Hill park and a man with a white shirt get into it. He stated the man had blood on his shirt. This seemed promising at first but when this potential witness was further spoken to his story changed and there were too many inconsistencies to pay any credence to his account. Another woman had rung in to nominate an ex-partner as being the murderer from a comment he made. This was bottomed out and her ex-partner had passed away in 2009 so that was that. A lot of time and effort is put into following up certain avenues which lead nowhere. With manpower being low, I had to streamline what jobs need prioritising.

*

That October, Detective Superintendent Mangan and Detective Garda O'Neill visited Cathy Wilson at her home in Donegal. During the meeting she was asked what she meant in her voice-mail on the night of the RTÉ documentary, and she replied that 'the times on the programme were all off'. When she was pressed on this, Cathy said she couldn't put her finger on it or say which parts, but that the times were wrong. She said she had fears for her own safety, adding: 'The times are annoying me.'

During this meeting, she also told gardaí that a person had previously mentioned to her that it would only cost €30,000 to have someone murdered in Dundalk. These comments, she said, were made before Irene was killed, but she refused to say who had said this or make a statement on the matter. Cathy told them that she would provide a further witness statement once she had concluded the civil court action she was taking. After speaking to Cathy, the detectives were left with the distinct impression that she had more to offer.

Gardaí were also continuing to receive intelligence from other confidential informants about the murder of Irene White. In 2013 a detective based in Dundalk was contacted by a man who sought a private meeting with him. During this encounter, the detective was provided with the names of three people who the informant claimed were involved in Irene's murder. One man was a member of the INLA from the Dundalk area and had previously been investigated over the Tallaght murder of David McGuinness in 2003. This individual also had a long criminal history, including firearms incidents, immigration offences, and making threats to kill, while he had also been previously linked to a bank robbery. He was another associate of the IRA man who it was claimed had been paid €60,000 to murder Irene.

As part of their recommendations, the cold case unit advised the investigation team to confirm if the garda's intelligence section, the Special Detective Unit, or the Criminal Assets Bureau had the criminal's mobile number, which could be compared against cell site records obtained during the original murder inquiry. It also emerged that the man had previously given a statement in 2006 as part of the murder investigation. At the time, he had told gardaí that he had been travelling along the M1 motorway on the day of the murder when he noticed a Garda Technical Bureau van driving in front of him before it turned off at the Dundalk exit. 'I thought something must have happened,' he said at the time. 'I heard about the murder then that evening. I know nothing about this murder. I have no information to offer, if I knew anything I would say so.'

The informant who contacted the Dundalk detective further alleged that the INLA figure organised the crime and paid a man called Seamus McMahon to plan how the murder was to be carried out. Seamus McMahon was well known within the Dundalk area for his involvement in organised crime and had been investigated in the past for firearms offences. In 2006 he had also been tried before the non-jury Special Criminal Court for membership of the IRA, having been stopped two years earlier in a car with his wife and son during which gardaí found ten 9 millimetre bullets wrapped in socks in the driver's door pocket. Despite the evidence of a chief superintendent that McMahon was a member of the IRA, he was acquitted by the three judges.

Anne Delcassian had previously stated during meetings with the Serious Crime Review Team that McMahon had acted as a local enforcer in the Dundalk area and had been intimidating Irene prior to her murder. It was also claimed by the informant that McMahon in turn hired another local criminal, aged 26 at the time of Irene's death, to carry out the killing. This individual had been on the garda radar since 1998 for a string of offences, including assaults, criminal damage – in one case of which he set fire to an ex-partner's car – and burglary. The informant detailed how McMahon drove this criminal to the scene, where he murdered Irene, and that his DNA would be found at Ice House.

There was no obvious link between McMahon and his accomplices and Irene White, but the detective believed the informant was genuine and had passed on the information in good faith. Unfortunately for the garda investigation team, following up with Seamus McMahon would be impossible. His life of crime had caught up with him on 21 March 2010, when he was shot dead while visiting a friend at a house in the Saltown area of Dundalk. Two gunmen burst into the house and ran upstairs, where they located McMahon and opened fire. He was struck multiple times before the hit team made their escape.

Other inquiries could be pursued, though, with the cold case unit recommending that the Dundalk crime branch try and establish if Alan White or Niall Power had ever employed Seamus McMahon in relation to recouping bad or outstanding debts, or if he ever acted for them in any capacity. They also advised that the investigation team should establish if Alan or Niall had been in phone contact with McMahon around the time of the murder. It transpired that neither had. While both the cold case unit and gardaí based in Dundalk had been attempting to exhaust all avenues to make sure that every line of inquiry was checked out, they weren't any closer to a breakthrough, and the real killer still hadn't been identified. However, a random phone call, from the other side of the world, was about to turn the investigation on its head.

12

AN ANONYMOUS CALL
FROM AUSTRALIA

Shortly after midday on 15 April 2013, the landline in the offices of the Serious Crime Review Team rang. It was Monday, and the team of detectives were preparing their workload for the busy week ahead. Detective Sergeant Frank Treacy was sitting at his desk in Harcourt Square that afternoon when he picked up the receiver, introducing himself and asking what the call was in relation to. On the other end of the line was a young woman who appeared nervous. Talking with an clear but audibly shaky voice, she asked to speak to someone about the murder of Irene White. Many calls had been received by gardaí about the case over the years, and while some were helpful, others led nowhere. This one would be different.

The woman said she was from County Monaghan and had been a student in National University of Ireland (NUI) Maynooth, but was now living in Australia. The caller refused to give her name and said she was calling from a payphone to make sure that her call couldn't be traced. Her reluctance to identify herself soon became clear; a friend, she said, had confided in her that he had murdered Irene White. Detective Sergeant Treacy's interest was piqued, and he began writing down exactly what the woman was saying.

The anonymous caller revealed how sometime in December 2005 she was at a social event when she met a friend who was from Castleblayney, and he later brought her back to her accommodation that night. The detective sergeant gently pressed the caller for more details, asking what the social event was and where she lived. The woman was careful not to reveal too much, though, and wouldn't tell him any specifics. Going on to describe that night, she recalled having a 40- to 50-minute conversation with her friend about the murder of Irene White. During this conversation, the man admitted to being the person who had murdered the mother-of-three in her kitchen.

She said her friend had worked in pubs and nightclubs in the Dundalk area back then and claimed he was approached by 'a number of bouncers to murder Irene White'. He was in financial difficulty at the time and was promised money for carrying out the savage act. The friend had also told her that on the day of the killing he had travelled to the UK to attend his girlfriend's graduation. Detective Sergeant Treacy asked the caller if she could provide any specifics about what her friend had told her about the murder, but she was frightened of possible repercussions if she said too much.

She had become extremely nervous after hearing her friend's confession and a short time later managed to convince him to leave her home. The man had been a regular caller to her house, but that was the last time he ever visited. The caller explained how she had told her parents about the man's admissions a year later and what had been said. Her father had remarked that a lot of what was mentioned by her friend wasn't public knowledge. Again, she was pressed for specifics, but she was too scared to reveal any more. At first her parents told her to go to the gardaí, but they later advised her not to tell anyone about the confession because of fears for her safety.

Throughout the phone call, Detective Sergeant Treacy assured the woman that anything she told him would be treated in the strictest confidence. She again declined to give her name, but did take his mobile-phone number in case she wanted to call back in the future. He asked her why now, some eight years later, she was revealing what her friend had said about the murder. The woman said she wanted somebody to know and decided to look up the number for the Serious Crime Review Team online. Having been on the phone for just over 11 minutes, she then said goodbye and hung up. Throughout the call she had repeatedly stated the name of the friend who had admitted to murdering Irene, even spelling it out to make sure that the detective sergeant was taking down the correct details. The friend's name was Anthony Lambe.

Detective Sergeant Treacy opened the garda PULSE system on his computer and typed in the name Anthony Lambe. It showed a man with that name living in the Castleblayney area of County Monaghan, with a date of birth of 22 May 1982. He compiled a report on the conversation with the anonymous caller, requesting that inquiries be carried out to verify if Anthony Lambe had featured in the murder investigation previously. The detective sergeant hadn't been directly involved in the Irene White case and wouldn't have had intimate knowledge of every name that came up during the inquiry. The investigation team in Dundalk, however, were very familiar with Anthony. He had come into the inquiry in the initial stages after Niall Power claimed he met him in Dundalk on the day Irene was murdered to pay him an advance on his wages. Over the course of several months, gardaí had also taken three statements from him, but there was never anything to indicate that he was involved in the murder. In the 85-page briefing document supplied to the review team, Anthony Lambe's name appeared only once, during a synopsis of the garda interviews conducted with Niall Power. The fact that it was now being alleged that he had confessed to being the killer came as a big surprise.

The cold case unit formed the view that the anonymous caller was genuine in the information she revealed and there could be real credence in what she claimed. The investigation was now centrally focused on identifying the mystery caller, while all available information was also being gathered on Anthony Lambe.

He had been born in Castleblayney to Michael Lambe and Bernadette Gorman and was the eldest of four children. He had sat his Leaving Cert in 2000, the same year he obtained a provisional driver's licence, before attending St Patrick's College in Drumcondra to study teaching. He studied there for a year, working part-time in the popular Cat & Cage pub near the college to finance his studies and social life. He had only attended St Patrick's College for a short time before dropping out, and he then returned to Castleblayney, where he worked in Hanratty's Pub for a year before getting a job in Ballybay as a machine operator. It was another term of employment that only lasted for around a year, before he worked driving tractors and agricultural machinery for a man in Kinnegad.

In or around August 2002, he began dating Castleblayney woman Annie Kane, whom he had flown with to London on the day Irene was murdered. In September 2003, he began studying civil engineering full-time at the Dundalk Institute of Technology, and a year later he got a part-time job with Niall Power at PPS Security. In early 2005, he began seeing a woman from Dundalk, despite still being in a relationship with Annie Kane. The other woman, Noelle, had also been spoken to previously as part of the garda investigation, after Anthony Lambe disclosed that he had stayed in her home the night before the murder. By 2007, both of these romances had ended, and Anthony began dating a woman from Bree in Castleblayney. The relationship appeared fractious on account of his volatile nature, and that May he appeared in court charged with assaulting his girlfriend after he hit her and threw her down a flight of stairs.

When gardaí examined their records, they showed that Anthony had been connected to seven incidents between 2005 and 2010. These included two road-traffic-related matters as well as two assaults, one in which he was the victim and the other being the attack he had carried out on his partner. A domestic incident was also listed on the garda database, again related to his relationship issues in 2007, as well as the theft of his mobile phone and loss of property.

The cold case unit had to establish where Anthony Lambe was now and what he was doing. Their inquiries revealed that in September 2011 he had commenced a BA degree at NUI Maynooth and was residing in student accommodation near the college. By 2013, Anthony Lambe was a member of the university's students' union as the Arts, Celtic Studies and Philosophy representative, and from a perusal of his social media accounts he appeared to be liked among his peers in NUI Maynooth. He seemed to be living a structured life, which was at odds with the profile of a callous killer who had stabbed Irene White 34 times in her home. Gardaí began gathering all files from the original investigation relating to him, with a view to looking back over his statements to see if his story matched up eight years on.

As this was ongoing, another unexpected call was made to the offices of the cold case unit. Shortly before 2 p.m. on 18 April 2013, Detective Sergeant Treacy was at his desk once again when the phone rang. He answered and on the other end of the line was the same woman who had called three days earlier. Over the past few days, she had thought more about what Anthony Lambe had told her, and she wanted to provide the gardaí with some further information. She said he'd made the confession sometime between Christmas 2005 and New Year's Day 2006, and this time said that he had called to her home drunk shortly before midnight while her parents were in bed. Anthony had told her that he 'knocked on the back door of Irene White's house' before motioning in a lunging fashion, re-enacting to his friend how he had attacked the housewife. The anonymous caller said she had asked Anthony Lambe what he had done with the weapon, to which he only replied: 'They should have found it.'

He also told the woman that he 'enjoyed the thrill of it', which she took to mean the act of murdering Irene. Anthony had remarked that a 'job had to be done' and referred to Irene White as 'a bad bitch'. The caller also revealed that he told her he was questioned by gardaí but scoffed that they 'had nothing on him'. She said Anthony had made reference to receiving €10,000 on the day of the murder, before he went to the UK, and claimed to have received a further €15,000 as a final payment at a later stage. Anthony had also told the woman that he was under financial pressure at the time and needed money.

The caller, still refusing to reveal her name, recalled that at some stage in April 2006, around the first anniversary of the murder, she read an article in the *Evening Herald* newspaper about the case. She sent a text to Anthony Lambe's phone, asking if he had read the paper, but got no reply. Two days later he eventually texted her back, simply saying that he had not seen the *Evening Herald* on the day she had contacted him. He didn't ask what had been in the newspaper and instead asked her how she was doing. She avoided any future contact with him but by chance ran into him in a gym they both used some years later. The woman couldn't recall when this was and refused to name the gym.

She did, however, provide more information about her connection to Anthony Lambe, saying that they first met in the Gaeltacht when she was 17 years old. They had become friends over the years but were never romantically linked. She was still friends with him on Facebook and was afraid to remove herself from his friends list, over fears that he would become suspicious as to why. The woman also confirmed further details that corroborated the garda belief that she was speaking about the same Anthony Lambe who had previously given three statements to the investigation team. She said he had studied in St Patrick's College and worked at the Cat & Cage pub but was now a mature student in NUI Maynooth while also class president of a society.

Speaking about Anthony Lambe's background, she said he 'was not liked by the other boys in Castleblayney when he was younger as he was very sure of himself', and revealing more discreet details about herself, she said that she was currently working in an office in Australia on a four-year visa. Detective Sergeant Treacy again queried why she was now deciding to disclose what she had been told after so long. The caller said she was away from her loved ones in Ireland and felt homesick, and she had sympathy for Irene White and her family. She had also recently been watching cold case programmes on Australian television, which led to her contacting the Serious Crime Review Team. At the end of the 24-minute call, the woman said she would be in touch again soon and on the next occasion might disclose her identity. The line then went dead. While her information was of huge significance, gardaí were frustrated that the woman wouldn't reveal who she was, with Detective Inspector Marry saying:

> This was a huge breakthrough in terms of new information relating to Irene's murder, but there was a stumbling block: the woman on the other end of the phone couldn't be identified. Despite their best efforts, the cold case team couldn't put a name on the lady. The incoming call from Australia had no number associated with it, only a code, which was no good in tracing the call location. She remained anonymous for the time being.

Some weeks later, a newspaper reported that an anonymous phone call had been made as part of the Irene White murder inquiry. Despite saying that she would call back and possibly reveal her name, the woman never phoned again. Inquiries were carried out with the Australian High Commission in London in the hope of identifying Irish women from County Monoghan who held four-year visas at the time of the call. Unfortunately, gardaí were told that, while Australian authorities appreciated the seriousness of the investigation, it would be incredibly difficult to identify the person from the information and parameters gardaí were working off. Thousands of Irish women had travelled to Australia over that four-year period with applicants being able to enter at any airport, meaning a person now living in a particular city would not necessarily have travelled into the country through the local airport.

In another effort to try and put a name to the caller, the Serious Crime Review Team looked up Facebook accounts with the name Anthony Lambe. They located a profile of that name that showed the user was also from County Monaghan, and they were happy they had the right account. A search of the profile's friends list showed he was connected with some 279 women on the account. One woman in particular appeared to match the profile of the anonymous caller. However, when investigators spoke to her, she denied having ever contacted the cold case unit. Given that the caller from Australia had refused to give her name, the Facebook friend had to be further looked into to conclusively rule her out as the anonymous caller. Detailed profiles were compiled on her and her husband, with a view to identifying any similarities between her and the woman who had called. This line of inquiry came to an end when NUI Maynooth confirmed that the woman had never attended there.

Gardaí continued carrying out an in-depth and arduous analysis of the other 278 women that were friends with the Anthony Lambe Facebook account. Despite some having similar details to those provided by the anonymous caller, the cold case unit were unable to identify her. The potential witness who could provide a significant breakthrough in the long-running inquiry would remain, for the time being, a mystery. In one of their fast-track recommendations at the time, the Serious Crime Review Team stated: 'It is of utmost importance that the anonymous female caller from Australia is identified and all details in her possession relating to Anthony Lambe and the murder of Irene White be relayed to the Senior Investigating Officer.'

*

While they couldn't pin down the name of the caller, they could look further into Anthony Lambe. The statements he had given now bore far greater significance almost a decade on. They were closely scrutinised, along with mobile-phone data and cell site records available to the review team, and when all of these records were compared, it showed there were glaring inconsistencies in Anthony's version of events.

When he first spoke to gardaí on 21 April 2005, he said he had stayed at the home of a friend named Noelle on the night before the murder, but claimed not to know her surname. There was good reason for Anthony Lambe to be coy about this detail, given that he was secretly dating her while going out with Annie Kane. He had met Noelle in a pub that night before going back to her home in Dundalk and staying over. Gardaí noted that this house was less than 300 metres from Marist College, where Irene dropped off Jennifer the next morning, and also close to Réalt na Mara primary school, where Irene spent close to an hour in the lead-up to her murder. Anthony had also said that when he rang Niall Power at 8.30 a.m., he wouldn't have done so in front of Noelle, and that he left for Dundalk Institute of Technology at this time. He further claimed that he arrived there between 9.05 a.m. and 9.15 a.m.

However, gardaí noted that this journey should only have taken 10 minutes at most, meaning that his timeline was off by at least half an hour. Anthony also said he ate breakfast in the canteen alone and didn't encounter anyone, raising the question of whether he had travelled to the college at all that morning, with no one able to verify his presence there. In a report compiled on their review, the cold case unit noted: 'There is a possibility that Anthony Lambe was conducting surveillance on Irene White and was not in Dundalk Institute of Technology.' The cold case unit also remarked of his affair: 'It is known that Anthony Lambe is capable of covering his tracks as he was living a double life with Annie Kane and [Noelle] however he was caught out towards the end of 2005.'

The flurry of phone calls on the day of the murder between Anthony and Niall, a man that gardaí had always believed was involved in organising the killing, now held much greater importance, given what was being claimed about Anthony. When speaking to gardaí in 2005, Anthony had said these calls were made when he was halfway home to his house in Castleblayney. If he was being truthful when claiming that he left Dundalk at 9.45 a.m., then this call should have been made at around 10 a.m. Phone data records, however, showed that the only calls between the pair were at 9.44 a.m., 10.13 a.m., and 10.14 a.m. Cell site data for the 9.44 a.m. call showed Anthony using the mast at Dundalk garda station, placing him in the town, with the call made around the time Irene was leaving Réalt na Mara to return home after the school drop-off. Eyewitnesses reported seeing a man running through Ice House Hill park at 10.09 a.m., who gardaí believed was the killer, and working off this theory, the calls between Anthony and Niall were made immediately before and after the murder.

His call data records weren't included in the initial cell site dump at the time of the murder, but because Niall Power's details were retained, gardaí could determine the location of any mobile phone he had been in contact with. This showed that Anthony's phone pinged off a mast at Dundalk's Oriel Park immediately after the murder, placing him closer to the crime scene than his home in Castleblayney. One witness had also seen a dark-coloured Peugeot outside Irene's home prior to the murder, and Anthony had driven a similar car at the time.

Anthony Lambe had also been in contact with another phone at 00.25 a.m. and 1.04 a.m. in the early hours of 6 April 2005. He again called the same number at 9.50 a.m., just as Irene had arrived home, and at 10.27 a.m., after the murder. However, gardaí hadn't been able to attribute the number to anyone. Given the timing of these calls, the cold case unit believed that 'the holder of that phone may have had a role in the murder' and the investigation team needed to identify this person.

There was also renewed significance to the events at Lannett Cross that morning. From the statements of people who were in the house, it was possible that Niall Power was there when he received the phone call from Anthony Lambe at 10.13 a.m. Cathy Wilson had previously described Niall as being 'in a tizzy' after he got off the phone, before leaving the house with Alan. Niall's phone records also showed that he received this call via a telephone mast in Carrickmacross, located near Vincent Dullaghan's home. Commenting on this in their report, the cold case unit said:

> The Serious Crime Review Team believes that Niall Power and Alan White may have known that Irene White was dead as a result of the 10.13 a.m. call. This call at

10.13 a.m. may have resulted in Niall Power and Alan White suddenly departing Lannett Cross and returning to Dundalk. It would appear that Niall Power and Anthony Lambe may have played a major role in this murder and their telephone records would cast further suspicion on them. Alan White, although he did not use his phone on the morning until 10.32 a.m., may have been in the company of Niall Power for the calls between Power and Lambe thus being aware of events all the time.

Another witness who could now have information of potential significance was Anthony's girlfriend at the time. Annie Kane had been with him after the murder, and although there was absolutely no suggestion that she had any knowledge of the crime, her recollection of events could further advance the circumstantial case that was building against her former boyfriend. On 13 October 2013, Detective Garda O'Neill and Detective Sergeant Treacy visited Annie at her home to take a witness statement from her. She recalled being in Dublin Airport that afternoon for their flight to London, which was due to depart at around 3 p.m. She described her boyfriend as being 'giddy, jittery in the airport, he was a bit jumpy in himself' and that this strange behaviour continued during the flight. Annie compared his demeanour to that of 'an excited child in the sweet shop' but put it down to him being on an airplane for the first time. However, the investigation team now believed that his peculiar behaviour could have been a direct result of a 'feeling of exhilaration in the immediate aftermath of murdering Irene White'.

Annie also detailed how on the day of the murder, and in the days after, Anthony Lambe appeared to have come into money and was overly generous financially. She said he was chatty in the airport and 'nearly forcing money' on her mother, who had bought the plane tickets. The following day, ahead of Annie's graduation, they went shopping in London, where Anthony bought a dress for his niece and a jacket for Annie. The family also had a photography session before the ceremony, with Annie telling gardaí she believed her boyfriend had paid for this. Later that evening they were going to a pub after dinner, and she recalled him being short of cash and that he went to an ATM. She also said how Anthony 'had words' with one of her friends that night, and she later made him apologise.

Anthony's ex-girlfriend also told the detectives that she first heard about the murder after arriving home from England, as it would have been on the news. She had discussed the murder with her then boyfriend but couldn't recall him making any specific comment about it, either in the days after the crime or during the rest of their relationship, which ended in December 2005. In her statement, Annie also revealed how close Anthony had become to Niall, with the relationship growing from an employer–employee dynamic into a friendship. She had met Niall previously along with his girlfriend Jane and knew they had since married because she was invited to the wedding with Anthony. She remarked that Anthony Lambe was even asked to be the best man at the ceremony.

Annie then recalled a particular occasion in or around September 2004 when they met Niall in the Phoenix Bar in Dundalk. Alan was also there, and they were later joined by one of Anthony's college friends, whose home they went back to having been refused entry into Ridley's nightclub. She recalled going to bed that night and leaving Alan, Anthony and his friend downstairs, before being woken at around

3 a.m. by the sound of raised voices. Annie came downstairs and walked into the sitting room, where she saw her boyfriend and Alan 'kind of squaring up to each other' and cursing at one another. She said that Anthony had his fist clenched and she thought he looked angrier than Alan. When Annie asked what had happened, her boyfriend told her 'that bollox did it', pointing at Alan. She stood between the men to separate them, before telling Anthony to go up to bed. This account by Annie Kane also highlighted another anomaly in Anthony Lambe's statements, in which he said he had only met Alan once some weeks before the murder. In one report, the cold case unit remarked that Anthony 'wasn't portraying an altogether accurate reflection of his association with Alan White' and that he 'may have been trying to distance himself' from him during his interviews.

A week after speaking with Annie Kane, Detective Garda O'Neill met with Anthony's former lover Noelle, who had already given a brief statement in 2005. What she had to say now could be of far greater importance. She gave another account to the detectives that married with her previous statement, but she was unable to provide much further information. One fresh detail she did recall was that Anthony drove a black Peugeot 205 van-type vehicle at the time and that they used to meet up once a week.

Another minute detail that now had greater importance attached to it was Anthony's declaration in his second witness statement that he had been in Ice House Hill park in the year before Irene's murder. Gardaí wondered why a young man who wasn't from the area and had absolutely no association with the town would be in that particular park, and specifically why he would place himself there in the months leading up to the murder, 'nosing around'. As a result of the anonymous phone calls from Australia, the inconsistencies in his statements, and his having appeared to have come into money around the time of the crime, Anthony Lambe was now cemented as the chief suspect for the murder of Irene White.

13

OLD-SCHOOL DETECTIVE WORK

The garda cold case unit formally concluded its review into the murder of Irene White on 20 January 2016. All documentation was handed back to gardaí in Dundalk, and members of the Serious Crime Review Team gave a presentation to the investigation team on their thorough findings. It included a staggering 271 recommendations for the detectives in Dundalk to pursue relating to suspects, witnesses, and mobile-phone analysis, on top of the 79 fast-track recommendations made during the course of their review. Detective Superintendent Mangan had moved to the Dublin Metropolitan Region (DMR) West in 2014, with Detective Superintendent Walter O'Sullivan taking over as head of the unit for the remainder of the review. Detective Garda Frank O'Neill had also been promoted, and his role as review officer was assumed by Detective Gardaí Frank Lambe and Tony Keane. The Serious Crime Review Team's final report named three people whom they classified as suspects in the investigation: Alan White, Niall Power, and Anthony Lambe. A further three people were described as witnesses and 25 as persons of interest, a category that is a halfway house between suspect and witness.

Several recommendations were made about Anthony Lambe, given that he had only been identified as a suspect during the review. The cold case unit advised Detective Inspector Marry and his team to confirm Anthony's shoe size to determine if there were similarities with the bloodied footprints left at the murder scene, while they should also locate a picture of him from 2005 to compare with the witness sightings near the scene. The review team also recommended that all CCTV footage covering the route Anthony claimed to have taken on the morning of the murder be analysed to confirm if his black Peugeot could be identified and corroborate, or dismiss, his account. They believed that if Anthony had admitted to the murder, as the Australian-based witness had stated, then he may have made similar confessions to other girlfriends or female acquaintances. 'Every effort should be made to identify and interview these females to establish if he ever mentioned similar facts to them,' the cold case unit wrote in its report. It was also recommended to consider obtaining the services of the National Centre for the Analysis of Violent Crime, based at the FBI academy in Quantico, Virginia, which provides expert analysis of murders. Contact should be made with the FBI, the review team said, 'with a view to acquiring their interpretation of the crime scene. Such a report may assist the Senior Investigating Officer in establishing a more detailed picture of the murder of Irene White.'

The central area of focus for the Dundalk detective branch would now be trying to identify the woman who had made the anonymous phone calls. One of the final recommendations made by the Serious Crime Review Team was that Detective Inspector Marry and his team should consider using Crime Stoppers Australia as a 'last ditch effort' to identify the anonymous female caller 'if all else fails'. Detective Inspector Marry was impressed with the investigative work carried out by his colleagues and began assembling a team of gardaí who would try and bring the matter to a conclusion.

It was an excellent review and presentation. I would not have expected anything less from Detective Superintendent Christy Mangan and his team. The review had several hundred recommendations to follow up on. Points had been raised about avenues being missed in the initial investigation and new lines of inquiry were also suggested. You had to be selective as to what, in my mind, were the ones to follow or not. There is no way my team could do 350 inquiries. I just didn't have the manpower and we were involved in other investigations, so I had to pick and choose. I guess as senior investigating officer you follow some of the recommendations which you believe are the best way to move the investigation forward.

I took charge and appointed Detective Sergeant Mick Sheridan as my incident room coordinator – a fine gentleman and solid as a rock, he had a great head for investigations. He had worked on the original investigation and knew the case inside out. I could always see Mick as a detective inspector some day; he has the qualities needed to solve difficult murder cases. I appointed Detective Gardaí John 'Bobby' Ogle and Rachel Reilly to the jobs team, two solid detectives who I held in high regard. Detective Garda Brendan Duffy was brought into the team as well – a most capable individual and a detective I relied on over the years. I looked for more personnel, but it was not forthcoming. The strategy was to run the cold case review team recommendations parallel with what I thought was the best way of progressing the case.

We started working away, just the five of us. It was a close team and I engaged in each and every conference with them. The only negative side was when management sat in and asked questions that were irrelevant. We always got a laugh out of their cluelessness. I often thought, 'How in God's name did he ever get to that rank!' The five of us concentrated on reviewing all the persons that came up during the investigation and the names that had been associated with the investigation from the start, including witnesses, persons of interest, and suspects. We needed to establish what people saw and heard and if this was going to be the same some 11 years on. Were these witnesses' descriptions and timings the same? We had to establish if the witnesses were credible then and now. I learned the hard way in previous cases that some witnesses come forward with a willingness to help, but what they have to offer is tainted or exaggerated. In all my investigations I liked to evaluate witnesses to get the measure of their testament.

I can never underestimate the value of statements being taken by experienced detectives who will corroborate the witness's version of events – invaluable work in any major investigation. So all statements taken were revisited, and I was happy that people who had made statements in 2005 were staying true to what they had said. There were a number of persons of interest and three suspects in the frame in the document submitted by the cold case review team. There was a full disclosure on the anonymous phone calls made by this mystery female from Australia, which was a key element to solving the crime. I was aware that the cold case review team had exhausted all avenues in trying to establish her identity. I guess if they had identified her, they would have travelled to Australia and held on to the case to solve, hence the completed report being handed to me to see what my team could do. You often hear the saying 'It's not the size of the weapon, it's the power of the shot.' Well, that rang true for the team on the Irene White murder investigation, as the five detectives were as tuned in as if it were ten detectives on the case.

The task of trying to identify the witness was handed to Detective Garda Bobby Ogle, who was based in Carrickmacross garda station but had been transferred to the investigation team on secondment. He began reviewing the Anthony Lambe Facebook profile that had been submitted by the Serious Crime Review Team, and he faced the daunting task of combing through the almost 300 females listed as friends on that account. However, something didn't sit right with the detective as he scanned the Facebook friends list, and he shared his concerns with his senior investigating officer. Recalling the conversation, Detective Inspector Marry says:

Detective Garda Ogle, a man I admired as a detective and an honourable gentleman, came to me and informed me that there was something wrong with the social media profile. I was all ears and what he said next was the start of the solving of the crime. Bobby noticed that the Anthony Lambe Facebook account he was reviewing was friends with quite a number of people from Monaghan

Town, Clones, and south Tyrone. This was unusual, as people from Castleblayney, where Anthony Lambe was from, would mainly gravitate towards Carrickmacross, Dundalk, and south Armagh, and mainly tend to socialise with people from those towns as well as Castleblayney. Bobby is a Monaghan man and knew the lie of the land.

The detective decided to conduct his own inquiries to satisfy himself that the correct profile had been passed on by the review team. He logged into the garda PULSE system and typed the name 'Anthony Lambe' into a search bar, showing all intelligence connected with the name. One incident that popped up was a search that had been conducted on a bus in Meath in 2005. One of the people who was travelling on the coach at the time was named Anthony Lambe. The PULSE incident included the name of the garda who had conducted the search, and Detective Garda Ogle contacted her to see if she could recall the incident. She remembered the search, as her partner was friends with that Anthony Lambe. When Detective Garda Ogle showed her a picture taken from the Facebook page he was reviewing, she confirmed it was the man she knew. The problem was that it wasn't the same Anthony Lambe who was now a suspect in the murder of Irene White, as Detective Inspector Marry explains:

Bobby informed me he had made contact with the garda who had dealt with that particular Anthony Lambe and realised we had the wrong profile. 'My God,' I said, 'is it a case of the cold case review team making a boo-boo in researching and doing a background on the wrong Anthony Lambe account?' Bobby replied, 'Yes, it appears that way.' The account submitted to us had the same name as our suspect and showed that this man was from Monaghan. The Facebook profile picture also wasn't very clear, as it was a group photo taken from a distance, and the man had similar features to our Anthony Lambe. I imagine this is how the error occurred.

The investigation had to locate the actual social media account but were essentially starting from scratch, and a search of Anthony Lambe on Facebook didn't bring up any matches for the murder suspect. They knew he was into health and fitness, and Detective Garda Ogle decided to make contact with a garda sergeant he knew from Monaghan who was involved in a sports club in the county. The detective asked his colleague if he knew Anthony Lambe, and by sheer coincidence, the garda sergeant said that he had only recently received a friend request from him. He was, however, using the Irish spelling of his name, Anton O'Lune, on social media. Detective Garda Ogle asked his colleague if he would accept the friend request and if the garda sergeant would give him access to the account so he could review the Anton O'Lune profile. Given the gravity of the offence being investigated, his colleague agreed.

Logging into the garda sergeant's Facebook profile, Detective Garda Ogle pulled up the Anton O'Lune account and clicked into the friends list. As with the last Facebook account, this profile also had close to 300 female friends, who would all have to be analysed and compared with the anonymous caller's details. 'Groundhog Day,' the detective thought to himself. It would take months, if not longer, to cross-reference the details given by the female witness and narrow down the list. Detective Inspector Marry says:

One thing she mentioned was that she had met Anthony Lambe at the Gaeltacht while she was a student. Inquiries were carried out with the Department of Education, but they had no record of Anthony attending an Irish language course while he was studying at St Patrick's College. Detective Garda Ogle was persistent, though, and he knew a school principal who had organised Gaeltacht courses in County Donegal. These would have been popular with students from County Monaghan. He made contact with the principal, who was sharp and remembered a young man by the name of Anthony Lambe attending his Gaeltacht. He said the records were on an old computer in his attic. A data request was served on the principal to get the names of every female from the Monaghan area who had attended the Gaeltacht between 1999 and 2002 while Anthony Lambe was there.

The principal duly obliged and printed off every name that matched their search criteria. The number of women who could be the potential witnesses had now been whittled down to 66. It was still a lengthy list, but another idea came to Detective Garda Ogle to try and reduce it further. If the anonymous caller was on a four-year visa in Australia, as she had stated, then she would have applied for a police certificate of character. The detective inquired with garda stations around Monaghan to confirm if they held any such records, which would help narrow down the search. One station didn't have any information of assistance, while another station had shredded all their records within a two-year period to keep in line with data protection protocols, much to the investigation team's frustration. Detective Inspector Marry explains his detective's next move:

> Trying to find this woman's name through her visa application seemed like a dead end. Bobby had another brainwave, though. He thought to himself that if a person was applying for a police certificate of character, then the garda filling out the form, if doing their job, would carry out inquiries to ensure that the applicant had no prior convictions. He searched through the intelligence tab on the PULSE system to see if any inquiries had been made relating to 'garda vetting' and 'Australia' in Monaghan. Bingo. A garda in one particular station had done exactly that some years earlier for a young woman from the town who was travelling to Australia on a four-year visa. It was a great bit of detective work.

Detective Garda Ogle then spoke with the garda who had carried out the vetting inquiry. In yet another quirk of circumstance, the garda confirmed that she could recall the particular inquiry as she knew the woman through her boyfriend. To get further information on the visa applicant, Detective Garda Ogle obtained a copy of her police certificate of character. It showed that she was now working in the financial sector in Australia and that she was similar in age to Anthony Lambe, again matching the anonymous caller's details. Importantly, it also listed an address in Australia where she could be located. In the space of a few weeks, the list had dropped from several hundred to just one.

Further inquiries also showed that this woman had attended NUI Maynooth in the 2000s, which tallied with the anonymous caller, adding further credence to the garda belief that they had now identified her. Given the seriousness of what was at stake, though, and the workload required to deploy a team of gardaí to Australia, the detective branch had to be sure beyond doubt. During her first phone call the woman had disclosed that she had encountered Anthony Lambe only once after he made the confession, at a gym several years later. Because Anthony Lambe lived in Castleblayney, there was one particular gym in the town that he was likely to have used. Detective Garda Ogle visited the fitness studio and spoke with the manager, inquiring if Anthony and the woman had been members there. Due to the investigation being at a sensitive and critical stage, and so as not to give away who they believed the witness was, the detective gave the gym manager a list of 21 names. While 19 of these were irrelevant, the other two were Anthony Lambe and the suspected anonymous caller.

Both were confirmed to have been members of the gym, and gardaí served a data request on the manager to establish on what exact dates they had used it. Every time a user entered the gym they would swipe in at the front desk, with each of these sign-ins logged. The records showed that Anthony and the woman were at the gym on the same day only once, at around 7 p.m. on 1 February 2009. Detective Inspector Marry says of this:

> Once we corroborated the story that the caller had only met Anthony Lambe once again after the confession at a gym, that was it. We were now 100 per cent sure that we had identified the woman, taking everything into account: the garda vetting inquiries, the Gaeltacht records, that she had attended Maynooth, her being

from a particular town in Monaghan, that she worked in finance in Australia, her age. All these inquiries resulted in the same name appearing time and time again. Being unwilling to share her name was a strange thing to do, given that she had relayed a lot of other information. But because of the diligent work of Detective Garda Ogle and the team, we had narrowed down the list in a few weeks rather than months or even years. The help provided by the school principal also can't be understated, as it kick-started the process of whittling down the list.

From our inquiries, in tandem with the findings of the Serious Crime Review Team, we were also confident at this point that Anthony Lambe was the killer. The statements he made during the initial investigation were scrutinised, and we did a timeline of Anthony's movements based off these. What was discovered was that when he was telling gardaí he was in Castleblaney that morning around the time of the murder, his phone was actually pinging off a cell site at Oriel Park in Dundalk town. He had lied and he was caught. This bit of information, along with his confession to the woman now living in Australia, placed him as the number one murder suspect. There had been appeals on TV for witnesses to come forward, while a vital piece of information in the form of the cell site data was there all along. The obvious next move was to approach the anonymous caller. We needed to go to Australia to interview her, as she held the key to solving Irene White's murder.

As a business-case proposal was being compiled seeking approval for the trip to Australia, Detective Inspector Marry requested a detailed examination of Anthony Lambe's background in order to get as much updated information on their chief suspect as possible. A decision was later made to also conduct covert surveillance on their target, so they could keep a close eye on him.

> Surveillance was something I had to consider now that Anthony Lambe was a clear suspect and I needed to know more about him. Sure, we knew his address, height, etc., but we did not know much about his current life. We did not know where he went while he wasn't working and if he was still living at home or who he socialised with. I knew I needed to gather information on him. I needed to be sure that, when it was time to make an arrest, I knew where I could find him. I had the luxury of having two men at my disposal who were fully trained in surveillance, and I extensively used their skill set during Operation Scale [a drugs investigation] in 2015. I tasked these two fine members of the force with locating Anthony Lambe and gathering as much information as they could about him – where he goes, who he meets, what are his hobbies, does he play sport, does he socialise? I needed a daily-life profile of Anthony Lambe. I instructed them to provide me with a report, verbal or otherwise, within a week.

The obvious location to begin watching Anthony Lambe was at his family home. This would prove difficult, as the house in Annadrumman was located on a small laneway off the N53, a national secondary road around 4 kilometres outside Castleblayney town. But gardaí got a break in the first hours of surveillance in 2016 when they spotted a silver 08-R-registered

Ford Mondeo pulling out of the laneway. Driving the car was a man who matched Anthony Lambe's description. The surveillance gardaí discreetly followed him in their unmarked vehicle, tailing him to a library in Castleblayney, where he arrived at 11.30 a.m. that morning. They watched as the driver got out of the car with a black satchel and made his way into the library. Two hours passed and there was no sign of the man emerging, so one of the surveillance gardaí went into the building to see what their target was doing. Detective Inspector Marry, recalling the account given by his colleague, says:

He went into the library and saw the man sitting at a desk, buried into his books. The impression the surveillance officer got was that he was a bit of a bookworm. It certainly put a doubt in his mind as to whether he was following the right individual. His demeanour was at odds with the profile of a killer. The surveillance garda began to wonder if he had tracked the wrong target, but the description and everything else matched, and he was satisfied that he now had eyes on Anthony Lambe. A short time later my team reported back to me on what they had witnessed. I told them to stick with it, it sounds interesting. Anthony returned to his home after some hours and there was no further movement that day.

Some days later, gardaí were carrying out further surveillance on the murder suspect when they once again spotted the silver Ford Mondeo driving out of the laneway near the Lambe family home. They took up a covert pursuit of the vehicle as it drove towards Ardee and made its way down to Dublin. The Ford Mondeo then drove onto the M50 southbound and took the Lucan exit at junction 7. The gardaí trailed Anthony Lambe as he continued onto the M4 and all the way to Maynooth, where he exited the motorway and drove to the university campus. They watched as Anthony got out of his car carrying the same black leather satchel that he had with him at the library in Castleblayney. Wearing a crisp blue shirt with the sleeves rolled up and black trousers, he locked his car and made his way into a building on the campus. One of the plain-clothes gardaí followed him from a distance, and as he walked into the building, the hallway was a hive of activity with students filing into classrooms. Describing the next sequence of events, Detective Inspector Marry says:

My surveillance garda didn't have a bag with him or anything of the sort that would help him blend in or look like a student. He hung back and watched the door of the classroom that Anthony Lambe had entered as people were milling around. One student caught his eye, and he brushed off him at the door, before asking him who was lecturing in that room. 'That's Mr Lambe's class, he's teaching history,' the student told my surveillance garda. He thought the student had misspoken or was joking and had to see for himself. He opened the classroom door and there was Anthony Lambe, a man who was the chief suspect in the violent murder of an innocent housewife, standing in front of 20-plus students. It was surreal. My surveillance garda later rang me in somewhat disbelief and informed me of this. I asked him, 'Are you sure?' He said he was, that Anthony was at the top of the class giving the lecture. It was later established that he had become a tutor in the History Department at NUI Maynooth.

The garda surveillance of Anthony Lambe continued, and several days later investigators shadowed him again as he made his way to the college. His day finished at 3 p.m., but instead of returning to Castleblayney, Anthony drove to an apartment complex in Tallaght, County Dublin. He got out of his car and tapped some numbers into the keypad at the front entrance to let himself into the building. The gardaí waited outside and 40 minutes later their target emerged, but this time he wasn't alone. Walking out of the apartment complex with Anthony Lambe were two school girls, under the age of ten, whom he guided into his car before driving to a fast-food takeaway nearby.

The description my surveillance garda gave was that Anthony was very attentive to the kids, he was looking after them and making sure they were okay at all times. It was quite the contrast when compared to the violent crime he was a suspect for. The surveillance garda had thought to himself 'what am I watching here' as he kept eyes on Anthony Lambe. I told him to stick with it, and he did just that. He managed to follow Anthony and the children back into the apartment block, and slipped into the building in order to identify the exact apartment Anthony went into. It was another key piece of information to help build a profile of our murder suspect and establish another property he had access too. It was top class work from the surveillance garda.

On another occasion, gardaí watched on as Anthony Lambe volunteered at a Big Tom country-and-western music festival in Monaghan, directing traffic and later engaging with revellers near the concert stage. Some evenings he would go to the pub, sit at the bar, and have two pints before driving home. Delving further into his background, a review of his school records revealed an intelligent student who did all honours for his Leaving Certificate and got 475 points. He then went on to St Patrick's College in Drumcondra to study primary teaching, where he started drinking heavily and later dropped out. He got into Dundalk Institute of Technology in 2003 but again succumbed to his over-reliance on alcohol. He also started regularly using cocaine and ecstasy and during this time met Niall Power. Anthony dropped out of college in May 2005, a month after the murder, without completing his degree. Between 2005 and 2011 he worked at a well-established business in Castleblayney, and in September 2011 he commenced a Bachelor of Arts degree at NUI Maynooth. He successfully completed his degree in May 2014 and then began a professional Master of Education programme at NUI Maynooth, which he completed in May 2016 before returning as a tutor at the same third-level campus.

Anthony Lambe fascinated me, as he was a graduate student in arts and his research was based around archaeology, experimental archaeology, and environmental archaeology. His interests were archaeology, Anglo-Saxon studies, early medieval Ireland, medieval history, Irish history, Irish studies, history, wetland archaeology, early medieval British archaeology, social sciences, philosophy, politics, and social and cultural anthropology. He submitted a paper titled 'Legislation in Early Ireland – Cain Domain' in late 2014. He was also president of the Mature Student Society in 2014. He came from a family of good standing who are well regarded in the local community and was considered an intelligent and well-educated man. We believed that his life had spiralled out of control by 2005 when he came under the influence of Niall Power.

Extensive inquiries were also carried out into Anthony Lambe's finances to determine if any large sums had been paid into his bank accounts around the time of the murder. There hadn't been, but they did show that on 21 October 2004 he had made an application for a €9,000 loan from his local credit union, while a year later he applied for a €1,000 loan from the same branch. The €9,000 loan for a new car, taken out five months before the crime, supported the claims by the anonymous caller that Anthony had complained he was in overall financial difficulty around the time Irene was murdered, and provided extra reassurance to gardaí about her credibility. Gardaí were now ready to travel to Australia and ask the woman to make a formal witness statement.

They had her home address, where her parents still lived, and consideration was given to speaking with them before approaching the witness. The investigation team, however, felt that this could jeopardise the case, as they believed her parents had advised her not to speak to gardaí out of fears for their daughter's safety. They spoke with the Australian Federal Police (AFP) and requested the woman's telephone data from April 2013, explaining that it was required to assist a murder investigation in Ireland. The data request needed approval, given that it related to phone records of a private citizen. Late one night, Detective Garda Ogle and Detective Sergeant Sheridan held a phone call with the office of the Attorney

General in Melbourne, outlining the seriousness of the case and the necessity of their request. The Attorney General's office was satisfied with the reasoning and the AFP promptly forwarded on the woman's call records. The information that came back confirmed Detective Inspector Marry and his team's suspicions about the anonymous caller.

The call records were sent over, and my question was answered as to why this lady did not give her name. The phone records showed that before and after each anonymous call to the gardaí the woman had rung her parents in Ireland. This told me a lot; the parents were still an influence on her, and they did not want her name out there even after she made the calls. It was also further corroboration of the woman's identity, given that these calls were made to her parents around the time of both anonymous calls. They had her best interests at heart, as it would turn out, and their fears were understandable given what she had heard. But it was now imperative that we speak to this lady face to face. I assigned Detective Gardaí Ogle and Reilly to travel to Australia to have this lady interviewed. Two applications for travel were forwarded to a senior officer.

At a conference, which this senior officer attended, I updated him on the progress in the investigation and informed him that we needed to travel to Australia. He requested we put it in writing. I informed him we had sent off two requests already and we would do a third. I told him we were travelling in a week's time; all was arranged but first we needed his approval. The business-case proposal was solid, and we needed to progress the investigation. What happened next still to this day defies logic and common sense.

I got a phone call from the senior officer who informed me that he wasn't allowing the trip to Australia. Our costings were out, he said, and he was concerned that the trip would all be for nothing if the witness wasn't there. I pleaded with him, but he wouldn't budge, and my team were understandably upset given the hard work they had put in to following up this vital lead. It was suggested we ring the woman to see if she would speak, but I told my team not to entertain this. We needed to cold call to this lady's home.

Two and a half months had passed and there was no change in the stance. I took the bull by the horns and informed senior management that I would tell the family and the media that we were being prohibited from solving Irene White's murder. The next day I was informed that the trip was sanctioned. Just like that. The AFP were very understanding and told us not to worry, they had people like that in their police force too. Anyway, the trip was on and a date set to interview this important witness.

On 19 August 2016, Detective Gardaí Ogle and Reilly touched down in Australia, in the hope of departing days later with a statement that would give them a breakthrough in the case. A mutual assistance request had already been arranged with the AFP, who were more than happy to help the investigation team. The protocol in place meant that local police officers had to make first contact with the woman and inquire if she consented to speaking with the visiting gardaí. That afternoon, Detective Gardaí Ogle and Reilly parked up outside a low-rise bungalow on the quiet residential street where they believed the woman was living with her partner. No one was at home, but they patiently kept watch over the property with their chaperone, AFP agent Hannah Speldewinde. The minutes turned into hours, but there was still no sign of anyone arriving at the house.

It had been a long few days for the garda detectives, having only landed in Australia after making the 16,000-kilometre journey from Ireland. They decided to wait until 6.30 p.m., and if the woman hadn't returned home by then, they would leave and try again the following morning. The clock eventually hit 6.28 p.m., and they were ready to give up for the day, when a car approached and turned into the driveway of the house they had been watching. 'This is it,' the detectives thought to themselves as a woman got out of the car and walked into the property. They were now moments away from potentially securing a vital statement that could finally solve Irene White's murder. However, the woman had refused to even give her name over the course of two anonymous phone calls, and they had no idea how she would react to gardaí showing up at her door three years later and unannounced. There was only one way to find out.

14

'WHAT KEPT YOU?'

The Australian federal agent walked up the driveway of the house, with the detective gardaí a few feet behind, and knocked on the front door. After a brief moment it was opened, and a familiar face peered out at Detective Gardaí Bobby Ogle and Rachel Reilly. They hadn't met her in person before, but they had spent months studying her social media profile and recognised her instantly. Agent Hannah Speldewinde told the homeowner that the man and woman standing behind her were Irish detectives who wanted to speak with her. Before the agent could explain the exact reason for their visit, the woman interjected and said: 'I know what you are here for, let them in.'

The detectives stepped into the house, asking her if she had made two anonymous phone calls to the offices of the Serious Crime Review Team in April 2013? 'I did,' she replied, adding, 'what the hell kept you?' Quick as a flash, Detective Garda Ogle humorously fired back, 'If you had given us a few more clues we might have been here quicker.' He asked if she would voluntarily accompany them to the local police station to be interviewed on camera about what she had disclosed three years earlier. 'I will,' she said, grabbing her handbag before walking out of the house with the detectives to be brought down to the local police station. Detective Garda Ogle phoned his detective inspector about the development and said he would call back once the statement was secured.

As they sat down in the interview room, the woman began describing the encounter she had had with Anthony Lambe over a decade earlier, telling a similar story to what she had disclosed in her phone calls. She had been friendly with Anthony in the early 2000s and would meet him every two months or so. He became a family friend of sorts and would be invited to her parents' home every Christmas. When the woman asked him to come over during the festive period of 2005, she didn't expect him to arrive drunk. Anthony pulled up to her house in his car and, although he was intoxicated, he wasn't slurring his words. They sat down on the sofa in her sitting room, and she could tell he was acting differently to his normal self. He had something he wanted to discuss.

Anthony asked if she had heard about the murder of Irene White, with the woman replying that she had. 'He told me "I did that",' she recalled, adding that she was dismissive of him at first. When he saw her reaction, however, Anthony's eyes widened, and he became more adamant. He was trying to convince her that he did indeed murder Irene and went on to describe the crime in graphic detail. She said that Anthony then re-enacted the moment he attacked Irene, standing up and making a cutting motion to the woman's throat. She said she got nervous at this point, so much so that she could hear her heart beating in her chest as Anthony Lambe was describing what he had done. Initially she had wanted Anthony to stay because he had drink taken and she didn't want him to drive.

After hearing what he had admitted, though, she was thinking of ways to get him out of her house. She told the detectives that Anthony admitted cutting Irene's throat at the back door of the house and emphasised how animated he was becoming reliving the murder.

He was describing the thrill of the crime and told the woman that 'it was the best feeling' he ever had. 'He kept on about the buzz that he got from it,' she said. Anthony told her how he had been hired for the murder through his work as a bouncer and that 'the reason he took it on was because he needed the money'. The witness said Anthony got paid before and after the murder and that he travelled to the UK later that day so he would have an alibi. He wasn't upset, the woman said, but rather trying his best to convince her that he was the killer, telling her he had been paid €10,000 and later €5,000 for the job. It was a slight variance on the figures she had mentioned in her anonymous calls. The woman said Anthony seemed excited about remembering the murder. When she asked him what he had done with the murder weapon, her friend tried to ignore the question, only telling her 'they should have found it'. Anthony then wanted her to research the murder on the internet, which he said would prove that he was telling the truth.

She was extremely unsettled by the shocking details being revealed to her and the vivid re-enactment in her living room. Eventually, she convinced Anthony to leave her house. As he drove off, she tracked the tail lights of his car travelling down the road until they were out of sight, making sure he was gone.

At the end of taking her statement, Detective Garda Ogle asked the woman if she would look through her old photos for a picture of herself and Anthony Lambe together if she was ever back in Ireland. She had no immediate plans to return home but said she would try. The detectives thanked her, and she was brought back home as Detective Inspector Marry was updated on the development.

After a few hours Detective Garda Ogle phoned me back to tell me that this lady made a full statement in writing and on camera about what Anthony Lambe had told her. We discussed the protocol of evidence, confessions of evidence, and the local police's role in the whole process. It was all legally sound and would stand up to scrutiny in a court of law. Detective Gardaí Ogle and Reilly did excellent work. During the recording of the statement, Detective Garda Reilly had to take over writing down the woman's account, as the AFP officer could not keep up with the witness's Monaghan accent. The right people for the job.

The woman had also been asked why she decided to only come forward in 2013 and make the anonymous phone calls. She explained that when she told her father of what Anthony Lambe had revealed, he wanted her to go in to the gardaí immediately. But when he thought about it more, he became concerned for his daughter's safety. Given that it related to someone being hired for murder in Dundalk, they feared there may have been subversive links to the crime. This wasn't the case, but her parents were terrified of what could happen to their daughter if she came forward.

Another reason was that she wasn't entirely sure if Anthony Lambe was telling the truth, as he had a habit of always bigging things up. He had told her that he stabbed Irene at the back door, but when she researched the case, she realised that Irene had been murdered in her kitchen. It cast doubt over whether Anthony Lambe was just making the whole thing up or not. Between this and her parents' concerns, she decided not to say anything. But Detective Gardaí Ogle and Reilly could see the relief showing on her face when they arrived at her house having held onto what she heard by not making a formal statement for 11 years. The weight lifted off her shoulders.

The detectives were impressed with the Australian-based witness, who came across as a very honest and well-intentioned person. They believed that, had it not been for her parents' concerns, she possibly would have come forward a lot sooner with the information. In a later report compiled on their interactions with her, gardaí noted: 'She is a very bright and intelligent person, and we believe despite the fact she did not provide her details when making the calls, she provided sufficient specifics over the course of the two calls that would enable investigating gardaí to identify her. She was somewhat tormented over the dilemma she found herself in, in that she didn't want to betray her parents' trust and advice by revealing her identity, but at the same time wanted to provide information to gardaí.'

Gardaí also approached the woman's family back in Ireland to take statements from them. Her father, though, reacted angrily to gardaí showing up at his door, making references to a press article printed in 2013 after his daughter had made the anonymous phone call. The newspaper report detailed how a caller in Australia had passed on significant information to the cold case review unit. Her father told gardaí that they couldn't be trusted and that his daughter's life had been put at risk by the call being leaked to the media. Despite his concerns, the man eventually made a statement to gardaí after speaking with his daughter. He had initially told her to go to the gardaí but then became seriously concerned that she may herself become a target of the people involved in the murder and strongly advised her against reporting it. The witness's father also told detectives that his daughter had told him that she was going to anonymously report what she had been told in 2013.

The woman's boyfriend in Australia was also interviewed, and he recalled her talking about Anthony Lambe's confession in the past. While he couldn't remember the specifics of what was said, she did mention that Anthony had arrived at her house drunk one night and brought up the murder of Irene White. The man said his girlfriend wasn't sleeping properly and was getting annoyed about it in recent years.

In November 2016, the witness returned home to Ireland unexpectedly and contacted Detective Garda Ogle. She had found a photograph of herself with Anthony Lambe taken at the Gaeltacht in 1999 and later handed it over to the detective. It was a further piece of evidence to corroborate her friendship with the murder suspect, and once again showed her willingness to assist the investigation team.

Gardaí now had sufficient grounds to arrest Anthony Lambe for the murder of Irene White, but they wanted to gather more evidence that could be put to him during his detention. A trawl of his financial accounts in the week of 6 April 2005 cast doubt over his claims that he urgently needed an advance on his wages that morning. On 5 April, Anthony withdrew €540 from his AIB account, leaving him with a balance of €126.27. The day after the murder he was paid €342.52 by PPS Security, and on 7 April he received his college grant of €148.80 into his bank account. Gardaí also discovered that the following week, his wages totalling €231 were lodged into his account.

While he had been in overall financial difficulty in the months leading up to the murder, that very week he had access to around €1,100. It called into question his pressing necessity to meet Niall Power at DKIT to get a €400 week's advance on his wages. The fact that his wages were also paid into his bank account the following day and again a week later raised further doubts over his story. The investigation team now believed that this meeting at the college was so that a sizeable portion of the murder purse could be handed over. They also believed that he'd committed the murder purely out of financial motivation, which was somewhat supported by the circum- stantial evidence within Annie Kane's statements, in which she described Anthony being unusually generous with his money in the days and weeks after the murder. On her birthday that May, Anthony bought her an annual gym membership costing around €650, two tickets for Meatloaf at Ardgillan Castle, a B&B stay for the night of the concert, and a bracelet. Annie also believed that he had paid a deposit of around €1,000 for an engagement ring in McGuigan's jewellers in Castleblayney in 2005.

This apparent lavish spending, gardaí believed, was consist- ent with what the Australian-based witness had said about Anthony Lambe spending money on his girlfriend. The pur- chases were also far in excess of the wages he was getting for his security work or his college grant money and had to have come from another source of income. In their investigative file gardaí laid out their suspicions, saying that he 'was funding this expense from the proceeds he received from the murder of Irene White'. They also believed that his ongoing financial burdens from his drug debts and credit union loans provided him with 'ample motive' to carry out the murder for a monetary reward.

The evidence against Anthony Lambe also confirmed garda suspicions around other suspects. They always felt that Niall Power had some involvement in the murder, and his phone traffic with the man who was now the chief suspect re-enforced that belief. In one investigative file, gardaí said they 'strongly suspected that these calls between Anthony Lambe and Niall Power directly related to the circumstances surrounding the murder of Irene White and the minutes immediately thereafter'. Niall had left Lannett Cross 'in a tizzy' around the time of the murder, and he later drove past Ice House without volunteering this to gardaí. They believed that he was checking up on the crime scene after the murder had been confirmed to him. The case against Anthony Lambe had to be proven in court, though – he was still only a suspect at this stage.

*

Detective Inspector Marry decided that a new media appeal should be utilised in an effort to bring more witnesses to the fore, people who had never come forward or who hadn't revealed everything they knew when spoken to initially.

One of the tools in the toolbox of the senior investigating officer is the media. They say paper doesn't refuse ink and that is true, but there is a lot more to dealing with the media. In this case, we suspected Anthony Lambe of being involved in the murder of Irene White. He had confided in the lady now living in Australia about what he did. My thinking at the time was had he confided in anyone else? I knew from dealing with other murderers in the past that they have a propensity to confide in someone to alleviate their own guilt.

I thought long and hard about how to approach the general public for information on this case, and I wanted our communication to have a sufficient impact on the investigation. I wanted to appeal in such a way that information received would assist us moving forward. I decided to do this through the long-established TV programme *Crimecall*, which highlights crimes across the country. I was also aware there had been several appeals with the media over the years, well before I took charge, and nothing of major interest was ever gleaned. We had to have an edge, something different, something real. We wanted to represent Irene White as a real person, a mother and a good woman, and needed to get in people's faces with this appeal.

Having viewed previous appeals, they were clinical and informative but didn't have the edge. Irene's sister, Anne Delcassian, featured in some of these appeals, and she was passionate about what happened to Irene and she wanted the killer caught. I decided I would ask Jennifer McBride to take part in the appeal. Secondly, I got Detective Bobby Ogle to walk the path in the park where witnesses saw a suspicious man on the morning of the murder. I wanted to bring home the reality of the crime and portray Irene as a mother going about her daily chores when she was murdered. Jennifer agreed to take part, and she gave a heartwarming and heart-wrenching appeal to the public for information.

On 21 November 2016, RTÉ's *Crimecall* programme aired a powerful segment on the murder of Irene White. Detective Garda Ogle took viewers through the events that unfolded at Ice House that day and the sightings at Ice House Hill park. In an emotional interview, Jennifer McBride recalled being told about her mother's murder and not believing it to be true at first. 'At that stage it didn't sink in. We had to drive past my house and that's when I saw the tape and all the gardaí. But it wasn't until I saw my nanny – she was in an awful state. And that's when I knew that it was real. Her kids were everything, so she devoted all her time and energy to all of us. I miss everything. There is a big hole in my heart, and nothing will ever fill it. There is a piece of me that died that day,' she told the programme.

In the heartfelt plea, Jennifer also told viewers: 'If anyone knows anything, no matter how big or small, please come forward. Any little thing could make all the difference, so please just come forward with information you have. I just want her to rest in peace. Some closure, some answers, that's all I want, that's all anyone wants. I want her life to have meant something.'

The appeal worked, and that night a man called in outlining that he knew a man living in Dublin who may have significant information about the murder. The caller claimed how, some months after the murder, he spoke with the Dublin-based man, who mentioned that his boss was asked to murder Irene White. He recalled that 'the boss' worked in the security business and also had an interest in martial arts. The man had worked for

PPS Security in the past and had given a statement in 2005, but nothing of interest was contained in his account. The new information had come at a timely juncture for gardaí, as they were focusing their attention on Niall Power, who they believed was the man being referred to as 'the boss'. They were also aware that the other man referred to had been known to Niall Power in the months before the murder.

On 29 November, gardaí met with the man in Dublin, and he recalled being present for several conversations in his house between Niall Power and Alan White. He said these exchanges were at times heated and references were made to money derived from the sale of Ice House. The man believed a figure of around €1 million had been mentioned and that, during one conversation, Niall told Alan 'she has to go'. When asked if he was ever approached by anyone to murder Irene White, the man categorically denied it, or that it was ever even suggested to him in any form. His statement once again reinforced the gardaí's suspicions around Niall Power.

The poignant appeal by Jennifer McBride also struck a chord with another viewer. Shortly after the *Crimecall* programme aired, a woman contacted gardaí to say she had information about Anthony Lambe that could help their investigation. On 5 December 2016, this woman was interviewed and recounted how, some months after the murder, she was in a pub in Castleblayney with her partner and Anthony. The trio were watching the television in the pub when a programme on the murder of Irene White came on the screen. The woman said Anthony turned to her and calmly stated 'I did that' before mentioning details about the crime. He had made reference to the rear wall of Ice House as well as an alleyway near the property. The woman felt at the time that he wanted to get it off his chest, given the way he made the confession, and decided to finally come forward after hearing Jennifer's appeal.

Speaking about the impact the programme had, Detective Inspector Marry says:

> I was very pleased with how the appeal went, and that another valuable witness – who said Anthony Lambe had confessed to the murder in a pub – was identified. Also, with public appeals there is a risk, and you have to be aware you don't divulge anything that would affect the investigation or that could become a legal issue or prejudice a fair trial. I believed I had all this covered and the aim was achieved. The late Keelan Shanley was the interviewer that night and she struck me as a highly intelligent woman. She came up to me after the show and said, 'You know who murdered her – I can tell from you and your appeal.' I remember telling her that time would tell.

*

Gardaí next decided to follow up on another of the Serious Crime Review Team's recommendations: it was time to speak to Cathy Wilson once again. On 6 December, Detective Sergeant Mick Sheridan and Detective Gardaí Ogle and Reilly visited her at her home. During their conversation, she maintained there were things she hadn't said in her initial statements as she wasn't specifically asked, and as a result certain aspects were not broached by her.

In a fresh statement, she outlined how in the months prior to Irene's murder there were regular meetings with Vincent

Dullaghan, Alan White, Niall Power, and herself about setting up a new monitoring company. According to her, this was to be funded by Alan White and Niall Power at an estimated cost of possibly €400,000. She said that a large portion of this would be financed from the sale of Ice House, and Alan White said he couldn't set up the company before the separation from Irene, as she would be entitled to her share.

She recalled how during one conversation Alan mentioned that he was on to 'top notch' solicitors in Dublin about the separation and that Irene was 'going to get nothing'. When speaking to gardaí in 2013, Cathy refused to say who had alluded to the price of getting someone murdered in Dundalk some years earlier. In her new statement, though, she confirmed this sinister comment was made by Niall Power, who remarked that 'it would only cost €30,000 to pop someone's clogs around here'. Cathy said she began having doubts about Niall's reason for leaving her house on the morning of Irene's murder, when he excused himself because his girlfriend was sick, as it didn't make sense to her. On several occasions she had asked Alan White where Niall was on the day of the murder, but she said she was told to 'quit asking those questions' because she would 'get some man in trouble'.

Cathy also felt that Niall was avoiding her after the murder. Before Irene's death she would speak to him at least twice a week, but after the killing she didn't see him much. He had also bought himself a new Crew Cab and had his house decorated later in 2005. When she saw the new jeep, she quipped to him 'did you have someone's clogs popped'. Cathy explained that she made this remark because she was annoyed with Niall for not giving her an explanation as to where he was on the day of the murder. She also said that after

Irene was killed there was no more talk about setting up the monitoring company.

She then told gardaí of a menacing incident she was exposed to at Ice House in the weeks after Irene had been murdered. Cathy recalled being with Vincent Dullaghan when he got a call to go to the house to do some electrical work, and when they arrived Niall Power and Alan White were in the back garden smoking. Alan had asked her to go into the house to get some clothes for his children, and while she was uncomfortable with this, she agreed. Cathy said she walked into the bedroom and saw the couple's wedding album laid out on the bed and Irene's wedding dress hanging on the door. The scene unnerved Cathy and she left the house momentarily.

When Cathy returned, she walked into the kitchen where the three men were now congregated. There was blood on the dishwasher as well as the floor, and the trio discussed possible scenarios of how the blood had got onto the dishwasher. She recalled Alan opening the appliance door and noticing a knife inside, remarking that gardaí hadn't done a great job on the forensics. In their investigative file, gardaí wrote of this encounter: 'The investigation team suspect that this exercise in bringing Cathy Wilson down to Ice House and exposing her to the scene and the manner in which Irene's wedding dress and album were displayed was an intentional and intimidatory tactic by Alan White and Niall Power on Cathy Wilson.'

The investigation team believed her fresh statement supported a conspiratorial element of the case, in that Niall Power stood to benefit from Irene's death in relation to finances being available for setting up the monitoring company, while his comment of having someone's clogs popped was also highly suspect.

Another person who had previously given a significant statement against Niall was his ex-girlfriend Ellen Johnson. The current investigation team hadn't dealt with her yet and decided to speak to Ellen themselves to both gauge her character as a witness and delve deeper into her previous comments. In December 2016, she was interviewed again, and her account was consistent with what she had told gardaí 11 years earlier. In her new statement, Ellen also repeated her previous claim that Niall owned a firearm in 2005 that he kept under his car seat. More damning, she said Niall had considered using the gun to murder Irene. Much of what he told her was in the evening times when they were at home and while Niall was under the influence of alcohol or cannabis. It was also Ellen Johnson's opinion that Niall was being brainwashed by Alan White and that he was under his influence to such an extent that he would do anything for him.

But Niall, she said, was getting angry with Alan in the months before Irene was murdered for not being focused on his work. Ellen described how an undertone developed of Niall wanting to get rid of Irene from a business perspective. She had spoken to Irene in the days before the murder and had never seen her so afraid. Ellen described Irene as 'petrified for her life' and that she was sleeping with a chair against the bedroom door for her safety.

A few days after speaking to Ellen Johnson, Detective Garda Ogle met Vincent Dullaghan at Carrickmacross garda station. He explained to Vincent that he wanted to reinterview him about events at the time of Irene's murder. Vincent engaged the services of a solicitor, and the following month he gave gardaí a prepared witness statement. He described how on several occasions he met with Alan, Niall, and Cathy to discuss the setting up of a monitoring company, but that his previous assertion that this was at an advanced stage was incorrect. 'What was being mooted was the possibility of the incorporation of a company called Superior Monitoring Limited,' he said, with a view to meeting the monitoring requirements of another business while engaging with new clients. If this came to fruition, Alan was to provide the finances.

Vincent said he had no recollection 'of anything being said that would cause me serious concerns or indeed any concerns for Irene's safety'. If anything of the sort had been suggested by Cathy then she was lying, he added. Vincent told the detective that setting up such a company would require €30,000 at most and that a large injection of funds wasn't necessary. He also said that, while he knew the relationship between Alan and Irene White was fraught, he had never heard Alan refer to his wife in vulgar or derogatory terms. He did say that Alan 'may have said words to the effect that she could rot in the Ice House as far as he was concerned and that he needed to provide a house for his children in any event'.

By mid-January 2017, a year after the case was formally handed back over to Dundalk gardaí, they had undertaken a significant amount of work. While suspicions hung over Alan White, and Niall Power even more so, they decided that nothing would be gained from arresting Irene's estranged husband or his business partner at this stage. This wasn't the case with Anthony Lambe, against whom a substantial amount of evidence had been compiled in the previous 12 months. The investigation team firmly believed that he had murdered Irene White and was the elusive figure seen running from the direction of Ice House after murdering Irene White on 6 April 2005. After months of keeping discreet surveillance on their chief suspect, it was time for gardaí to step out from the shadows and confront Anthony Lambe about what he had done.

15

THE KILLER

The team of gardaí gathered at Dundalk garda station for their final briefing. It was the morning of 20 January 2017, and the plan was to travel to Annadrumman in Castleblayney, County Monaghan, for the purpose of arresting Anthony Lambe. A day earlier, Detective Sergeant Mick Sheridan had obtained a district court warrant to search their prime suspect's family home, having outlined to a judge that he believed evidence connected to the murder of Irene White could be obtained at the property. The gardaí, split into an arrest team and a search team, set out in convoy, arriving at the home of Anthony Lambe at 11.15 a.m. His sister answered the knock on the door and was shocked to see a group of detectives standing in the driveway. Detective Sergeant Sheridan explained the reason for their unexpected visit and showed her the search warrant, before being granted access to the house.

As they walked in, Anthony Lambe came down the stairs to be greeted by ten gardaí standing in the hallway of his home. He didn't show any signs of shock or bemusement. Before the investigators even had a chance to explain to him why they were there, he remarked: 'Of all days, lads.' His parents were still in the house, and he didn't want them to see him being arrested. He led gardaí up to his bedroom, where he pointed out a number of electronic devices belonging to him. At 11.19 a.m. Detective Sergeant Sheridan arrested Anthony under Section 4 of the Criminal Justice Act 1997 for an arrestable offence, namely the murder of Irene White. He was handcuffed and placed into an unmarked garda car. As he was driven to Dundalk garda station, a search team led by Sergeant John Moroney continued a trawl of the property for any further evidence.

After arriving in the garda station, Anthony Lambe was fingerprinted and photographed, and buccal swabs were taken from him to compare with DNA recovered at the murder scene. He was then led into an interrogation room with his solicitor where, at 3.22 p.m., Detective Gardaí Ogle and Reilly sat down with him to begin their first interview. They cautioned Anthony, informing him that he wasn't obliged to say anything unless he wished to do so, but anything he did say would be taken down in writing and could be given in evidence against him. Anthony had no intention of staying silent. Having held onto a dark secret for nearly 12 years, the time had finally come for him to tell gardaí what he had done.

Anthony said that back in 2004 he was drinking heavily on a daily basis and his life had spiralled out of control. Shortly after he started working with PPS Security, he became friendly with Niall Power, often receiving money from him on top of his wages to feed his binge drinking and drug habit. He told the detectives that, in or around Christmas of that year, Niall approached him and asked him if he would murder Irene White. Anthony said he was reluctant at first, but his boss was incessant and raised the matter two or three times a week.

'These conversations didn't seem real,' he explained, with Niall Power insisting 'you will, you should'. He said he was to be paid 'thousands' for carrying out the murder but couldn't recall exactly how much was offered. Eventually, he relented and agreed to murder Irene White.

He said that one night at a house party, in either February or March 2005, he met Alan White, who he claimed made a vague threat against him. Alan, he stated, told Anthony he was aware of what he had been tasked to do, and if he didn't go through with it, 'they would find someone else'. Anthony said he was also told that he would be the only other person who knew, which would make him a loose end. He took it to mean that he would be next and felt like there was 'no way out' for him. In early March 2005, Niall Power informed him that Irene was a member of the gym at the Carrickdale Hotel in Carrickcarnan, County Louth. He said that Niall provided him with a knife and got him to drive to the hotel, with the plan being to attack Irene as she came out of the gym. Anthony, however, said that he couldn't go through with it and drove home, discarding the weapon as he left the gym.

He told the detectives that in the last week of March 2005 he had asked Niall for €1,000, who in turn told him: 'if you do what was asked, you will get even more'. Anthony was told that any debts owed would be written off and that he could get a further €3,000 or €4,000 for murdering Irene. As the murder conspiracy was crystallising, Niall told him that he could say exactly when Irene returned home from the daily school run. As part of the planning, Niall had also shown him around Ice House Hill park, Anthony claimed, which included pointing out what gate led to the rear wall of Irene's home and which route wasn't covered by CCTV cameras.

Detective Garda Reilly produced a number of aerial photographs of the scene to get a better understanding of exactly
what locations Anthony was referring to. Anthony pointed
out the exact route that his boss had told him to walk, which
led him to the rear wall of Ice House. Anthony explained that
on a previous occasion Niall had actually walked around the
park with him as part of a reconnaissance exercise before the
murder, and he'd advised him to stab Irene in the chest. 'Once
or twice should do it,' he was told, and he would later say of
the recce:

While there, Niall laid out how I was to get into the
house from the park. He walked me through the park and
showed me it. It was daytime. He actually took me over
to the wall and showed me the drop on the other side. It
was the house where Irene lived in. I had never been in
that park before this. Niall had told me that the cameras
in the house and around the back of the house would not
be working. I was supposed to do it the week he showed
me, but I didn't. He gave me the knife that day too, the
day he showed me around the park. He had given me a
knife for the hotel too, but I threw it away.

I'd say this day in the park, the murder was a week and
a half or two weeks after. It was two weeks after. I was
looking for money off Niall to go to Annie's graduation
and Niall told me I had a job to do. I was all over the
place. I didn't want to do it. I spent most of the time off
my face – drink, coke, ecstasy. I was afraid about what he
said to me and my family.

How could I go home and say I had been hand-picked
for a murder. I could have gone to so many other doors

that morning and that woman would be alive but try telling him that. Niall had given me a rough outline of the school and how she would do her bit. I know Niall pointed out her car to me one day at the house. He did mention her mother was there. He did mention that it had to be a day the children weren't there, early enough, so it had to be at that time. I don't know where Alan White was to be.

Anthony had been informed that Irene was security conscious and reluctant to answer the door to a stranger. The ruse to lure her outside, he said, was to knock on the door and say that the side gates were swinging open, as they had tended to do in the past. On the morning of 6 April 2005, Anthony drove to DKIT and aimlessly hung around, not knowing what to do for a while, and described himself as being in a daze and stressed out. He admitted that the calls between himself and Niall that morning related to the murder. In one phone call, Niall warned him that he wouldn't get any money 'until the job was done'. When Anthony was in situ at O'Hanlon Park, the housing estate beside Ice House Hill park, he again rang Niall to confirm that he was going to get his money if he did the job.

It was confirmed that he would be paid and that Irene was now at home. Their phone records showed two calls between Anthony and Niall at 9.44 a.m., the second of which lasted 39 seconds and matched the time Irene would have left Réalt na Mara primary school nearby. While sitting in his car, Anthony took out a small ziplock bag containing cocaine, emptied a dash of the white power out onto his finger, and sniffed it. He then got out of his car and walked through the park, making his way to the back of Ice House. Asked by the detectives to describe what he was wearing, Anthony said it was probably dark jeans and a jacket, a hoody, a ski mask and woollen gloves. He couldn't recall what footwear he was wearing, but if it was runners, they would have been Asics or Nike branded. When later detailing what happened next, he said:

After the final contact with Niall, I believed then there was no alternative. I jumped the wall. I can't remember if the gate was closed. I did as Niall said. I knocked on the door, Irene looked out the door. I said the gate swung out. I think she opened the door a bit. I didn't know her to see. I had never been shown a photo of her. She opened the back door then. I stabbed her there at the back of the door. I stabbed her in the chest, and she fell back in the door. I'd say it was once at that stage. I'm left-handed. I was using the knife Niall had given me. I can't remember how many times I stabbed her. I got so afraid. She shouted at me. She said, 'Stop, why are you doing this?' I can't remember anything about her. I remember her face, that's it. I still remember her face. At that stage I broke down in the middle of it, but I knew it was too late. I didn't even remember cutting her throat. I can't even remember the layout of the place. She was lying on the ground. She was finished at that stage.

Anthony Lambe detailed how Irene was trying to get a hold of him as he attacked her, but said she 'didn't have a chance'. Detective Garda Ogle then asked Anthony if he kneeled beside Irene after stabbing her. He said he had, to say the 'Our Father' prayer, before picking up the knife and running out of the back door. He had the weapon tucked under his arm as he fled through Ice House Hill park before getting back into his car. 'I was afraid then because of that morning, the way Niall spoke to me and because of the threat from Alan,' he said. 'I realised because I did this, I was a loose end. After I done it, I rang him and he said, "We'll meet you with the money" and I got scared. I said I'd go home first.'

Anthony also claimed that during this call Niall inquired if Irene was definitely dead. Anthony said he left Dundalk by driving out past the Lisdoo Bar and Restaurant, along the Armagh Road, then headed for Castleblayney. Asked what he did with the knife, he said he threw it into a field somewhere along the way. 'My knees were bloody. I was bloody enough, I wasn't destroyed. I discarded the gloves with the knife. I fired them out of the window down that back road. I didn't stop the car. I threw them out the driver's window. I was in the North. I couldn't tell you where, it was before I got to Crossmaglen. I told Niall I'd meet him at the college before the airport.'

He met his mother when he got back to the house in Castleblayney, still wearing the bloodied clothes, having murdered Irene less than half an hour earlier. Anthony told her that he'd come across a young man that had been involved in a motorbike accident, and then he threw the bloodied clothes into the washing machine on a boil wash. He showered, got dressed, and went into Castleblayney town to buy new clothes. 'You have asked me what the necessity was to get money off Niall. It was for drink. After I bought clothes in Castleblayney I picked up Annie and headed up the road to meet Niall.' When later asked about the meeting with Niall Power at DKIT, he said:

It was a bit weird. He had the money for me, €1,000, he gave it straight away. Me and Niall got out of the cars and walked away. He asked me if it had gone to plan, and I said it did. He asked me why I didn't meet him earlier and I said I was bloody and wanted to go home and get changed. He seemed angry earlier when I wouldn't meet him. At that stage he already knew how many times she had been stabbed. He asked me why I stabbed her so many times, and I told him I panicked. He had a number. I didn't even know how many times I stabbed her. That was it. The €1,000, he gave it in cash.

Niall, he claimed, was also aware that Irene's throat had been slit and asked him why he had done this. He was angry that Anthony had made 'so many mistakes' during the murder, with his main bone of contention being that the knife hadn't been left at the scene, as he wanted the killing to look like a robbery gone wrong. Detective Garda Ogle then asked Anthony if he'd ever told anyone about what he had done. He believed he'd told an ex-girlfriend, who would 'throw it back at him' when they argued. When the name of the Australian-based witness was put to him, Anthony had no recollection of ever telling her. With that the first round of questioning was done and the murder suspect was given a short rest.

At 7.47 p.m. that evening, Detective Gardaí Ogle and Reilly took up the interrogation of Anthony Lambe once again. The name of his female friend now living in Australia was put to him again, and while he couldn't recall admitting anything to her, he didn't deny what was contained in her statement. He put this down to the fact that he was functioning on a cocktail of alcohol, ecstasy, and cocaine at the time. He revealed how, around three years after the murder, Niall Power approached him and asked if he had ever told anyone about his dark secret, but he told Niall he hadn't.

The detectives then began trying to build a clearer picture of what exactly had been discussed in the phone calls with Niall that morning. Anthony said he didn't have a great recollection of the sequence of events, so Detective Garda Ogle attempted to summarise the calls from what Anthony had told the gardaí already. 'So you remember the call at 8.30 a.m., from you to Niall Power, a second one from Niall Power to you at 9.44 a.m. for 39 seconds. You believe that's him telling you she's home or on the way ... Another call after you murdered her, you got scared and decided not to meet him and went home by the Lisdoo Bar and Restaurant, and much later another call when you were on the way up to Dundalk at 11.39 a.m. to collect the €1000?' Anthony agreed with the summary, adding that Niall told him he didn't have the money on him and that he would have to get it.

This was significant, as at 10.41 a.m., after allegedly being told about the murder, Niall Power withdrew €1,000 from the Permanent TSB in Dundalk town centre. This was less than 30 minutes after getting off the phone to Anthony and matched the initial purse he was to be paid. Later, discussing how he coped with the burden of carrying the murder in the days and weeks that followed, Anthony said:

> I was up and down in the UK. After drinking over there I just wasn't right. But it was my first time on a plane, so I thought I got away with most of it. I think I came back the Friday, the day after the graduation. There was media and press about it. I think I spoke to Niall that weekend.

It feels like I slotted back in straight away. That's the way it feels looking back. I was worried but Niall told me to stick to the story that I needed the money for the wages and was paying it back. He reiterated that a few times. He asked how I was and asked if I told anyone.

Anthony also said that he got paid another €1,000 later that summer, which was the last instalment he got for carrying out the murder. He told the detectives that he and Niall had been good friends and that he looked up to his boss, but later began to resent him. 'I don't know what pressure he was under either. I was at his wedding and stag party. I am godfather to his eldest son. It was a good way of keeping me close. I would die for family and friends,' he said. Asked why he didn't distance himself from Niall Power after the murder, Anthony explained that Niall 'kept ringing me', telling him never to discuss the murder on the phone or around the car. He agreed with the detective's suggestion that Niall had essentially groomed him for the murder and that, as part of his efforts to convince Anthony, Niall had admitted to doing something similar himself a few years earlier. The investigation team believed this was a reference to murdering an RUC member in Northern Ireland, which Niall had also told Ellen Johnson about.

Asked about the arrests of Niall Power and Alan White in 2006, Anthony confirmed that he had spoken to his boss about it afterwards. 'He said "they think it's me, but they are barking up the wrong tree because I have an alibi for the day". Then he would go over my story for the day. I can't recall telling anyone I did the murder. I was shocked when you read [the Australian witness's] statement. It was the Christmas after it. I was practically cooked,' he said of his admission. When questioned about what knowledge Alan White had of the plan, Anthony believed that Alan was well aware, but added that the only time the topic was mentioned between them was at the house party. Speaking about his own life after the murder, Anthony said he managed to keep down a job but that 'the first couple of years were rough'. He had also attempted to take his own life a couple of times but managed to get off drugs, completed the Dublin marathon in 2011, and started a higher diploma course. 'Before I started the master's in 2014, I stopped outside the barracks in Dundalk for a couple of hours but hadn't the courage to go in. It was guilt. I don't know what it was. I was going to kill myself someday. I never saw myself growing old. I was going to do it when I was 40. Since 2005, I thought I didn't deserve to live.' The second interview then concluded for the night, and Anthony Lambe was taken to the custody suite to rest. Recalling leaving work that day, Detective Inspector Marry says:

> All investigations throw up elements that stick with you and which you are not going to forget. When Anthony Lambe was in custody being detained for questioning, I remember getting ready to leave the station that night. I decided to look in at Anthony Lambe in the cell, just to see if everything was in order. I opened the hold, and he was standing up, walking around. He said to me, 'You were the detective in the *Crimecall* programme looking for information.' He told me he returned home the night the *Crimecall* programme was on. He said he was sitting with his parents watching it and got a shock when Irene White's daughter came on to talk about Irene. He said it was Irene he saw, not Jennifer; her voice was the same

as Irene's. He told me that, when he stabbed Irene, she said, 'Why are you doing this?', and that it was the same voice as Jennifer's. Anthony told me he got up from the couch, went to bed, and cried constantly for six hours solid thinking about what he had done. He said that in the years since the murder he was doing voluntary work to see if he could right the wrong. 'But you can't,' he said.

At 9.47 a.m. the next morning, gardaí began their third and final interview, focused on the other people involved in the murder conspiracy. Anthony Lambe said that in a debrief of the attack, Niall Power was unhappy with the volume of phone traffic between them. Detective Garda Ogle asked if there was ever mention of a firearm, to which Anthony said that his boss did admit while drunk in a pub one night that he had a gun. This was another piece of information consistent with Ellen Johnson's statement, while Anthony said that figures between €4,000 and €10,000 were 'bandied about' by Niall for the murder contract.

Niall had also warned Anthony that they would be arrested over the murder, but if they stuck to the story about his wages, it would be fine. Even though €1,000 was handed over, Niall believed a figure of €400 would be a more believable number to tell the gardaí. Anthony was also shown photographs of the gates at Ice House. He confirmed that they were pointed out to him by Niall as part of the ploy to coax Irene out of her home. He also told gardaí that after being handed the €1,000 for the murder, he asked about the rest of the money. 'We'll see about that,' Niall told him. At the end of the interview, Anthony was asked how he felt about what he had done. 'A teenage girl went to school that morning and returned to no mammy,' he told the detectives, breaking down and becoming extremely emotional once again. Recalling the conclusion of the interrogation, Detective Inspector Marry says:

> I have never seen it before, but when Anthony Lambe made his admissions and before leaving the interview room, he spontaneously hugged one of the detectives. I could see in this gesture that he was nothing but honest with us and had told the whole truth of how he came to murder Irene White. He was ecstatic to finally have been given the opportunity to get the monkey off his back.

Throughout the interview, Detective Inspector Marry was liaising with the Office of the DPP. The legislation under which their prisoner was being detained meant that he could only be questioned for a total of 24 hours. Given what he had revealed, it was more than enough time. Following the third and final interview, an oral direction was given by the DPP to charge him with the murder of Irene White. At 1.05 p.m., Detective Inspector Marry put the charge to Anthony Lambe, who replied: 'I'm very sorry.' A special sitting of Dundalk District Court was convened, and a garda escort brought Anthony Lambe to the courthouse. The convoy made the short journey across Dundalk town, where Detective Inspector Marry and Detective Sergeant Sheridan then flanked the accused murderer as they led him up the steps and into the building. The press photographers and camera crews who had waited patiently for his arrival were unable to get a clear picture of him, as he held a jacket over his face while walking up the steps.

A number of locals had also arrived at the courts complex and jeered Anthony Lambe as he was being led in, with some shouting 'scumbag' at him. Wearing a maroon jumper and blue jeans, he sat quietly in the dock and stood up as Judge Denis McLoughlin entered the court. Detective Inspector Marry gave evidence of the earlier arrest, charge, and caution, and he applied for the accused to be remanded in custody, to appear before the court again the following week. The request was a formality, as on a murder charge, an application for bail can only be granted by the High Court.

Anthony Lambe's solicitor also applied for free legal aid, saying his client was a student with no fixed income. This request was granted, while his legal team also asked that he be placed into protective custody. When the judge inquired if there was a perceived threat against Anthony, Detective Inspector Marry informed the court that he 'may be a vulnerable person at this stage'. He had himself seen Anthony Lambe's emotional state over the previous two days in Dundalk garda station, and he was aware that during his garda interviews, Anthony had admitted having contemplated taking his own life in the past. With that the hearing was adjourned, and Anthony Lambe was led out of the building to a further chorus of abuse from onlookers as he was placed into the garda car and driven off to prison. After nearly 12 years, a person had finally been charged with Irene White's murder.

16

AN UNEXPECTED VISITOR

While gardaí had secured the first charge as part of the long-running murder inquiry, other avenues had to be fully explored for the investigative file being submitted to the DPP. The detective branch also had to prepare themselves for a potential trial, even though this was an unlikely prospect given Anthony Lambe's detailed admissions, as Detective Inspector Marry explains:

Regardless of your feelings, if someone was going to plead guilty, and indicated as much, you'd never take a chance or shortcut right up to the day of a trial. We had to prepare in full for a not-guilty plea and trial process, and this included preparing the book of evidence and handing over disclosure to the defence. In the UK they call this 'serving the case'. Disclosure is providing the defence with all copies of all material accumulated during the course of the investigation. They must have access to all materials that they can use to undermine the prosecution case. Anthony Lambe had always indicated he would plead guilty, and I had no doubt this is what he would do.

I have dealt with several murderers and would say all but Anthony Lambe were psychopaths. He was different in that he expressed full empathy from the time of his interview and had genuine remorse for what he did. He acknowledged the pain and suffering he caused. He had the clear ability to distinguish that he had done wrong and knew the difference between right and wrong. What he did was evil, but his behaviour over the following years after the murder was in keeping with social norms. He continuously volunteered, did charity work, and helped his community as best he could, but as I told him in Dundalk garda station that night, there's no balancing the books for murder.

Gardaí began tracking down the other women Anthony Lambe had been in relationships with over the years to establish if he had made confessions to any of them. On 20 January 2017, Gardaí James Kilgannon and Connor McCaughey interviewed an ex-girlfriend of his at her home in Tallaght. She had been involved with Anthony between 2012 and 2016 and was shocked by the call to the door. In a brief statement, she had nothing but good things to say about her ex-boyfriend, having trusted him implicitly with her daughter too. The woman said he had never revealed anything, be it about the murder or any other criminality, that led her to have any concerns about him.

That same day, the gardaí interviewed another former girlfriend, who had gone out with Anthony for several months in 2009. The woman also didn't have any derogatory remarks to make about him, revealing how they had remained friends after their relationship fizzled out. She did recall one occasion in 2009 when he told her that he was interviewed by gardaí about the murder of Irene White, and she remembered think-ing to herself 'oh, shut up'. The woman didn't believe the Anthony she knew would be capable of hurting anyone, and he never brought up the murder again. He had only texted her weeks earlier on New Year's Day, saying, 'I'm glad to say 2016 is over, tumours removed, heart breaking, stress and anxiety, with a little bit of mental health problems to sweeten the deal. I speak to a counsellor from time to time and I now teach mental wellbeing.'

The following day, Gardaí Kilgannon and McCaughey interviewed the girlfriend that Anthony Lambe had been charged with assaulting several years earlier. She portrayed an altogether different picture of the accused murderer in comparison to the glowing references given by the two other ex-partners. Their relationship began in 2005, lasting two years, and was a violent one. She said Anthony Lambe would become particularly aggressive when drunk and that he regu-larly assaulted her. He was jealous and controlling, she said, and in one particularly vicious attack he threw her down the stairs of her home.

On Valentine's Day 2007, he took her to Paris as a surprise, but throughout the weekend subjected her to violence and locked her into her hotel room while he went out one night. On another occasion, back in Ireland while she was on a night out at a disco, she noticed Anthony trying to discreetly follow her. During the night he approached her, put her finger in his mouth, and removed her ring with his teeth, leaving bite marks. Later that night, he also assaulted her back at her house and gardaí were called. Anthony Lambe was arrested and charged, but the woman dropped the complaint on the condition that he never trouble her or speak to her again.

The only reference she recalled him making about Irene White's murder was when she collected him from Crossmaglen in South Armagh one night. They got into an argument, and he started pulling her hair, with the woman shouting at him 'you're going to fucking kill us' while demanding he get out of her car. Anthony, she said, angrily fired back by warning her 'I'll do the same to you as what happened to the woman in Dundalk'. The chilling threat was made less than a year after Irene White had been murdered, and she knew exactly what her boyfriend was referring to. It was the one and only time he ever brought it up.

While the statements didn't advance the investigation much further, it showed the volatile character Anthony Lambe was and that he seemed to have reformed in his later relationships. His mother was also spoken to because her son had said he had encountered her at home after the murder. Bernadette Lambe, though, couldn't recall anything specific about the day, only remembering that her son had come home one time after coming across someone involved in an accident.

The garda liaison officer appointed to Alan White also kept in contact with him. He had been informed prior to the court hearing that a suspect had been charged with his wife's murder, and he attended the hearing when Anthony Lambe appeared on 20 January. Weeks later, gardaí would be in touch with him again, but this time it was after they had received an unusual phone call.

On 10 February, an ESB employee was working at the power station in Ballykelly, on the outskirts of Dundalk town, when he noticed someone walking around the perimeter fence. He recognised the man as Alan White, who was a distant relation of his. The ESB employee thought that Alan looked slightly disoriented, and he appeared to be looking up at the large pylons inside the fence. The man approached Alan, who began asking him about the strength of the voltage from the electrical poles. The ESB employee became concerned about Alan White, given what he had asked about, and called a garda he knew in Dundalk. The strange encounter was passed on to the investigation team, and the following day Detective Inspector Marry and Detective Sergeant Sheridan went to Alan White's home in Knockbridge.

They were invited in, but before the detectives had a chance to bring up his presence at the power station the previous day, Alan began asking them about Anthony Lambe, the status of the case, and the issue of bail. He believed that a man charged with murder surely wouldn't be released from custody pending trial and that, because Anthony Lambe had admitted to the murder, the case could be disposed of quickly. From his comments, Detective Inspector Marry believed that Alan White had an appreciation for the murder suspect's academic qualifications, as he also said that his profile did not fit that of a murderer. Alan was twice asked if he knew Anthony Lambe, but denied that he did. He said he tried to look at him in court and saw a picture of him on social media, but didn't recognise him. He then pressed the detectives on why Anthony Lambe had murdered his estranged wife, being told that they could not discuss the specifics of the case. Detective Inspector Marry then specifically asked him if he had met Anthony previously. Alan again denied that he had. Throughout the conversation he seemed lucid and, in contrast to his apparent demeanour the previous day, did not appear in any state of distress or anxiety.

Finally, the detectives got around to asking him to account for his presence at the power station. Alan explained that he had a very keen interest in power lines and voltage. When they explained that they were concerned he was going to do something stupid to himself, or had something preying on his mind, he rubbished their suggestions, saying that if he was going to do something to himself, he would 'go somewhere a lot handier'. The investigators then left, with Detective Sergeant Sheridan immediately returning to Dundalk garda station to write up contemporaneous notes of the encounter.

Alan White had good reason to assume that the man charged with his estranged wife's murder wouldn't get bail, given that he was accused of carrying out a vicious murder. However, in early March 2017, Anthony Lambe successfully applied to the High Court to be released from custody while awaiting trial. Several strict orders were imposed on him as part of his bail conditions, including that he reside at his home and obey a curfew between 10 p.m. and 6 a.m. and that he would make himself available to gardaí during those times. He was also ordered to stay out of Dundalk and not have any contact with witnesses in the case. The following month, the book of evidence was served on him, which outlined the overwhelming material supporting the charge that he had murdered Irene White. The most damning piece of evidence was his own admissions, while there were also the statements from the two women he had confessed to, the discrepancies in his original accounts, and cell site data placing him in Dundalk around the time of the murder.

In their investigative file submitted to the DPP, gardaí noted the hold Niall Power had had over Anthony in getting him to carry out the murder. They also wrote that if Niall were to be interviewed, 'he may well depict Anthony Lambe to be a more willing accomplice than Lambe would have the investigation team believe'. The garda file also highlighted the admission made by Anthony to the Australian-based witness, in which he referred to Irene as a 'bad bitch' and said that a 'job had to be done'. Given this, gardaí wrote, 'maybe Anthony Lambe wasn't painting an altogether accurate account of matters during his interviews after arrest'.

> However, notwithstanding all of this, nothing can excuse the ferocious and vicious manner in how Anthony Lambe murdered a defenceless woman in the kitchen of her own home in a frenzied knife attack that resulted in Irene White being stabbed 34 times, one of the injuries being the slitting of her throat. Anthony Lambe lived with this for nearly 12 years and who knows for how much longer he would've done but for his arrest. He has made a full and frank confession to his part in this atrocious crime and appears to have genuine remorse for what he did. He is resigned to the fact that he must pay his debt to society and is facing a mandatory sentence of life imprisonment. Anthony Lambe indicated a sense of relief upon his initial reaction to seeing the gardaí in his house on the morning of his arrest. He accepts that he has ruined a lot of lives and has to carry this for the rest of his life.

In the end, as predicted, there was no need for a trial. On 29 January 2018, Anthony Lambe appeared before the Central Criminal Court in Dublin and was arraigned on the sole count on the indictment that he murdered Irene White at Ice House on the Demesne Road, Dundalk, on 6 April 2005. After the charge was put to him by the court registrar, the 34-year-old stood up and simply replied, 'Guilty, Judge.' His sentencing hearing that afternoon was a formality in terms of the mandatory life tariff imposed for murder, but it also gave a chance for Irene's family to show the devastation his actions had caused. In her victim impact statement, Jennifer McBride said that the murder of her loving and gentle mother had caused 'tremendous pain, sorrow and devastation'. She described Irene as 'great fun' and 'the life and soul of the party', but that as she went to school that morning, she didn't know it would be her 'last goodbye to my mam'. The thought of her mother dying in a pool of her own blood would haunt and torture her forever, Jennifer said, adding that her and her siblings' world had been turned upside down after the murder.

She said their home had been filled with peace, tranquillity, love, and laughter, but that was all taken away when she was called out of class that morning and told that her mother had passed away. Jennifer described how she felt shock and numbness and that she was left completely heartbroken. She said her mother's murder was 'frenzied, uncontrolled and an act of sheer brutality'. Jennifer went to live with her grandmother after the killing and was separated from her two siblings. Further tragedy hit six months later when Maureen McBride died 'from a broken heart', having never recovered from discovering Irene's body. It left Jennifer isolated and homeless, with no immediate family to support her.

Detective Inspector Marry outlined the facts of the case to the senior prosecuting counsel, Sean Gillane, and described Irene as a respected member of her community who was savagely murdered. The Central Criminal Court heard that Anthony Lambe was asked by an individual on behalf of another person to kill Irene White and that he received a relatively small sum of money for this. The person who approached him also gave him details of the layout of Irene's home and her movements. While not named in court, it was a direct reference to Niall Power's suspected role in the conspiracy. Detective Inspector Marry told the judge that Anthony Lambe showed genuine remorse for what he had done and that he was sorry and broke down on several occasions during his garda interviews. He said the defendant came from a 'very well-respected, decent family' who had been distressed on learning what he had done. At the conclusion of the hearing, Justice Patrick McCarthy handed down the mandatory sentence of life imprisonment.

That afternoon, Anne Delcassian walked out of the court complex proudly displaying a photograph of her younger sister. Addressing the media gathered on the front steps of the Criminal Courts of Justice, she said:

It's been a long time coming, but the murderer of my sister has got life today and I'm absolutely delighted. My sister Irene McBride was murdered on 6 April 2005. She was home alone on that day. She had just returned from leaving her three children at school and that was the last time her children got an opportunity to see their mother. He gave my sister a horrible, horrible, death. It was a brutal death. Lambe stabbed her over 30 times. This was a callous act. He had no thought for Irene or her family. My mother came across from her mobile home for her breakfast and found my beautiful sister murdered in such a savage way on the floor.

Alan White also attended the court case and was approached by members of the media as he walked out of the building and along Parkgate Street. Referring to the evidence that Anthony had been paid to kill Irene, her estranged husband said he was surprised that someone had ordered the murder. 'I am shocked about all the information,' he told reporters. When asked to comment about rumours that he was in some way linked to his wife's death, Alan replied: 'You can't speak for what people believe in.' He said he didn't know who'd ordered the murder but was confident that gardaí would continue working on the case to bring the other people involved to justice. 'This doesn't surprise me, that it has taken a long time to come about, but in the end it did. We were waiting for this stage to come.'

Speaking about the first conviction in the large-scale inquiry, Detective Inspector Marry says:

It's usually the family of the victim that come to you after a sentence hearing to thank you. In this case, Anthony's father approached me to shake my hand and thank me for treating his son the way we did, from his arrest right to its conclusion. It can't have been easy for Anthony's family – they were decent people who were shocked to the core about his past. I had a degree of sympathy for him, given he was undoubtedly manipulated and persuaded into the evil deed at a time when he was young, vulnerable, on drugs and drink, and in financial difficulty, at a time he was carrying demons in his head of a different nature.

After giving his reaction to reporters outside the courts in Dublin, Alan White was approached by *Sunday World* journalist Patrick O'Connell at his home in Knockbridge and questioned about his suspected involvement in the murder. He said he understood why people thought he was a suspect but maintained that he had nothing to do with the murder. When asked if he would be surprised if he was arrested for a second time in connection with the investigation, Alan responded: 'Nothing would surprise me anymore. In a way I wish they would because I might get some answers.' In a previous article he had referred to himself as the prime suspect, and this time around he said: 'That [the suspicion] has always sort of been there. But what your man [Anthony Lambe] said on Monday, I was gobsmacked by that. One door closes and you think you're finished and then another one opens, and you don't know now whether you're worse off than ever.'

The reporter then directly asked him: 'Did you pay Lambe money to kill Irene?' to which Alan White responded: 'No, I didn't even know the fucking chap! I'm gobsmacked why that simple line has been accepted. Here you have a guy up for murder and the focus has actually gone off the murderer because of the comment he made that he was paid to do it. And the gardaí are singing his praises.' Although Alan denied knowing Anthony Lambe or that he had any involvement in his wife's death, the garda investigation team still had their suspicions about Alan's potential involvement. In their investigative file submitted to the DPP in respect of Anthony Lambe's case, the gardaí noted:

Despite the frustrating lack of supporting evidence at this remove of the investigation, the investigation team are in no doubt that the ultimate benefactor following the murder of Irene White was to be her husband, Alan White. The original investigation sought to prove this same belief but no matter which angle this investigation is to be looked at, the recurring and obvious focal point as to the origins of the motive, is the sale of Alan White's house, Ice House. It could be argued that although there were inherent marriage difficulties that existed between Alan White and Irene White prior to the offer from Eircom, this apparent offer of €925,000 proved to be the catalyst that was to drive a deep sense of resentment through Alan White towards Irene White and her perceived entitlement to her fair share of the sale.

Gardaí also wrote in their investigative file that plans to set up a new remote monitoring company in 2005, which they believed would have been far ahead of its time, promised real potential in the form of financial reward once under way. For Niall Power, gardaí said that getting this venture up and running became 'a consuming influence' on him. The main source of finance for this new firm was apparently to come from Alan White, and it was obvious to Niall that Irene was proving to be a major obstacle for them. If she were to succeed in securing a considerable portion of the proceeds from the sale of Ice House, this could seriously affect the available capital for investment, jeopardising the business even getting off the ground. This, gardaí felt, represented motive for Niall, while adding:

It was an extremely unfortunate encounter for Anthony Lambe, meeting Niall Power when he did. They seemed to become very friendly in a very short space of time. One must consider did Niall Power have an ulterior motive from the outset in regard to his relationship and friendship with Anthony Lambe who by his own admission was in a bad place at the time. His vulnerable and impressionable demeanour was to provide Niall Power with an attractive target to influence and groom for his nefarious motives. As soon as Niall Power floated the idea with Anthony Lambe of murdering Irene White, and for whatever reason was not immediately met with complete refusal from Lambe, he continuously and unrelentingly kept on at him about doing it, three or four times a week he'd mention it, saying things like not letting the opportunity pass him by, that he must do it, he should do it, etc. Such mind games employed by Niall Power were akin to virtually brainwashing Anthony Lambe. Niall Power was also aware that Anthony Lambe had financial problems and promised him a significant sum on completion of the job.

Ultimately Niall Power orchestrated the murder of Irene White through his influence over Anthony Lambe. Following the aborted actions in Carrickdale, Niall Power's actions seemed to intensify. He expressed anger and annoyance towards Anthony Lambe for not going through with the attack at Carrickdale. In the months and years that followed, Niall Power exercised cunning in his effort to keep Anthony Lambe close to him and on side. He maintained a relationship with him and even asked him to be godfather to one of his children.

Gardaí felt there was now sufficient evidence to arrest and detain Niall Power for the murder of Irene White, but they were concerned that the specifics of what Anthony Lambe had revealed could not be used as evidence against him until they were recorded in a formal witness statement. If Niall were to exercise his right to silence in garda custody, such allegations would be futile from a prosecution perspective. Detective

Inspector Marry believed it would be a much more prudent exercise to let the court process conclude, in order to 'cleanse' Anthony Lambe as a witness, and then approach Anthony to make a comprehensive statement. Explaining this, Detective Inspector Marry says:

> Comments made during a person's arrest cannot be used as evidence against another person. New statements – witness statements – would have to be acquired once they were serving a sentence. We call this cleansing the suspect. They must be dealt with by the courts before any approach could be made to make witness statements.

In their file, gardaí conceded that the case against Alan White wasn't that strong. Anthony Lambe had only said that Alan made comments to him about knowing what he was meant to do and that he would be a loose end. The investigation team began planning their next move in relation to Niall Power, as Detective Inspector Marry explains:

> He was a clear suspect and I had encouraged having Niall Power arrested when Anthony Lambe was detained for questioning, but the constraints of other investigations had caught up with me. Niall Power was for another day. It is strange how investigations take turns you were not expecting. Following Anthony Lambe's conviction I knew we had to pursue matters to see if we could secure enough evidence on others believed to have been associated with the crime. This included taking a formal witness statement from Anthony Lambe. Little did I know how things would change so quickly.

Less than 24 hours after Anthony was sentenced to life imprisonment, the investigation was turned on its head once again. At 1.25 p.m. the following afternoon a middle-aged man walked into Dundalk garda station and asked to speak with the member in charge. He appeared frazzled and concerned, saying that he urgently wanted to speak with the detectives investigating the murder of Irene White. The dishevelled man standing in the foyer informed the garda at the counter that he would sit down and wait patiently until the investigation team were ready for the unexpected visitor. After nearly 13 years of holding in a dark secret, it was time to finally clear his conscience.

17

'I AM THE MIDDLEMAN'

Niall Power was visibly upset and trembling as he stood in the lobby of Dundalk garda station on 30 January 2018. Garda Seán Murphy was at the front counter. He told Niall he had to leave momentarily to get one of the detectives working on the Irene White case and asked him if he was okay waiting for a moment. 'I'm not going anywhere until I get this off my chest,' Niall replied. The garda went to inform his colleagues, before returning to tell Niall Power that someone would be down shortly. 'That's great, thank you,' he politely replied.

Moments later, Garda Connor McCaughey and Sergeant John Moroney walked into the public office and spoke with Niall, who agreed to accompany them to an interview room. Sergeant Moroney had been connected with the case since 2005, having been one of the gardaí tasked with securing the crime scene in the days after the murder. Just as they sat down with Niall, he blurted out, unprompted, 'I want to put my hands up, I'm going to ruin a lot of lives here.' Sergeant Moroney immediately cautioned him, informing Niall that he was not obliged to say anything but that whatever he did say would be taken down in writing and could be given in evidence against him. Niall was also advised that he could consult with a solicitor, that he was not under arrest, and that he could leave at any time. Niall said he understood the caution and, wiping away tears, declined the presence of a legal representative.

The rest of the investigation team had to be informed of Niall Power's impromptu visit, so the sergeant left to speak with Detective Inspector Marry. Garda McCaughey remained in the interview room as Niall broke down and began crying again, babbling that he had suicidal thoughts about what he was about to reveal and the impact this would have on his wife and children. As Garda McCaughey tried to calm him down, Niall told him that another man involved in the murder may hurt his family. A cup of water was brought in for him, and as he took a sip from the plastic beaker, he began talking about Irene White. He told the garda that she was a 'lovely girl' and again made a vague reference to another unidentified man having a hold over him. Recalling that afternoon, Detective Inspector Marry says:

> I was notified that Niall Power was in the station and wanted to speak about the murder. I was under severe pressure with other investigations at the time and I was preparing to chair a conference where the garda commissioner and other high-ranking officials would be attending. I was informed Niall Power was downstairs and he wanted to see me, but I told Sergeant Moroney, 'Tell him to come back, I am busy.' Sergeant Moroney replied, 'No, he says he wants to get it off his chest, his part in the murder of Irene White,' and I told him I would be straight down. Niall was nervous but calm and a man

who had made up his mind to come clean. I asked him if his family knew he was here, he said no. I asked him if I could contact them for him, but he declined.

He had by this stage made verbal comments to other gardaí about his involvement in Irene's murder. I needed to make sure that his rights were being catered for, given his verbal admissions. I instructed the member in charge to come to the interview room where Niall Power was. The member in charge asked Niall Power a number of questions, which he noted in his notebook. Niall Power was asked if he was at Dundalk station to speak to the gardaí in relation to the murder of Irene White. He confirmed that he was, and immediately the member in charge informed Niall Power that he had come to the garda station voluntarily and that he could leave at any stage. Niall Power understood this and stated he knew he could leave at any time. These notes were read back to Niall Power and he agreed with what was asked. He signed these notes as did I, Sergeant Moroney, and the member in charge.

It was a busy time in Dundalk garda station, with the crime unit preparing to arrest Crossmaglen man Aaron Brady, the chief suspect for the murder of Detective Garda Adrian Donohoe during the armed robbery at Lordship Credit Union in 2013. Brady, then aged 27, was serving a custodial sentence for road traffic offences and was due for release from prison soon. He would later be convicted of the detective's capital murder. Detective Inspector Marry was finalising plans for the arrest operation and tasked his investigation team to deal with Niall Power.

We made a very good profile on him, and we could connect him to the murder. His parading himself at Dundalk station, looking back on it, was fortuitous. We had our homework done and were in a position to question him with all the nitty-gritty details of his involvement. I left Sergeant Moroney and Detective Sergeant Sheridan, two very capable investigators, to deal with Niall Power. Detective Sergeant Sheridan had worked with me relentlessly on the Irene White murder investigation and knew all the ins and outs of the case. I knew they would not make any mistakes in this chapter of the investigation.

Detective Sergeant Sheridan walked into the interview room that afternoon and introduced himself to Niall Power. He told him that they would listen to what he had to say and that they would conduct a voluntary interview with him, which would be recorded. Niall was once again advised that he could consult a solicitor and, no sooner had the investigator taken his seat, than the businessman began outlining the circumstances surrounding the killing. Detective Sergeant Sheridan (MS) then asked him how he was involved in the Irene White case.

NP: Around 1996/1997 I met Alan White, and he asked me to do some building work. I was hoping to set up a security firm and Alan White became my friend and encouraged me to set up the business. We became good friends over a two-to-four-year period. I was the director of the business, as was my father. The office was behind the house at Ice House Hill. I got to know Irene very well and the family. Then things turned between him and her. I can't remember the year, 2003 or 2004 maybe, he was put out of the house, and he took it bad. We were going to a conference, and he asked me to sort her out. I thought he was joking. He kept going on about it. I knew straight away that he meant he wanted her dead.

Detective Sergeant Sheridan then cautioned Niall Power, advising him of his right to silence, before asking him to continue.

NP: I thought he was venting on me when he was saying it and he kept saying it. He was pushing for maybe five or six months. He said I'd be nothing without him and he was talking about moving on, walking away.

MS: Did you ask what he meant?

NP: No, I knew by the tone of his voice he wanted her dead. It went on for three or four months easy. I remember around 2004, the nurse's college was after being built and we had the contract. He came up to me and he was very angry. I was afraid of him. I didn't think I could come up here. I felt it would wear out and that he was just an angry man venting his anger.

MS: Did he stop?

NP: No. It got worse. It got to the stage that he was on about it every day. I said I couldn't do that myself, meaning kill Irene. I can't remember if I mentioned the words kill, but I took it that she was to go. I know it sounds desperate but that's how I took it. That went on for two or three months. One day I was up, I worked security on the door at the college bar in DKIT. You got to know a lot of people. I got to know Anthony Lambe very well. He was a nice guy. I know this sounds weird. It was like I owed Alan White something.

MS: Did he make you feel that, or did you think that yourself?

NP: I suppose it was but I'm not a very smart guy. I wasn't great at school. It's not that difficult to run a security firm. My wife does the books. I'm no dumb-dumb but I can organise people for work, and I get on with people. The following week I was back at the college, the Tuesday or the Thursday, and they were up saying it was good to have me back. Anthony Lambe came up to me and asked me was I alright. I told him I needed to talk to him. I don't know why it was him. I needed to talk to somebody, but I told Anthony the craic. He told me he would get it done. I told Anthony Lambe that day in the college for the first time that Irene had to be done. That was the first time I said it to anyone. For some reason, Anthony was a fella you could talk to, a normal fella. I felt a bond with him. It sounds a bit gay. We connected. I didn't go up that day to say it to Anthony, but it just happened.

MS: What did you say the first time?

NP: I told him a man was pressuring me into doing something I didn't want to do. I told him a man wanted his wife killed. He said like 'whoa fuck' and then the next sentence he said was 'I can get that done for you'. It kind of went on from there. It felt like the pressure was off. Until he was arrested, I didn't know he did it himself.

MS: It's time to be honest.

NP: I'm going to lose my family. I'm being honest, I felt relieved. It was like pass it on, good luck. All I can do is give you my part of what's happened.

MS: What happened after you told him?

NP: As far as I can remember everything is blurry after that. The day Irene was murdered – we didn't know it was going to happen that day. I didn't know. I don't know if there was something going on behind my back. I don't think Alan knew that day, unless there was something behind my back. I've heard that Anthony Lambe was addicted to drugs and all that, but I wouldn't buy that. Far too sensible and against drugs. The day he told me he could get that done we were outside the college. It felt like it was not my problem anymore.

MS: Did you say this to Alan?

NP: I did. I told him I was talking to a guy, and he could look after it after that.

MS: Did you tell him who?

NP: The following week, Tuesday night I think, I introduced Alan to Anthony in the Phoenix Bar. I'm not playing down my role.

Niall Power stood by his previous statement about not wanting to go to the security expo in Dublin because he wouldn't make it back in time to meet workers at a site in Dundalk.

He recalled being in the car with Alan at around 10.45 a.m., after leaving Vincent Dullaghan's home, when he received a phone call from Anthony who informed him 'that job is done'. When he asked what he was referring to, Anthony told him Irene's murder. Niall began to panic and said that Alan White told him to 'calm the fuck down'. In an attempt to explain the role he'd played in the murder conspiracy, he told gardaí, 'I am the middleman', but maintained that he didn't know Anthony had carried out the murder himself. 'I'm not the big instigator in this. If I got 25–30 years I don't care. Maybe there's things I'm forgetting. I'm doing my best. I'm not looking for a clap on the back. I'm going to lose my business, wife, kids, house, not to mention what it will do to my mother and father. Part of coming here today is to take part of this off you. Alan White is wrong, Anthony Lambe is wrong, and I'm wrong.'

He also insisted that he didn't pressure Anthony Lambe to carry out the murder and that he didn't know his employee had committed the crime himself. 'Two weeks after the murder, two heroin heads landed to the college looking for Anthony, and I thought it was them,' he said, adding: 'I didn't think he had it in him. 34/35 stab wounds, that's an animal.' Niall said that he didn't feel threatened by Alan White personally but did on a business level. 'I'm not a bad person. I wouldn't hurt a fly. I was afraid of losing the business,' he said as he became teary-eyed again.

MS: You said Anthony asked for money twice. Tell us how much and where?

NP: I don't know, and I don't want to know. I woke up the day she was murdered, and I was part of something I didn't want to be part of. The only love or feeling I have is for my wife and kids. I keep people away from me.

MS: Why?

NP: Look what happened with Alan White who I thought was a really good friend. I don't let people get close. I never thought I would be sitting in front of you. I didn't see this coming. I knew it was wrong.

MS: Why do you think Anthony did it? Where was the pressure coming from?

NP: Not from me. I had nothing to put pressure on him, I don't believe Anthony being on drugs. If I had known Anthony Lambe done this, do you think I would make him godfather to my first-born child?

MS: Tell us about the money.

NP: Alan White gave me the money about a week after the murder. As far as I remember Anthony rang me to get on to Alan White about money, a payment. Alan gave me money the next day and said to pay him. I told Alan I didn't want to be part of it even though I was. I can't remember how an agreement came to money in the first place. I don't remember any time that me, Alan White and Anthony Lambe sat down at a table ... the money was handed over at the Saltown site. I don't know how much money; I didn't even have fingerprints on them. I wore gloves.

MS: What was the turning point for you to come in today?

NP: I think it was finding out Anthony done it himself. It was like I threw the ball, but the fella broke the window. I was like venting and I said it to the wrong person, and they acted. I don't know if I wanted it to happen. It was months of pressure from Alan White. I thought it was about the kids, but I found out afterwards it was money for the house. When you look up to somebody and then you find out that you were being used. I'm sorry it took so long. Maybe a better person would have dealt with it better.

While Niall said his motivation to become involved in the murder was so that Alan White wouldn't leave his business, he claimed not to have gained anything financially from the murder. The detectives, though, felt that Niall was downplaying his important role in the murder and weren't convinced that he had only realised Anthony was the killer when he'd pleaded guilty. Detective Sergeant Sheridan then asked Niall to elaborate on describing himself as 'the middleman' and was told: 'I allowed myself to be the middleman, talking 13 years afterwards. It's hard to think you let a man you looked up to do this, would grooming be a right word. When I got the call from Anthony, I thought "how did I let this happen".' Asked if he thought that he didn't have any part in planning the murder, Niall replied 'course I did', saying he was under no illusion that Irene was to be killed. He couldn't remember the exact figure offered to Anthony Lambe but believed it was around €10,000.

He said he'd hoped gardaí would come for him after Anthony was arrested. When the detectives put it to him that they had been at his door before, he said, 'I know, and I was that close, and I tried but I'm here to give my best description.' He said that Anthony Lambe's sentencing hearing the previous day wasn't the reason he decided to come in, but added: 'It didn't help.' Speaking about the time he was under arrest on suspicion of withholding information, Niall said: 'I was so close to telling Adrian Donohoe, God rest him. I'm glad I'm sitting here talking to you.'

The detectives then queried whether he had arranged any meetings between Alan and Anthony or if he could say how they were introduced. Niall told them, 'Don't ask me when it was, I haven't a clue. It wasn't a set up meeting. It was after Anthony said to me he would get it sorted. Alan made a statement to Anthony that night, "are you the man who is getting the job done", and I was like "fuck me". It was getting real. That was a few months before.' Sergeant Moroney put it to Niall that he was under no illusion that Irene was to be killed. 'Absolutely,' he replied, becoming tearful and emotional once more. 'I'm so sorry. I didn't want to hurt anyone, but I've no sympathy for Alan White.' Shortly after 4 p.m. he was permitted to take a cigarette break, and when he returned, his statement was read over to him. He agreed that it was accurate. For the gardaí, it was only the beginning of their questioning. Following the conclusion of the voluntary interview, Niall Power was led back into the public office at 5 p.m. where he was arrested on suspicion of the murder of Irene White. A solicitor was organised for him while his fingerprints and DNA samples were taken. Sergeant Moroney and Detective Sergeant Sheridan then returned with him to the interview room to formally question him about the murder.

He was asked again why he thought he was the middleman in the plot. 'Because I was put in a position where Alan White would say one thing to me and I'd have to go over and back,' he said. 'I didn't want to be there. It's like he put his problems on top of me and I'd move them on, and I'd have to go back to him. The man more or less used me and me being an eejit went with him.' Niall claimed that he didn't pull out because things had 'gone too far', and he told gardaí that when he got the phone call that Irene had been murdered 'something left me'. Sergeant Moroney (JM) then asked Niall if he would accept that his role didn't end when he mentioned the murder to Anthony Lambe at the college.

NP: No. I wanted it to end but nothing was going to be good enough for Alan until Irene was dead.

JM: What form did your role take on?

NP: I'd say two or three occasions easy Alan got on to me asking why wasn't this happening and then I got on to Anthony. I'd say two or three times, saying that he was getting on to me about why this wasn't done. I didn't know it was happening on the day it did.

JM: But you were of the belief it was going to happen sometime?

NP: Yes, now but back then, no.

JM: When was this?

NP: This was after. I was afraid before because he was getting on to me but really after it happened, I said 'well what am I?' I'm not trying to use excuses.

JM: Do you think that if you wouldn't have mentioned this to Anthony Lambe or indeed kept at him about doing it, if you hadn't done it, do you think Irene White would be alive today?

NP: Without a doubt, unless he got another one.

JM: Would you then accept that you were complicit, involved in Irene's murder?

NP: Yes. I don't like to say that but yes.

JM: Did you ever discuss it with Anthony Lambe, how this job was to be done? Think carefully, he was no hitman for hire. He was an amateur.

NP: We all were.

JM: You came to him and asked him, did he not come to you for direction?

NP: I said it to him. I didn't ask him. I said it. He was amazed.

JM: But he seems to have offered to have done it very quickly. 'Whoa fuck', and then offering. He was a young guy who never knew anything.

NP: He did. It was like something that was never going to happen. When I said it to him it was like, it's not my problem anymore.

JM: Did you classify him as a soft touch?

NP: Definitely. He's not a smart lad.

Asked if Alan wondered if the killer could be trusted, Niall said: 'He wasn't concerned. I was his little puppet. I don't think he cared so long as it was done. I did not know it was going to happen that day,' he insisted once again. 'You can nail me to the wall and beat it out of me, it's still the same answer. I don't know if he knew. I didn't wake up that morning thinking I was going to have a murder on my hands and be talking to you 13 years later. It's not me but it was me. If I could go back now knowing what I know now, I'd hammer the living daylights out of myself.' He also said that Anthony didn't seem to need much persuasion to carry out the murder.

Niall didn't think there was much, if any, direct contact between Alan White and Anthony Lambe. Niall felt Alan had a grip on him and that his former business partner 'got a weakness in me, I can't understand it, but if he told me to jump in the sea, I would have done it, for some strange reason'. The detectives were perplexed as to how Niall Power, a grown man, could claim to have been put under a trance by Alan White? 'I don't know either, I'm not a bad person. It's despicable, I couldn't have done what happened to Irene. If one of my family cut their finger, I'm not able to handle it,' he replied.

He said when his relationship with Jane McKenna got serious, he eventually got free from the 'shackles' of Alan White, in or around 2008, and that they hadn't spoken since. The questioning then moved on to the events surrounding the murder. Niall said he collected his van from St Malachy's Villas after being told by Anthony that Irene was dead, and he then drove to Muirhevnamore to collect Jane. He insisted that he didn't know Irene White had been murdered at Ice House when he drove past the scene at 11.48 a.m. that morning.

> NP: Can I say something? If Alan White was so careful, why am I here right now? Why did he use me?
>
> MS: Why is right.
>
> NP: If you ever find out let me know.
>
> MS: Maybe to distance himself?
>
> NP: There it is. Eejit here.

By this stage, Niall Power had been in Dundalk garda station for nine hours, and the questioning was suspended until the next day. His period of detention was also extended by Christy Mangan, the former head of the cold case unit who had been appointed as chief superintendent for the Louth division in 2017. Throughout the night a garda checked on Niall Power every half-hour to ensure that he didn't try to harm himself. Detective Sergeant Sheridan and Detective Garda Rachel Reilly took up the interrogation the following morning, and they began by trying to establish the motive for the murder. They spoke about PPS Security and Alan White's role in the business, before the questioning moved on to the setting up of a remote monitoring station.

When the detectives put it to Niall Power that the €925,000 from the sale of Ice House would be great money for the new company, he told them: 'No, I see where you are going, definitely not. You are saying Irene was killed for that. No, that's totally wrong. Why wasn't the money used when Irene was killed?' He also told them: 'It was beyond my capabilities, I hadn't the money. I came in here. I'm pleading guilty. The monitoring thing doesn't come into this. Everything I told you the last day is why Irene was killed.' He described as 'too bloody obvious' the suggestion that Irene was murdered in order to get the full proceeds from the house sale and put this into the new company. For Niall, his motivation was so that Alan White wouldn't walk away from PPS Security, as opposed to the risk of losing out on a large injection of cash for the monitoring station if Irene got half of the Ice House sale money.

The statements made by Ellen Johnson were then put to Niall Power, which included his involvement in a plot to seduce

Irene and that he'd considered using a gun to murder her. 'I never had a gun in my life. So, I was going to seduce Irene, shoot her, record her? That's nonsense.' He also denied the claims that he had admitted to murdering an RUC member or that he was a member of any criminal organisation.

In the next interview, the detectives informed Niall that they were going to go through the details contained in Anthony Lambe's account of the murder. 'Is this bad?' he asked them. 'I need to prepare myself.' When it was put to Niall that he had contacted Anthony on the morning of the murder to relay Irene's whereabouts, he said: 'Sure how would I know where she was? I wasn't following her. I didn't know she was going to be murdered that morning. I got the phone call to say the job was done. I dropped [Jane's child] to school and went up to Alan White's mother's house. If I knew more, I would tell you more. I don't.' He again claimed that he believed Anthony Lambe 'was getting boys to do it' and rejected the claim that he'd provided the knife used in the murder.

While Niall accepted that he had told the killer at what time Irene's children would be out of the house, he again denied giving him real-time updates on Irene's movements. 'I also told Anthony it wouldn't be a good place, Mo lived at the back. The last thing I wanted was the kids or Mo to come in on it. I didn't know how it was going to happen. I know I'm going to do life. I was passing it on.' He also rejected the detailed account given by Anthony Lambe of the two men doing a recce of Ice House Hill park prior to the murder. When the detectives asked Niall why Anthony would implicate him to such an extent, Niall surmised, 'A grudge, I brought him into it.' Describing meeting Anthony Lambe at the college after the murder, he said, 'there wasn't a bother on him. He was as cool as you are now. That day I met him at the DKIT I thought he was passing on a message. I didn't realise he did it himself.'

Niall denied giving Anthony €1,000 at the college, saying it was roughly €400, but maintained that this was for an advance on his wages as he had previously claimed. 'He was not jittery that day when I met him at the DKIT. He was heading to her graduation. He thanked me for the money. Were her parents going? He told me they were, and he was going to buy them a drink at the airport. I know it looks bad, me giving him wages that day. I have done it before for other employees.' Niall also stated that he only found out about the severity of Irene's injuries from media reports, not from Anthony Lambe, and that they never discussed the killing. He whined that Anthony's account was 'making me look the worst of it here' and that there was no mention of Alan White in the killer's version of events.

At 8.30 p.m. that night, Sergeant Moroney and Detective Garda Reilly commenced the final interrogation of Niall Power. They took him through his garda interviews when he was arrested in 2006. 'Kells was tough because I was telling lies,' he said. 'I nearly said it to Adrian. I can only apologise. You have to be me back then.' He professed that he was 'close' to telling Detective Garda Donohoe the whole truth but that another detective came into the room whom he didn't like, and he decided to say nothing.

Niall was then taken through CCTV footage that tracked his Ford Fiesta van travelling around Dundalk on the morning of the murder. At 11.39 a.m. he had received another call from Anthony Lambe, and at 11.48 a.m. his car was seen travelling past the Carroll Village shopping centre on the Long Walk towards Ice House. 'I didn't know Irene was in the house at that stage, I would have stayed away,' he said. While Niall accepted that he knew Irene was dead, he was adamant that he didn't know where she had been killed and 'didn't want to be associated with it'. Sergeant Moroney asked him if he wanted to add anything to what he had already said, putting it to Niall Power that they believed he was more involved than he had let on over the previous two days. 'I wasn't, I came in here to tell the truth,' Niall replied. The fourth and final interview then concluded, and Detective Inspector Marry had to decide on the next course of action to be taken.

> I was in direct contact with the DPP's office during Niall Power's detention and appraised them of the developments in the case. While detained, he admitted to his involvement in the murder of Irene White and, when asked would Irene White be alive today if it wasn't for his suggesting it to Anthony Lambe and his influence over Lambe, he replied 'without a doubt'. He openly admitted to his complicit involvement in the murder. I have often thought about this, and I guess his conscience and the guilt he was feeling got the better of him. He also knew we had caught Anthony Lambe and he suspected, rightly so, that we would raid his home and arrest him. He may have been trying to protect his wife and children from this.
>
> I gave him every opportunity to have a solicitor or family present, but he declined. He was adamant that this was something he had to get straight between himself and the gardaí. Niall Power, to us in the investigation team, was always the middle man, the man who coerced Anthony Lambe to commit murder for money that

Anthony Lambe never got in full – having been promised thousands but only being paid €2,000 in two separate payments. It was a first for me where a suspect walks in off the street and wants to confess to a murder you are investigating. They say there is none as quare as folk. I have to say I was delighted he made his confession, which saved the team a significant amount of work preparing for a raid, and they did great work given the quick turn of events. I relayed all the admissions made during his interview to the DPP, who gave a verbal direction to charge Niall Power with the murder of Irene White.

At 10.40 p.m. Detective Sergeant Sheridan marched Niall Power out into the public office of the garda station and informed him that he was being released from custody relating to his detention. The investigator then immediately arrested Niall Power and informed him that the DPP had directed that he should be charged with murder. While he had talked away in the interview room over the past two days, this time Niall Power had nothing to say. He was detained for the purposes of charge and kept in Dundalk garda station that night.

The following morning, 1 February, he was led out into an unmarked patrol car and driven to a sitting of Dundalk District Court. Dressed in dark clothing, he used a red jumper to hide his face from the assembled press photographers and camera crews, as he was brought into the court building flanked by Detective Sergeant Sheridan and Sergeant Moroney. During the brief sitting, evidence was given of his arrest, charge and caution, while Niall Power's solicitor applied for free legal aid. He said his client was a 45-year-old man and a father-of-four, who was currently earning around €450 a week. Judge John Coughlan acceded to the request, and Niall Power was remanded in custody to appear in court again the following week. There had been no charges in the first 13 years of the investigation but now, in just 12 months, two suspects had been brought before the courts over Irene White's murder. However, the investigation was far from complete, and there was still a third suspect to be pursued.

18

THE MASTERMIND

Six days after Niall Power was brought to court, one of his former PPS Security employees arrived at Dundalk garda station to speak with members of the investigation team. Gerry Ross had read an article online earlier that week in which Alan White was quoted after Anthony Lambe had been sentenced to life imprisonment for Irene's murder. Gerry had important information that he wanted to share with the detectives.

He recalled the headline saying 'I'm innocent, I didn't even know the chap', with the comments attributed to Alan, claiming not to know Anthony. He told gardaí that he knew this claim to be false and that Alan did in fact know the man who had murdered his wife. He agreed to make a statement, outlining how he was drinking with both men one night in a Dundalk pub, before they returned to a house in the Garybawn estate. He explained how the mood changed later that night and Anthony Lambe began arguing with him. 'Anthony threatened to burn my house down with my family in it. I don't know if this was something he said because he was drunk or he meant it,' Gerry told gardaí. 'I believe the mood changed because they didn't want me there. When the row was going on I looked to Alan for support, thinking "help me out here". Alan was stone-faced and cold towards me; he didn't offer me any support.'

He believed that this row happened before Irene was murdered and didn't attach any significance to it until he read the newspaper article the previous week. For gardaí, it was a further indication that Alan White had lied about not knowing Anthony Lambe, both when Detective Inspector Marry and Detective Sergeant Sheridan spoke to him after Anthony was charged and in the comments attributed to him in the newspaper article.

Anthony Lambe had by this stage also been cleansed as a witness, as the criminal charges he was facing had concluded, and gardaí visited him at Mountjoy Prison in Dublin, where he was serving his life sentence. He agreed to give them a witness statement and on 21 February 2018 he sat down with Detective Sergeant Sheridan and Detective Garda Ogle. Anthony gave an account that was consistent with what he had revealed during his garda interviews a year earlier and gave several additional pieces of information, among them corroboration of the row with Gerry Ross in front of Alan White.

Myself and Gerry had a row of sorts, silly shite. I don't remember what it was about. It was a physical fight. I don't know how it started. After the row Alan spoke to me. I don't remember if Gerry stayed. Alan told me that he knew what Niall had asked me to do. He was more forceful about it. He indicated I owed money to Niall, and it could be to him. I don't know how much. He told me that he wanted it done and that if I didn't do it, I would be next. Alan White said to me at this house party that he knew Niall had picked me to kill Irene and if I didn't, I would be next and any of my family that stood in the way. This was the only occasion Alan White said this to me.

The convicted murderer also recalled another night, prior to Irene's death, when the men were drinking in the Phoenix Bar in Dundalk.

Alan was there, Niall, myself and maybe Jane, but she may not have been in our group. Niall was excited about it, like he was looking for Alan's approval. He seemed to be out to please or impress Alan, like I was with Niall. I can't remember the specifics of what Niall said but this was going ahead, and the money owed would go away. I wouldn't be stressed about Annie, and Niall said as he always did "that I can get things going". Alan silenced Niall. I can't remember the specifics of what he did. That was the third or fourth time I met Alan and one of those was the party which wasn't a positive experience.

Anthony said that he never spoke to Alan White after carrying out the murder, and he told gardaí he believed he was going to get caught when they spoke to him in 2005.

I had a bit of a panic attack when I had to make a statement. I knew to stick to the story as I was afraid they had got me. I was interviewed two or three times by the guards. After the garda interviews, Niall did a debrief with me, what was I asked, what I said and how I said it. There was another sum of money, in the summer of that year ... I gave it to Annie to buy furniture for her new house in Castleblayney. Niall gave it to me. I can't remember being told what this money was for but what else was it for. I knew I should be getting more money, but I never asked for it. I withdrew from Niall.

He also gave a further insight into the pressure being put on him by Niall Power to carry out the murder, saying it was mentioned to him several times a week in the months leading up to the killing. 'At times I would draw back from it but he would ring me and he was good craic. It was intense for a period of time – just the constant referring to what he wanted me to do. I was a mess at the time through drink and cocaine. There was shame leaving St Pat's and not going to college in Dundalk. I backed myself into a corner,' he said. 'After a period of time, with the pressure, I did say to Niall I would do it. The pressure he was applying on me, you could see he was transferring the pressure. At the start he was overjoyed and over the moon when I said I would do it.' Giving a further insight into his thought process on 6 April 2005, Anthony claimed he had no specific plans to murder Irene that day. It was only when Niall told him that he wasn't getting money until the job was done that he made his way to Ice House. He also said he rang Niall Power minutes before the murder 'begging him not to let me do this' but was told 'now is the time, she is home from the school'.

Discussing what life had been like since it became public that he was the killer, he told them: 'There isn't really any relief. It's not just my shame, it's my family's shame.'

The statement was included in the investigative file being prepared for the DPP in relation to Niall Power's case. In it, gardaí discussed Niall's confession and their belief that he wasn't admitting the full level of his involvement.

Niall Power obviously felt the weight of pressure on him when the facts of the case were outlined in the Central Criminal Court on Monday 29 January 2018. When the media published specifics as to what Anthony Lambe revealed regarding a third party to have her murdered, Niall Power's conscience finally got the better of him and he succumbed and took the unprecedented step of presenting himself at Dundalk garda station on the following day of the court case, looking to confess to his part in this case.

The admissions made by Niall Power throughout his interviews are quite damning. However, despite this, what's of some concern is the fact that he would not accept the level of his involvement as suggested in the memos and fresh statement of Anthony Lambe. Maybe Niall Power wasn't as influential as Anthony Lambe paints him, but although Niall Power wanted to confess, it could be the case that it's a damage limitation exercise to him and he doesn't want to present or portray himself as a major player in the overall enterprise. He certainly couldn't offer any explanation regarding the level of phone calls between Anthony Lambe and himself on the morning of the murder.

Commenting on Niall Power's motive for conspiring to murder Irene, the garda file noted it was always their belief that this was done entirely from a business perspective and centred around the potential setting up of a remote monitoring company. Although Niall Power denied this, their suspicion was grounded in statements made by Cathy Wilson, Vincent Dullaghan, and Ellen Johnson, and it was somewhat galvanised and justified in the witness statement provided by Anthony Lambe after his incarceration. They pointed out the comments made by Niall to his employee, in which he told him, 'I could get the whole thing going if this person was out of the way' and 'if only I could get someone to do a job for me, I would be set up'. Anthony Lambe's understanding of the murder conspiracy was also that it was done from a business perspective, as Niall Power had mentioned to him that Niall had 'money tied up but couldn't get at it and she was the reason they couldn't get at it'. The gardaí submitted in their file that Anthony's vulnerable and impressionable demeanour provided Niall with an attractive target to groom and influence for his nefarious motives.

> He cunningly and deceitfully would give money to Anthony Lambe in order to let Lambe finance his drink and drug habit at the time. Power then let Lambe build up this debt and then used this as a means of a control mechanism over Anthony Lambe. Such mind games employed by Niall Power were akin to virtually brainwashing Anthony Lambe, who looked up to Niall Power, and Niall Power used this to his advantage and to manipulate Anthony Lambe. Ultimately, Niall Power orchestrated the murder of Irene White through his influence over Anthony Lambe.

While awaiting trial for murder, Niall Power applied for bail, which was granted despite garda objections. His marriage had broken down since his arrest and charge, and he moved in with his parents as he waited for his case to come before the Central Criminal Court. There was significant evidence against Niall Power, mainly from his own admissions but supported by the meticulous case built against him, and in the end there was no need for a trial. On 8 July 2019, over 14 years after playing an integral role in the murder of Irene White, the middleman arrived at the Criminal Courts of Justice on Parkgate Street in Dublin. Shortly after 10 a.m., his name was called, and he took his seat in the dock. When the registrar read out the charge of murder, Niall Power, then aged 47, stood up and replied, 'Guilty.'

The sentencing hearing was again a formality, given that he was facing a mandatory life term, but gave gardaí another opportunity to outline the facts of the case and for Irene's family to again show the trauma they had suffered. Detective Inspector Marry had retired by this stage, and Detective Sergeant Sheridan provided a summary of the murder to Justice Michael White. He told the judge that Niall Power had come to know Irene through another man 'not before the court' and that he became emotional in his garda interviews while admitting his involvement. Detective Sergeant Sheridan said this other man asked Niall to 'sort out' Irene, which he took to mean that he wanted her dead. This was repeated to Niall Power almost every day for several months until she was killed.

His defence barrister, senior counsel Michael Bowman, offered some brief mitigating points, telling the court that this other man had a hold over Niall Power that made him feel 'like a puppet'. He said his client had lost his family, his business, and his home because of his involvement in the murder and had been living with his elderly parents since being granted bail. Under cross-examination Detective Sergeant Sheridan agreed that Niall Power came from a very decent family and was the last person one would expect to be involved in such a crime. Michael Bowman also informed the court that he was instructed to offer Niall Power's deepest apologies to all those who had been affected.

In her victim impact statement, Jennifer McBride told the court: 'This time around it is even harder than the first as the man who stands before the court, Niall Power, is not a stranger to our family but is in fact a person who was at one time a close family friend and would have not only been trusted but also welcomed into our home, not only by myself and my siblings but by our mam.' Justice Michael White described the murder as 'an unspeakable crime and a great tragedy'. He noted that the family had been waiting for justice for over 14 years and were 'still waiting'. Niall Power gave little reaction, only nodding to the judge after being informed that he was being sentenced to life imprisonment. Irene's estranged husband was also in court for the hearing but didn't provide a victim impact statement as part of the proceedings. As he walked out of the court complex, Alan White briefly spoke to press reporters, saying he had hoped for years that Irene's killer would come forward.

Anne Delcassian, who had worked tirelessly to get justice for Irene, was too ill to attend court as she was bravely fighting her own battle with cancer. Her husband, Kenneth, was accompanied to court by their solicitor, Kevin Winters of KRW Law, who told reporters after the hearing that the DPP now had sufficient evidence to prosecute the 'mastermind' who they believed orchestrated the murder. This unnamed individual, he said, remained elusive, but they believed gardaí had sufficient evidence to now charge him, given that two full books of evidence had been prepared to convict Anthony Lambe and Niall Power. 'We would say there is sufficient and ample material within those books of evidence, and additional information and material that points towards a decision to prosecute,' the solicitor said. 'Sadly, given the life-limiting nature of Anne, that is probably just far too late for her.' His final words sadly rang true less than a month later. On 9 August 2019, Anne passed away at her Louth home surrounded by her husband and daughters. She wouldn't be alive to see if gardaí would be able to prosecute the man they suspected had ultimately ordered the murder of her sister. Speaking about how the investigation would proceed at that point, Detective Inspector Marry says:

Anthony Lambe always maintained he was put under pressure to kill Irene White by Niall Power, who in turn maintained he was put under pressure by someone else to have Irene murdered. You might think it would be easy to nail the third suspect, but not so. Now that Niall Power had been cleansed as a witness, an approach would have to be made to ask him to give a statement that could be used in evidence, as had already been done with Anthony Lambe.

While there were serious suspicions over Alan White, the evidence against him wasn't strong enough from a prosecutorial point of view to establish that he had a role in his wife's murder. In an interview with the authors, he has denied that he was the mastermind behind his estranged wife's murder or that he had any involvement in her death. While a number of new statements indicated that Alan did in fact know Anthony Lambe, gardaí noted in one investigative file that this 'is of limited significance in isolation from a prosecution perspective'. In a file to the DPP ahead of Niall Power's guilty plea, gardaí had also stated:

> The substantial planks of evidence in building a solid prosecution case against Alan White rests for the most part in the potential evidence that Niall Power can provide by way of a cleansed witness statement. If Niall Power provides such a statement in keeping with what he revealed during his interviews regarding Alan White being the instigator and the driving force behind the plot to murder Irene White then, coupled with the statement of Anthony Lambe and the entire circumstantial evidence regarding the violence between Alan and Irene White, the subsequent separation and the complications surrounding the sale of Ice House, we should be on a much more solid grounding for a case against Alan White.

The investigation team believed that any plans to detain Alan before Niall Power provided a witness statement could jeopardise the investigation, with gardaí noting:

> If Alan White were to make no admission, of which there exists every possibility, then there would be little or no evidence to ground a charge and the likelihood would be that he would have to be released without charge. However, if we are patient and await the outcome of proceedings against Niall Power and he subsequently agrees to make a statement, then to exercise such patience

would be a much more prudent strategy in the overall scheme of things.

Despite making admissions about his own involvement in garda interviews and alleging that Alan White told him to 'sort out' Irene, Niall Power has to date refused to provide gardaí with a formal witness statement. The investigation continued, and in early 2023 a file was submitted to the DPP in respect of Alan White. The garda file contained all the evidence that had been gathered as part of the 18-year investigation and in its conclusion recommended that Alan White should be charged with Irene's murder. He was subsequently approached by the media and asked to comment on the fact that gardaí wanted to charge him.

Speaking to Paul Healy of the *Irish Daily Star*, Alan White said it was 'quite a shock' and 'so out of the blue'. Asked directly if he was the 'mastermind' being referred to in media reports, Alan White replied: 'No, I don't think I'm the mastermind of anything.' He said that he was maintaining his innocence and that he would defend this in court if charged. 'They're not telling the truth, you know what I mean? That's why I'm saying I'm surprised. I don't know how long this is going on.' He also said that he couldn't fully understand how Niall Power or Anthony Lambe got involved in the murder, telling the reporter: 'I don't know because I find it hard to even understand how that came about. So obviously there was a lot going on that I wasn't aware of, so I don't know, I can't figure it out. I'm angry that everything is sort of left wide open to interpretation. And you know the public, they take their own interpretation on it. But I've been lucky to have a lot of support from people. So that end of it hasn't affected me.'

Following a lengthy review of the investigative file by a senior counsel, the DPP came to its decision on the matter in November 2023, ruling that there was insufficient evidence to charge Alan White as had been recommended by gardaí. Irene's daughter Jennifer and brother-in-law Kenneth Delcassian were notified of this and, despite subsequent attempts to have the DPP reconsider, the decision remained that Alan White should not face any prosecution. It marked the end of the road of the long-running saga, or so it seemed.

EPILOGUE:

'SUSPICION ALWAYS FALLS ON THE HUSBAND'

Five years after his former business partner was sentenced to life imprisonment, Alan White was in a reflective mood. Sitting on the couch in the sitting room of his home, he was relaxed, dragging on a cigarette and occasionally sipping from his mug. He won't face any prosecution for his wife's murder, which he has always denied having any involvement in, but, at the same time, he could see why the finger was pointed at him. 'I can't remember where I heard it from, I think it was the paper – that suspicion always falls on the husband. Even to this day, I don't understand any real logic to it. I have my own views on it.'

It was October 2024, and Alan White agreed to speak with the authors and discuss certain aspects of the investigation into Irene's murder. Months earlier, Niall Power had brought a legal challenge to the Court of Appeal against his murder conviction. While sitting in Dundalk garda station in January 2018, Niall had openly admitted to his role, accepting that he was 'going to do life' and was facing '25–30 years'. The prospect of spending the next few decades behind bars suddenly didn't seem that appealing, and the middleman had a change of heart. The fact, though, that he pleaded guilty to the very conviction he is now appealing means he has a difficult case to argue. The solicitors he approached seem to be of the same view.

Appearing before the Court of Appeal in June 2024, he informed Justice George Birmingham that he had been unable to secure legal representation. 'I've tried, no one will take me on,' he whined. 'I've rang 20 or 30 different ones, and no one's interested because of the position I'm in.' Justice Birmingham remarked that there were many solicitors on the legal aid panel who were very anxious for work. 'What can I do? I'm in prison, my hands are tied here,' the convicted murderer replied. 'I can't personally force a solicitor to take me on. If I can't get one, what am I supposed to do?' He was told that the case would be put back for several months, by which time he would have to find a legal representative or the matter would 'come to an end'. At the time of writing, Niall Power's case is still on the Court of Appeal list, yet to be heard.

Alan White has his own thoughts on his one-time close friend's legal challenge. 'Initially when I heard about the appeal, quite recently, from the little I know, it didn't make sense. How can you appeal what you said earlier?' Alan is now in his 60s and living a quiet life in the rural village of Knockbridge. Despite the garda suspicions about his involvement in Irene's murder, he won't face any prosecution as part of the investigation. While this position would be reviewed if Niall Power were to make a formal witness statement, that prospect is unlikely, and Alan White remains an innocent man.

But there are many unanswered questions that still needed to be addressed. While saying he didn't want to comment in any great detail, he did give some of his thoughts on certain aspects of the case. The claim by Anthony Lambe that Alan approached him at a house party and told him he knew what he had been tasked to do relating to the murder was put to Alan White. 'I don't really want to get into it, but what I will say is that was put to me in garda interview,' he responds. 'And I don't remember any house party in fact, my memory isn't great anyway, but to try and recall I asked the guards when that was, and they couldn't tell me. And again, trying to rack me brains. It must have been a hell of a party,' he says, laughing. 'I then asked where was it, and they couldn't tell me either. Just couldn't recall. I don't particularly want to comment anyway, but just explain that to give you some sort of background.'

The authors put it to him that there were issues within his marriage and around the sale of Ice House, which is why gardaí focused on him from the beginning. He avoided the question, replying: 'My memory is awful and the last time the guards were here some detective, don't ask me his name, I didn't even recognise him, seemingly I was speaking to him previously. And I just copped the name. I didn't actually take much notice at the time; it didn't really register with me, you know.'

Did he threaten Irene prior to her murder, warning her that she wouldn't know the hour or the day, but that she would be got, and that he would have an alibi? 'I've actually heard that before. I heard that from Irene's sister, Delcassian. There's something curious there because she claimed she had diaries and stuff, Irene's diaries, and I would have assumed that they would have been passed on to the guards. If what she said was true, why wouldn't she pass it on. That's what I thought.' Asked again if he'd made these threatening comments as alleged by Irene, he says: 'No, I never said that, no.' When told that this threat was alleged to have been said by him in April 2004, after gardaí were called to Ice House, he says: 'That's news to me.'

The allegation made by Niall Power in garda interview that Alan asked him repeatedly to 'sort out' Irene is also put to him. 'I don't know, there was a lot going on at the time. From what I since discovered, I wasn't aware of it, but there was a link to drugs and that. And I detest drugs. From what I hear your man Lambe [took drugs], but then I heard that Niall was sponsoring it or covering debts or supplying, I don't know. I was very surprised at that.'

Does he think Niall was trying to shift the blame away from himself and on to Alan by saying he pressured him to arrange the murder, or was there truth to this claim? 'Well, I have my own theory about his motives, which I'm not going to say. I don't know what he's thinking, saying this. That's what I'm saying, a lot of it doesn't make sense to me. It was true about the drugs then so, was it? I don't really know, but the thing that got to me was, there seemed to be a link between Niall and Lambe – there was obviously a link – but the link with either finance or supply of the drugs for Lambe. I couldn't believe it. I don't think Niall was ever a user, not to my knowledge anyway, and he knows how strong I am against it.' Again, the specific claim made by Niall, that he was put under pressure by Alan to have Irene murdered, is put to him. 'Yeah? I've got my own ideas on that.'

The subject moved on to the garda suspicion that he was involved in the murder and to his arrest in 2006. 'I remember the media attention at the time, it was relentless, so it was. I suppose it's their job but it's not pleasant when you're on the wrong end of it. The kids were much younger, and you don't really know what they're going to hear in school you know. Then you don't know if the press is going to approach them, now in fairness they didn't, as far as I know.' The children, Damhan and Dairine, were only young at the time of their mother's murder and are now in their 20s. Alan talks about how proud he is of them and the success they are having in their respective careers.

Going back to the garda investigation and the recommendation that he should be charged with murder, Alan says, 'It wasn't really like that from my memory. Every time I spoke to the guards it was okay, there was nothing hostile or anything like that. Just having a conversation and even when I left, there wasn't a whole lot said. And then reading about it in the newspaper, there thinking, either I'm dumb to the whole lot, or they just seem to know more than I do. I must have walked out an eejit, to tell you the truth, not realising the severity of it from what you read, like. I tell you, it's not like what you see in the movies, or any of these things. It's just mad, you know. I don't know what the books are like,' he jokes. 'It's weird. Initially in the early days it takes every minute of your day, you are literally racking your brains. But you don't know what to believe anymore.'

Reference had also been made to a mastermind who orchestrated the murder and he is asked what he thinks about the inference that he is that mastermind. Laughing at the suggestion, Alan says: 'I'm glad they think I've the intelligence for it. I heard another phrase in the paper I laughed at, underworld. There again, it can just be headline grabbing you know, I suppose that's what sells. They have to make a living I suppose.' Asked about the ongoing suspicion that he was involved in the murder, he says: 'It was very frustrating at the time, you can't really avoid it because if you don't comment, they'll print what they want anyway, even if you do comment. So, you're in a no-win situation, you know.'

The conversation in Alan White's sitting room drifted momentarily to other topics: his life growing up in St Malachy's

Villas, his interest in model trains, and the cost-of-living crisis, which he attributes in part to Brexit. When the issue of Irene's murder is returned to, and he is asked if he has anything more to say on it, he responds: 'Not really, to tell you the truth, for one it's hard to remember. I tell you what happens, because you're furious, and you're listening to opinions from friends and relatives, they're all trying to help out, in the end you don't know what to believe. You're thinking "did I remember that or was I told that". It gets very confusing. Initially, you go mad, you're thinking day and night, and I don't know. It would put you mad.'

When he heard that Niall Power was pleading guilty to the murder, he was in shock. 'You're just numb. You're trying to gather information, much like yourselves, and you get bits and pieces. Some fits into what you were thinking, and some is just outrageous, and you just dismiss it. But the amount of energy it takes, trying to process this. It is head wrecking, like. The last I heard was something on the news about Niall looking to appeal the case.' The matter of Niall implicating Alan in the murder conspiracy, saying he was putting pressure on him to arrange Irene's murder, is returned to again. 'I heard that yeah. It's all mad. I don't know. You're trying to analyse every word you can get. I don't know what's true, what's not. I thought Niall was trying to take the attention off himself. I'd say he regretted going into the garda station, he since had time to think about it, hence the appeal.' At the end of our conversation, he was asked if he still denies any involvement in Irene's murder. 'Oh yeah, yeah.'

Anthony Lambe was the man who mercilessly stabbed Irene White 34 times in the kitchen of Ice House on Demesne Road, Dundalk, County Louth, on 6 April 2005. He is now quietly serving out his life sentence in Mountjoy Prison in Dublin, where he works on the internal grounds. Despite his remorse and attempts at contrition over the years, the savagery Anthony Lambe used in murdering an innocent housewife means it will be a long time before he will be considered for release.

As matters stand, with what has been proven in a court of law, the only other person who was criminally responsible for Irene's murder, by orchestrating her death and planning her demise, is Niall Power. While he awaits the fate of his appeal, he is also serving his life sentence in Mountjoy Prison. He too is considered a compliant prisoner, causing no issues for staff, and works as a cleaner on the committal landing of the jail. The modest jailhouse role is a world away from the successful business he once ran. Unsurprisingly, the convicted killers don't communicate with one another behind bars, with Anthony blaming Niall for involving him in the murder and Niall blaming Anthony for his ultimate downfall.

Reflecting on the status of the case, and the work by his team, Detective Inspector Marry concludes:

The investigation is at a standstill until new evidence can be secured. Looking back, I am very proud of the work done by the investigation team, which numbered five when I took over the case: Detective Sergeant Sheridan, Detective Gardaí Ogle, Reilly, and Duffy, and myself as the senior investigation officer. You can't replace hard work and commitment, and I was honoured to have worked with these fine detectives, true investigators and honest gardaí. Along with the work of the original investigation team and the Serious Crime Review Team, we ensured that two people have been brought to justice for the murder of Irene White.

ACKNOWLEDGEMENTS

Firstly, we would like to acknowledge the innocent victim at the centre of this case, Irene White, whose life was taken in the most cruel and senseless way. Irene was a caring mother who was deeply loved by her friends and family, and this was always at the forefront of our minds when writing this book. We also wish to acknowledge the dedicated work carried out by members of An Garda Síochána over the years, which ultimately led to two men being brought to justice for Irene's murder. We would like to express our sincere gratitude to everyone who made this book possible, many of whom cannot be named here. A thanks to the foremost expert on Irish libel laws, Kieran Kelly of Flynn O'Driscoll, for his legal guidance with this project. Thank you to our talented copy editor Emma Dunne, who is always a pleasure to work with. Many thanks to publishing agents Simon Hess and Declan Heeney of Gill Hess Associates for their continued help and support. Sincere thanks to Atlantic Books and MD Drummond Moir, and a special word of thanks to Atlantic group's associate publisher Clare Drysdale for putting her faith in us once again.

Robin:

Thank you to Mediahuis Ireland for their support and giving me time to work on this book – editor-in-chief Cormac Bourke, group head of news Kevin Doyle, news editor Gareth Morgan and the team. I am also grateful to my colleagues across the media industry, of whom there are too many to name. Those that I need to mention though are Ken Foy, Philip Ryan and my former *Irish Independent* colleague Niall O'Connor. Thank you, lads, for all your guidance and friendship. A special mention also to John Hand, crime correspondent with the *Irish Sun,* for always giving his time to provide advice on this project. Thank you for your patience, John. To my mam, dad and sister, thank you for always encouraging me, and for always offering words of wisdom when needed. To my in-laws, thank you all for your constant help and support. Finally, a special thank you to my wife and our baby boy for your love and support, and for your understanding during the long weekends and late nights while I worked on this book.

Pat:

This case would not have been solved but for the dedicated gardaí who worked tirelessly to ensure that Irene White got justice. To my own team that took over in 2013, we were only five but what a five it was. I want to acknowledge Detective Sergeant Michael Sheridan, who knew the case inside out and was a fantastic incident room coordinator. A true investigator who is solid as a rock, thank you Michael. I worked with Detective Garda Bobby Ogle on a number of major investigations, and it was his determination and skill that led to the breakthrough in this case. An honourable person and an admirable detective, it was a pleasure to work with you, Bobby. Detective Gardaí Rachel Reilly and Brendan Duffy brought valuable experience and dedication to the investigation which ensured that two people were brought to justice. They are utmost professionals, thank you Rachel and Brendan.

I also must acknowledge the work of the investigation teams involved prior to us taking over. In particular I want to pay tribute to the work of the Serious Crime Review Team under the stewardship of Chief Superintendent Christy Mangan. They are a very dedicated and professional outfit and An Garda Síochána is lucky to have them. I would also like to say thank you to the members of the Australian Federal Police who were of invaluable help in progressing the investigation. In particular I want to acknowledge the assistance of Agent Hannah Speldewinde who shepherded the investigation team on their journey to Australia to secure what was a most critical witness statement and provided the breakthrough needed in this investigation.

Finally, to my wife Niamh, thank you for your support and patience, and to my daughters Cheryl, Jade and Doireann, who always encourage me.